DRIVING HUNGRY

DRIVING HUNGRY

A Delicious Journey from

Buenos Aires to New York to Berlin

LAYNE MOSLER

Vintage Departures
Vintage Books
A Division of Penguin Random House LLC
New York

FIRST VINTAGE DEPARTURES EDITION, JUNE 2016

I have changed the names and identifying characteristics of some of the people in this
book to protect their privacy. For the sake of narrative momentum, I have condensed a
period of several years into one year, and in some cases I have rearranged the order of
events. In two instances, I have not written about persons who were present in a scene,
as I felt their presence would have distracted from the story. Other than that, I have
told this story to the best of my memory.

Parts of Chapter 7 have appeared in different form in *The Best Women's Travel Writing*
under the title "Passion and Pizza" in 2011. Other parts of the book have appeared in
different form on the author's blog, *Taxi Gourmet*.

Grateful acknowledgment is made to the following for permission to reprint
previously published material:

Duke University Press: An excerpt from *Paper Tangos* by Julie Taylor, copyright © 1988
by Duke University Press. All rights reserved. Reprinted by permission of
Duke University Press, www.dukeupress.edu.

Valorie Hart: An excerpt from "Balada para un loco" by Horacio Ferrer, translated by
Alberto Bernardino Paz. Reprinted by permission of Valorie Hart.

The Library of Congress has cataloged the Pantheon edition as follows:
Mosler, Layne.
Driving hungry : a memoir / Layne Mosler.
pages cm
1. Mosler, Layne—Travel. 2. Food writers—Germany—Biography.
3. Food writers—United States—Biography.
4. Restaurants—Anecdotes. 5. Taxicab drivers—Anecdotes. I. Title.
TX649.M68 A3 2015 641.5092—DC23 [B] 2014043506

Vintage Books Trade Paperback ISBN: 978-0-345-80267-5
eBook ISBN: 978-0-345-80268-2

Book design by Betty Lew

www.vintagebooks.com

Printed in the United States of America
10 9 8 7 6 5 4 3 2 1

For Leroy and Virginia

I beg you ... to have patience with everything unre-
solved in your heart and try to love the questions themselves as if they were locked rooms or books written in
a very foreign language. Don't search for the answers,
which could not be given you now, because you would
not be able to live them. And the point is, to live everything. Live the questions now. Perhaps then, someday far
in the future, you will gradually, without ever noticing it,
live your way into the answer ...

—Rainer Maria Rilke, *Letters to a Young Poet*

———————————•———————————

PART I

Buenos Aires

First, one must know how to suffer
Then to love, then to leave,
And finally to wander without thought . . .

—Homero Expósito, "Naranjo en Flor"

I

"Where can I take you?" said the taxista, picking up the *mate* gourd in his lap and taking a quick sip through a metal straw as he glanced at me in the rearview mirror.

I flipped through my planner, wishing I'd thought to memorize my new cross streets. "Avenida Santa Fe y . . ." How many times had I looked at that map on the internet? "Santa Fe, y Bulnes," I said, brushing a bead of sweat off my temple. I rolled down the window. January was to Buenos Aires what August was to Miami, and stepping out of Ezeiza airport and into the ten a.m. sunshine felt like walking into a sock, or falling into a vat of broth.

"Bueno." The taxista nodded. "Santa Fe y Bulnes." He pulled away from the curb, cruising past the other cabs parked in the arrivals area—mostly Fiats and Renaults, yellow on top, black on the bottom, they looked like toy cars that might be swept away by a strong wind. "Santa Fe y Bulnes," the taxista repeated, glancing at me again in the rearview mirror, a coy smile hovering in the lines around his eyes, which were deep-set and dark brown. "We might get caught in a traffic jam, *¿sabés?"*

I slid closer to the open window, wondering how he could stand to be wearing a long-sleeved shirt. *"Bueno . . ."*

"Bueno no es," said the taxista. Good it's not. We pulled up to the parking booth. *"¡Che, Juan! ¿Como estás, viejo?"* He handed the attendant a few pesos, and the wooden barrier arm rose in a slow, unsteady upward slice, as if reluctant to let us leave the airport. "The *piqueteros,"* he said to me, waving around his *mate* gourd as we drove away from the parking booth and coasted along the curves of the road to the airport exit, "are marching downtown."

"They are?" I stuffed my planner back in my purse. "Do you know why?"

"Who knows?" The taxista sipped his *mate*—the green-tea-like beverage that takes up more shelf space in Argentine grocery stores than coffee and tea combined—through a silver *bombilla* until he made a slurping sound. "*Piqueteros* have a right to express themselves," he said, setting the *mate* on the console, in front of the gearshift. "But I also have a right to drive the streets of my city in peace, don't I?"

He grinned at me in the rearview mirror, where he had hung a wooden rosary, and a ribbon in Argentine blue and white that fluttered when he merged onto the *autopista,* which was empty but for a few other taxis. I gazed out at the pampa, shimmering in the midday heat, an ocean of tall grass stretching to the blue-brown horizon. I could comprehend its vastness no more than I could comprehend that I was here, at last.

"What are you doing in Buenos Aires?"

I looked out the window, not knowing how to answer him. We were driving past a *villa miseria* (shantytown), where the sun glinted off the corrugated tin roofs and clotheslines sagged between cinder-block huts. Just beyond the *villa* was a billboard with a slogan painted over the stripes of the national flag: *"Argentina: un país en serio."* Argentina: A Serious Country.

I wiped another drop of sweat off my temple and thought back to the Night of the Inviolable Oysters.

"You're too *slow!*" the Sorceress shouted at me from the pass-through window, her normally stoic brown eyes magnified and wild behind her rimless glasses. "You can't even shuck an oyster!"

The Sorceress was a forty-year-old, stringy-haired, pot-bellied chef who was addicted to painkillers and probably under their influence when she decided to name her high-end San Francisco French-Asian fusion restaurant "Vertigineuse." I called her the Sorceress because anything she cooked—white gazpacho, foie gras with mango butter, seared hamachi wrapped in shiso leaves—was impossible to stop eating, whether I was hungry or not.

Now she was trying to woo a dozen VIPs at table 11, starting with oysters on the half shell. I tried to wedge the knife into the shell's wavy crease without mangling its contents, but the oyster kept its mouth shut, tightening its seal. The Sorceress rolled her eyes. In that unshuckable oyster, she was seeing all of my ineptitude.

"What are you going to do," she said, pressing her palms into the small of her back, ignoring the plates the other line cooks were setting before her for inspection, "when we *really* get busy?"

I had no idea. I swept a dozen oysters into my apron, grabbed the shucking knife (short, thick, and dull, designed to pry, not to cut), left three fig-gorgonzola-caramelized-onion flatbreads in the pizza oven, sprinted past Bob at the sauté station (who was pirouetting between foie gras on the flat top and corn nage on the stove), past Rob at the grill (roasting racks of lamb, finishing wild salmon), and past the Sorceress, who hissed at me—"You have one *min*ute!"—as I flew by.

I raced down the hall, into the prep kitchen. "Raúl!" I said, holding out my apron to show him the oysters. *"¡Ayúdame, por favor!"* Raúl was our lead prep cook. He put down his boning knife, pushed aside the cutting board with the tuna he was filleting, and scooped the oysters out of my apron and onto the stainless-steel counter in a single motion. Like everyone else in the kitchen, he pitied me—I *was* too slow. Unlike everyone else in the kitchen, Raúl was kind.

He should have been where I was, cooking on the line, learning the cold station, plating salads and desserts. Raúl had played semi-professional soccer in Guadalajara until he tore a ligament in his knee. He never wasted a movement. His knife skills were equal to or greater than Bob's and Rob's. Yet after three years working two jobs in San Francisco kitchens, he didn't speak more than a few words of English—so he stayed in the back of the restaurant, prepping. But he could shuck a dozen oysters in forty-five seconds, a screaming chef in the background, a placid smile framing his perfect teeth.

Hours later, after the VIPs left, the Sorceress went home, and Vertigineuse closed for the night, I was sitting at the bar, sipping Johnnie Walker Black that Ray, our freckle-faced, swan-necked headwaiter, was pouring as though he owned the place.

Everyone adored Ray. Every night, before opening, he would make espresso drinks for the entire kitchen staff, to each person's specifications. He could sweet-talk any cook on the line into redoing a dish if a customer was unhappy, and he could take the temperature of a table in seconds. My grandma would have called him a caviar personality.

"What happened in there tonight?" said Ray, looking down at my hand, which was wrapped in an Ace bandage.

I sighed. "Same thing that happens every night. I burn flatbread. I mess up the *tuille*. I overdress salads. Or underdress them. And this"—I pointed to the bandage—"is from the blowtorch. I'm not allowed to do crème brûlée anymore."

"So," said Ray, half smiling, raising one of his bow-shaped eyebrows, "you want to fire yourself?"

I tried to laugh as I turned away from my red-faced reflection in the mirror behind the bar. "The Sorceress hasn't paid me in two months, so I'm kind of fired anyway."

"What do you mean she hasn't paid you?"

"You know the restaurant is losing money," I said.

Ray nodded. He knew, and he wasn't worried. He would always be able to wait tables somewhere.

I leaned over the bar, lowering my voice. "She asked me if I could wait to get paid, and I told her yes. I didn't think it would be two months, though." I downed the rest of the whiskey, closing my eyes as the boozy warmth of it spread through my stomach.

"Oh, girl." Ray clucked his tongue. "That ain't good!"

"You know I'm not gonna be a line cook. *I* know I'm not gonna be a line cook. I probably don't even deserve to get paid." I drummed what was left of my fingernails on the side of my glass. "But I'm trying to learn every job in the business, so I'll know what I'm doing when I open *my* restaurant."

"You sure about that, honey?" Ray glanced at the Ace bandage again as he refilled our glasses. "You really want to open a restaurant?"

I had gotten the idea to open a restaurant—rather, I had fallen in love with the idea of opening a restaurant—in the middle of a dismal semester of graduate school in New Jersey, where I was working toward a master's degree in community development and spending several hours every day watching the Food Network and testing recipes on my roommates. On my birthday, I took myself to Philadelphia and splurged on lunch at the White Dog Café, Judy Wicks's restaurant cum social change project. Halfway through a bowl of green garlic soup, I was ready to follow in Ms. Wicks's footsteps. *To hell with SWOT analysis and human development indicators,* I thought. I could do a lot more immediate good in the world by feeding people Dad's milk bread, or Grandpa's fennel sausage (which, as a professional butcher, he only knew how to make in hundred-pound batches), or our New Year's lasagne, from a recipe Grandma got from an Italian grocer in L.A. and only gave to Mom after my parents had been married for five years.

By the time I blew out the candle on my sour cherry cheesecake, I had a vision: my restaurant, as a West Coast riff on the White Dog. We'd grow our own herbs. We'd serve wine from the barrel, like they did in Italy, in little glass pitchers. Customers could pay what they wanted. And all the tables would be round, so conversations could flow.

"All that education, to work in a restaurant!" said Mom.

"You sure that's what you wanna do, kid?" said Dad.

I put my master's degree on hold, moved to San Francisco, and dove into the restaurant business. I washed dishes. I waited tables. I worked as a barista at Java Supreme, where I learned how to properly use an espresso machine. I became a hostess at Greens, the San Francisco Zen Center's "world-famous" vegetarian restaurant, where the customers didn't mind when they found worms in their salads ("Well, now we *know* it's organic!"), where I worked my way up to managing Greens to Go, their takeout café.

Meanwhile, I filled notebook after notebook with ideas for my restaurant: we would put cheese and olives and marinated vegetables on the table as soon as guests sat down, like they did in Portugal, so people would have something to munch on while reading the menu. We would organize recipe contests for customers, and add the winning dishes to the menu for a month. And I would make focaccia, in a wood-burning adobe oven in the center of the dining room. I thought about applying to the California Culinary Academy.

"Before you spend fifty thousand dollars on cooking school," said a chef named Nano, who drove me down Lombard Street on his motorcycle and introduced me to the glories of Super Quesadillas Suizas (giant flour tortillas griddled to order with avocado, sour cream, queso fresco, carne asada, and as much tomatillo salsa as we wanted) at El Farolito at one a.m., "you should cook on the line."

Nano helped me get a minimum-wage job in the Sorceress's kitchen at Vertigineuse, where he had once worked as a sous-chef. It was a location in limbo, between the old money on Nob Hill and the drug-addicted poverty in the Tenderloin. In the last ten years, three restaurants had failed in that very spot.

"All that education, to chop mushrooms!" said Mom.

"As long as you enjoy what you're doing," said Dad.

I hoped Vertigineuse would be the last job I took before I wrote my business plan and started raising money for my restaurant. (I was still searching for a name. "Gusto" was the best I'd come up with so far.) Yet ten months into cooking on the line, instead of getting that crazy high that made Bob and Rob cackle with glee when they were slammed with orders, I was still panicking, losing what little ability I had to prioritize. One night, Bob, who always looked ready for a fight, even in clogs and checkered chef pants, took me aside, trying to help. "When you're in the weeds, you gotta focus," he said. "Take thirty seconds, look at everything you gotta do, and figure out what has to happen first. Make a plan. Then *go!*" It sounded easy. "OK!" I nodded. "I'll make a plan!"

But everyone needed their chawan mushi and their spicy eggplant napoleon and their oysters on the half shell *now*. Ten months in, I had to face facts: Bob and Rob moved at a different speed than I did. As much as urgency inflamed them, pulling them into that high-pressure kitchen dance that line cooks live for, it paralyzed me. *So I'm not a line cook,* I thought. *That doesn't mean I can't run a restaurant.*

However, on the Night of the Inviolable Oysters, with the burn smarting under the Ace bandage as I pedaled my three-gear beast of a bike down Nob Hill, through pockets of fog and over asphalt glistening with two a.m. dampness, I thought about Ray's question—"You really want to open a restaurant?"—hoping the answer was still yes, willing it to still be yes, but knowing it was no.

. . .

"I want to write about Buenos Aires," I said to the taxista, as we cleared the last toll plaza on the highway from Ezeiza airport.

"Eh?"

The traffic on the *autopista* was heavy now, within the city limits, and he was hunching over the steering wheel as if bracing for an attack. *"Mira,"* he said, "if you tell people the truth about this place, no one will believe you. But what do I know?"

I glanced out the window at the sun-bleached sprawl: the city looked like a built-up extension of the surrounding plains, with skyscrapers as afterthoughts.

"Actually"—I turned to the taxista, smiling at his profile—"I'm really interested in the food here."

"¿Cómo?"

"I want to write about gastronomy."

"Astronomy?"

"No." I laughed. "*Gas*tronomy—food, restaurants, that kind of thing." After the Night of the Inviolable Oysters, and the subsequent realization that I had spent the better part of a decade working toward the wrong dream, I began to search for a new vocation, jumping from job to job, from lease to lease, moving back and forth across the Bay, growing more restless and more jaded each time a novel scenario became reduced to a routine. Meanwhile, my friends in San Francisco were buying real estate and planning their weddings, earning law degrees and accounting degrees, and master's degrees in public health and social work. *Everybody's serious but me,* I thought. But I believed choosing one path meant eliminating too many others. I didn't want to "make a living." I wanted to live everything. Taste everything, go everywhere I could. I wanted passion, and an all-consuming occupation—and I wanted it to involve food.

The taxista sat up straight, cinching his eyebrows as he studied me in the rearview mirror. "Where are you from?"

"Guess."

"Colombia?"

I shook my head.

"Venezuela?"

"Nooo."

"México?"

"Close," I said. "California."

"California?"

I nodded.

"Ay, Caleefooorneeeya." He sighed as if recalling an old fling. "I lived in L.A. for a year, *¿sabés?* From 2002 to 2003. After *la crisis.* I painted cars in L.A. When I came back here, I had dollars in my pocket, but I made some bad investments, so here I am. Driving a taxi." He sighed again, raising his *mate* in a mock toast. "*La crisis.* What are you going to do?"

La crisis, the way the taxista explained it, was the collapse of the Argentine economy at the end of 2001, which was sparked by a recession, and massive international debt, and the rumored devaluation of the peso, which led to a run on the banks, which led to the freezing of bank accounts, which led to massive *cacerolazos* (pot- and pan-banging street protests), which escalated into riots that killed twenty-five people, after which the president resigned, fleeing the Casa Rosada in a helicopter, after which an interim president declared a default on the country's debt and stepped down after a week in office, after which another interim president devalued the peso, after which thousands of people lost their savings, their homes, and/or their jobs.

"How long are you staying in Buenos Aires?" said the taxista.

"Indefinitely."

"Do you have family here? A husband?"

"No. No husband."

"How old are you?"

I laughed. "Thirty-one."

"Do you have friends here? A boyfriend?"

"No," I said, knowing how strange and sad I must have sounded to a man who came from a culture where love and friendship rule a person's life decisions. "I've been here once before," I told him. "With my best friend. And I fell in love with the city. So—"

"You fell in love with Buenos Aires?"

"*¿Cómo te lo puedo explicar . . . ?*" How can I explain it to you?

Was it some combination of steak and empanadas and dulce de leche, and streets named for poets and philosophers and tango composers, and bookstores on Avenida Corrientes that stayed open well past midnight? Was it the musical, Italian-inflected cadence of *rioplatense* Spanish? The way the entire city had erupted—*GOOOOOOOOOOOOOOOOOOL!*—when the national soccer team scored in a World Cup qualifier against Uruguay? Was it the newspaper *kioscos* on the sidewalk, positioning Neruda and Shakespeare alongside the latest issues of *Hello!* and *Hustler?* Was it the edginess of the city, urging me always, always to pay attention? The chaos of the traffic on the grand *avenidas,* which seemed to mirror and dwarf my own? Or was it the feeling that the city was just beginning to emerge from *la crisis,* and that the food here might be changing, too? Here, I told myself, was a place where I could start something new. Here was a place Borges called "a land of men born as exiles, of men nostalgic for the distant and the different," a place where people seemed to believe their treasure might be buried somewhere far away.

The taxista pulled off the *autopista*. Were we driving north or south? I couldn't tell. I didn't see any *piqueteros*. The air smelled like overripe peaches and diesel fuel. My back was drenched with sweat. There were signs in red block letters—LAVANDERÍA, PAPELERÍA, HELADERÍA, EMPANADERÍA—and men in tank tops drinking Fanta, and women with tanned legs in short skirts who strutted over the craters in the sidewalk.

I asked the taxista what he thought of Borges.

"Borges?" he said. "No, no, no, no, no, no, no. If you want to understand Buenos Aires, don't read Borges. He's not even *buried* in Argentina! If you want to understand this place, you have to know the tango. Forget Borges! Forget astronomy!"

"Do you dance tango?"

"No," he said. "My parents did. When I was young, tango was what the old people listened to, *¿sabés?* We were listening to the Beatles. And rock 'n' roll. But now that I'm older, I wish I would have learned. And now I like the music." He reached over and opened the glove compartment, where there were two neat stacks of cassette tapes, "Do you know Julio Sosa?"

"No. But think I've heard the name—"

"*¡Qué voz!*" he said. What a voice! "Here, listen to this."

He popped a cassette into the stereo. Julio Sosa's baritone, commanding, weighty, laden with irony, seemed to fill the speakers to capacity. The taxista turned up the volume. "That *voice*! Listen to what he's saying. This tango is called 'Cambalache.' Listen!"

I tried to translate the lyrics as I listened. I couldn't understand a lot of the song.

"This song was written in the 1920s, but what he's saying is still true! *Increíble*. Listen!" He rewound the tape to the beginning. "He says, 'The world was and will be filth in the year five hundred six and in the year two thousand, too!' He says, 'Today everything is the same, nothing gets better, to be ignorant, a genius, a pickpocket, a swindler.' It's all the same."

We sped through a yellow light and braked behind a bus. The taxista pulled a metal thermos out of a satchel on the passenger seat and refilled the *mate* gourd. He was almost shouting over Julio Sosa now. "He's talking about a lack of respect, a loss of reason! How full of problems the twentieth century is! If you don't cry, you don't get fed! If you don't steal, you're a fool!"

"What do you think?"

"I'd be a fool to think otherwise," he said. "Not just a fool. A starving fool."

Julio Sosa sounded like he was savoring the pain by the time he got to the final verse of "Cambalache," and I was catching the gist of the lyrics: The idiot lives off his job, and the smart guy lives off the idiot. And we'll all see each other in hell.

The taxista veered around the bus, *mate* gourd in hand, and turned onto Avenida Santa Fe. "Where should I drop you off?"

I looked out the window, squinting at the street numbers. There was my building: five stories of 1970s concrete sandwiched between a Burger King and a cell phone store. My stomach clenched, in a deadlock between doubt and fear, when I realized it was time to get out of the taxi. I was about to move into a studio apartment I had only seen on the internet, I had three months of savings to live on, and my emergency contact person was ten thousand miles away.

2

Everything I did on that first jet-lagged day in Buenos Aires was a blur—the city was sweltering and half empty, and *porteños* (literal translation: people from the port; local translation: anyone from or living in Buenos Aires) with means had fled to the coast or to the mountains. Restaurants were closed. Banks, some of whose windows were still cracked from the protests after the peso crash three years before, were closed, too. I stood alone in the tropical heat of the subway platform, blotting the sweat off my forehead and gazing at a TV monitor tuned to the tango channel: a young couple, dark-haired and dressed in close-fitting red and black, was dancing on the screen, legs whirling in sync with the staccato strokes of a violin.

I had been curious about tango long before meeting the taxista who loved Julio Sosa, long before I had been to Buenos Aires. Each year since I was seven, I had watched every round of the World Latin Dance Championships on PBS. I loved the sunlit energy in the salsa and the samba, and the big stomping drama of the paso doble, but the tango was what fascinated me most: I stared at the couples with slicked-back hair, scowling at each other, pulling apart, seizing each other again—they were so fierce, so emphatic—and I promised myself that someday, somewhere, I would learn that strange, beautiful dance.

Not long before I left San Francisco, a tango-dancing friend of a friend had told me about La Catedral, one of the most popular underground *milongas* (tango clubs) in Buenos Aires. "On Mondays," he said, with a wistful smile, "they teach tango for beginners." *Perfect,* I thought.

La Catedral was in a middle-class barrio called Almagro, fifteen blocks and a realm apart from the fancy shoe stores and the fresh pasta shop and the organic German bakery near the little studio apartment I was renting on Avenida Santa Fe. As I walked to the tango club, munching on a pair of beef empanadas with sweet paprika, the street-lights thinned out, the cracks in the sidewalk widened, and the smells of dog poop and garbage—strewn over the pavement, spilling into the gutter—grew stronger in the muggy night. I put away the empa-nadas and held my breath for long intervals. When I got to where La Catedral was supposed to be, I found a rusty metal door and no sign. A teenager in a Che Guevara T-shirt opened up when I knocked.

"*Hola,*" I said, hoping he wasn't noticing the rings of sweat under my arms. "Is there a tango class here tonight?"

"*Arriba,*" he said, pointing to the concrete staircase behind him.

A headless mannequin in a G-string greeted me at the top of the stairs that led to the ballroom, which looked like a cross between a film noir set and a flea market. The wooden ceiling must have been forty feet high, and the unpainted walls were crowded with used bike tires, empty picture frames, hubcaps, a single dusty tango shoe, and corroding fans that halfheartedly pushed the hot air around the room. Stray cats slept between the mismatched chairs bordering the dance floor, which was lit by a handful of bare bulbs in primary colors. It was dim, it was filthy, and it might have been on the verge of being condemned. I couldn't have conjured up a more romantic place to learn tango.

A tall woman in red stilettos strode to the middle of the dance floor and clapped her hands. "*¡Vamos, chicos!*"

I'd been fantasizing about this moment. I'd had time for only one tango on my first trip to Buenos Aires—with a dancer on staff at a steak house in La Boca—and it had been more than awkward, but I told myself it was because our tango had lasted all of forty-five sec-onds. Though I knew I would never be a professional dancer—that hope was dashed when I was four years old, in my first ballet class, when the teacher told me my torso was too long in relation to my legs—nothing could stop me from imagining that I might be some kind of tango prodigy, that I might take to the dance quickly, naturally, uncannily. Someday, I thought—piggybacking on the fantasies of the lead actress in a film called *The Tango Lesson*—I might even tango for an audience at the Teatro Colón (Argentina's Carnegie Hall).

I edged into the circle of students surrounding the *profesora*. Most of the women were wearing high-heeled dancing shoes. Others wore ballet slippers. The men were dressed in everything from ties to T-shirts. The *profesora* looked us up and down as she twisted her frizzy chestnut hair into a bun. When she got to me, she fixed her eyes on my feet.

"How the hell do you expect to tango in those?"

Heads turned. The *profesora* shifted her weight from one long, slender leg to the other and pointed a long, burgundy fingernail at my flip-flops. The cigarette smoke that had been drifting through the air seemed to hold still.

"I'm sorry," I said, "I don't—"

The *profesora*'s partner, who was shorter than she was, stepped into the middle of the circle of students, slipping his arm around her waist. He looked at me, and there was pity in his dark eyes. "Are those the only shoes you have?"

I nodded, my face burning.

He turned to the *profesora*. "Gisela," he said, "it's her first class. She'll get some shoes."

I was still nodding. *Yes!* I wanted to tell them. *Yes, I'll get some shoes!* A pair of Argentine girls in strappy tango sandals started to giggle. I wanted to disappear.

"*Bueno,*" said Profesora Gisela, pursing her lips, double-clapping the class to attention again. "*¡Vamos, chicos!* Time to walk. Look at me!"

She slid into line in her red stilettos, her ballet-dancer arches hovering above the soles of her high heels. I watched my classmates glide over the warped wooden floorboards, doing a very good job of mimicking Profesora Gisela's feline walk. I struggled to follow them. It took only a few steps to realize that I was most certainly *not* a tango prodigy.

The *profesor*, who told us his name was Luis, pressed Play on the boom box. Now we were supposed to do the feline walk in time to music. My flip-flops refused to stay on. Gisela bit her tongue. I felt as though she could see right through me, as if she were well aware of all the unrealistic notions I'd brought to her class. I was too mortified, and too sweaty, to be disillusioned.

Profesor Luis stopped the music.

"OK, *chicos,* pick a partner!"

Oh, no.

I stepped to the edge of the dance floor and watched my class-mates pair up, greeting each other with happy kisses on the cheek. A man about my age was walking in my direction. I had noticed him, and his wavy black ponytail, and his carefully trimmed goatee, at the beginning of class—he could have played a sword fighter in an Errol Flynn movie, or a pirate in a Disney one. *"Hola,"* he said with a half smile. "I'm Daniel." His eyes were the color of tawny port.

"I'm Layne." I held out my hand.

"E-la—?"

"Like Luisa Lane. You know—Superman's girlfriend?"

He grinned, holding my hand more than shaking it.

There were dimples on either side of his goatee. I glanced at his white dress shirt, perfectly pressed, without a drop of sweat. He was as elegant as I was unkempt. I tucked my hair behind my ears. His beauty flustered me. He smiled again. I thought about the empanadas I had eaten on the way to class, and smiled back with closed lips.

Gisela and Luis demonstrated a step sequence. They moved with-out effort, turning and sidestepping, their torsos joined, their feet in a nimble dialogue. They were not as flashy as the couple I had seen on the tango channel in the *subte* station, but they were every bit as sensual.

"Es lindo, ¿no?" said Daniel. It's beautiful, isn't it?

"Sí." I nodded. *"Muy lindo."*

Gisela and Luis repeated the sequence, deconstructing the steps, making them look simple.

"Vamos," said Daniel, leading me to a corner of the dance floor. "Let's try it."

We tried it. Every time I took a backward step—which was most of the time, since most steps for the woman in tango involve some variation of walking backward—I either lost a flip-flop or nearly lost a flip-flop. But my problem went deeper than my shoes: I did not have a dancer's memory. No matter how many times I watched Gisela and Luis repeat the steps, I could not translate them into my body. It looked like the other couples could, though—circling the floor in the low light, flirting a little as they found their way into the sequence. They were glowing, as if their movements were making them radiant, while I continued to drip, on the insides of my elbows, on the backs of my knees. I wanted another empanada.

"Luisa Lane?" said Daniel.

"I'm sorry. I don't know what to do."

"Don't worry," he said. "Just follow me. *Yo te llevo.*"

Yo te llevo. I'll take you. It sounded lovely. Take me where?

We attempted the sequence a few more times before Daniel paused, in mid-turn. "What are you doing in Buenos Aires?" he said, taking a step away from me.

I ran my fingertips over my eyebrows, wiping away the sweat. I could have told him what I had told the taxista, that I had come here to write, but it would have been a lie to call myself a writer. "It's just a feeling," I said, crossing and uncrossing my arms, "that this is the right place to be."

"If you want to learn tango, this is the right place," said Daniel, who told me he was a *porteño,* born and raised and planning to die in Buenos Aires.

Meanwhile, Profesora Gisela was moving from couple to couple, darting around the dance floor like a nymph in high heels, making corrections as she went. Daniel and I tried the sequence again. We stopped when she got to us.

"This arm"—Gisela grabbed my right biceps—"is like flan. We don't want flan. How are you going to feel his lead? Put some tension in it. Here! Like this."

She raised her dry palm to my clammy one. "Don't push! You want some tension, but never, ever, ever, *ever* push the man's arm in the embrace. You want him to know you are there. But you do *not* want to make his arm sore!"

My head understood perfectly what she was saying. Getting my arm to take it in was something else.

Daniel's eyes lingered on Gisela's legs as she walked away. "Gisela's tough, but she's a good teacher," he said. "She just wants to make sure you're serious about tango."

I looked down at my feet. "I see."

"*¡Vamos, chicos!*" Profesor Luis called us to the center of the room, and Gisela walked into his arms, her body softening as if she were climbing into bed.

"They always end class with a tango for us," said Daniel. "Then we can stay after and dance if we want."

Someone pressed Play on the boom box.

Daniel closed his eyes. " 'Paciencia,' " he said. "This is a very beautiful tango. Listen."

The music was jaunty—violins flitting between the quick beats of what sounded like an accordion. (I learned later it was a *bandoneón,* the cousin of the accordion that came to Argentina via Germany, the instrument that gives tango its signature searching sound.) But the lyrics of the tango, or what I could understand of them, turned quickly from sweet ("Last night my eyes saw you again . . .") to bitter (". . . in the end we were two strangers . . . why fake it?").

"Do you understand?" Daniel whispered. "It's about admitting you don't belong with someone, but you can't help wanting to be with them anyway."

This was the way Gisela and Luis moved to "Paciencia," holding each other like doomed lovers drowning in their last tango. Watching them felt like trespassing on territory that might have been too intimate.

The song ended. We clapped. Gisela curtsied, and Luis touched her shoulder. The lesson was over.

"Are you staying?" Daniel looked at his watch. *"La noche está en pañales."*

"The night is in diapers?" I laughed. It was midnight. I looked around: The *milonga* was just getting started. Men were lining up at the bar, lighting cigarettes. Women were walking in, alone or in pairs, taking the first seats they could find, quickly changing into tango shoes. Two couples were dancing to a tango waltz, the men cradling the women's backs with one arm, the women closing their eyes as they circled the floor, and circled their partners.

What they were dancing, and what Gisela and Luis had danced, bore no resemblance to the tango I had seen on PBS: there were no straight arms, no swiveling heads, no roses in the women's mouths. This tango was more reflective than dramatic, more about surrender than struggle—it was gorgeous, and it was sexy (that nearness!), and yet, if I was reading the serene expressions on the dancers' faces correctly, there was something contemplative about it, too. I wanted to move like that, to feel whatever it was they seemed to be feeling. But this was impossible in flip-flops. I told Daniel I had to leave.

I was almost out the door, about to bid a silent goodbye to the headless mannequin in the G-string, when Profesor Luis stepped into my path: *"No te vayas."* Don't go. He took my arm. *"Vamos a bailar un tanguito."* Let's dance a little tango.

"What?" I said. "No. *No puedo bailar."* I can't dance. I pointed at my flip-flops.

"Then we'll walk," he said. "Come on."

He led me between the dancing couples, to the center of the floor. "Relax!" he said. "*Ya sé.* You're worried about everyone looking at you. They don't care."

"But—"

"*Vamos.* Walk with me. Pretend we're wandering through a forest."

He held out his arm, and I took it. Side by side, we walked a few steps forward, a few steps back. It was too ridiculous. I laughed, trying not to care, hoping Daniel wasn't watching.

"Don't think about tango," said Luis. "Just walk."

I closed my eyes, trying to picture the forest. Luis turned to face me, taking my right hand, wrapping his other arm around the middle of my back. I took a backward step, lost a flip-flop. We paused to retrieve it. Then he pulled me into a close embrace—our chests together, our heads side by side. His cheek was cool. I let out an unsteady breath. So much touch was a shock to me, coming from the U.S., where contact with strangers was limited to handshakes or limp hugs. But more frightening was not knowing where or how the *profesor* wanted me to move.

"Don't anticipate," he said. "That's the first thing you have to learn. Don't try to guess where I'm going."

"What?" Unless I was eating, I was always anticipating. In the absence of something delicious—something along the lines of Grandma's potato salad, or a fish taco from Mariscos Sinaloa in Oakland—thinking about the future, and doing everything in my power to prepare for it, was my default setting. In that moment, I was willing the tango to be over, hoping I could make it to the empanada parlor before it closed. I dug my toes into my flip-flops, imploring them to stay on.

"Breathe," said Luis.

He caught me in mid-exhale and stepped forward, and left, and left again, and somewhere in a nanosecond of not thinking, I found his lead. I didn't know where he was taking me, and I didn't need to know. My mind gave way to my body, to his body, to instinct, to *that* instant. The music struck triumphant chords. My shoes stayed put.

Violins announced the closing notes of the tango. I began to sweep my leg into a final pose, pointing my toe and dragging it over the floor in a half circle, the way Gisela had, at the end of her tango, but I bumped into Luis's leg, and he tripped. I was sorry for breaking the spell.

"Never apologize," he said. *"Lo tenías."* You had it.

For maybe a verse I'd had it. And it was clear to me, in that moment, why I was in Buenos Aires, why I had come to this tango class, and why, despite the *profesora,* and my natural clumsiness, and the difficulty of the dance, I would show up again next Monday: I had so much to unlearn.

3

After that first lesson, I began to immerse myself in tango. I tried other teachers. I bought a pair of dancing shoes—open-toed stilettos with thin straps and three-and-a-half-inch bronze heels—and I carried them around in a satin bag, rarely leaving the apartment without them. I went to afternoon *milongas,* where my teachers told me the old masters were happy to go through the basics with clueless foreign women, especially if they were young. It was at one of these *milongas* that I met Liliana, a psychiatrist in her fifties from Lomas de Zamora who had blue eyes lined in silver and a glorious head of wavy blond hair.

"Buenos Aires is a Freudian city," said Liliana, between *tandas* (song sets), fluttering a black lace fan at her high forehead as we sat at one of the tables next to the dance floor. "We have the highest number of psychiatrists per capita of any city in the world."

"More than New York?" I offered her a bite of empanada. The empanadas at the *milonga* usually came out of a microwave, but I had started making a ritual of ordering two or three when I went dancing.

"Many more than New York," said Liliana. *"No, gracias."* She smiled, shaking her head at the empanada. "We like to say there are two therapists for every Argentine."

I laughed, and she stood up to join a thin-lipped man in a lilac shirt who was waiting for her on the dance floor. They chattered like old friends, letting the other couples dance around them before they leaned into each other and started on their own counterclockwise path around the floor.

"Tango," said Liliana, after the *tanda* with the thin-lipped man, who escorted her back to our table when it was over, and bowed to both of us before he returned to his, "is the most psychological dance of all."

"Why?"

"It's the embrace," she said, picking up her fan. "How can I explain it? It's like you're communicating with someone. But not in a traditional way. In a very, *very* intimate way. It's like an emotional dialogue." Liliana told me she had been dating a fellow tango dancer for four years. "Be that as it may"—she snapped her fan closed— "I always tell my patients it's a bad idea to get involved with a man at the *milonga*."

Between *milongas,* I was writing my first food articles. Mostly I gravitated toward offbeat topics: the new wave of vegetarian restaurants in the Metropolis of Beef, for example, or a group of nineteenth-century anarchist bakers who invented a series of pastries (including *bolas de fraile,* priest testicles, and *suspiros de monja,* nun sighs) to poke fun at The Church. But my favorite piece, inspired by a dinner prepared by a young chef named Lucas Mallmann, was about the birth of the Slow Food movement in Argentina. Mallmann's food—onion and wild mushroom soup with Torrontés, trout pâté from San Martín de los Andes, goat cheese from Santiago del Estero, marinated beef from Bariloche—was an ode to the flavors of the Argentine provinces. And when Mallmann, who was the nephew of Francis Mallmann, one of Argentina's best-known chefs, came out of the kitchen at the end of the meal, stroking his thin mustache, blushing at our applause, saying, "Please, when you applaud, you should be clapping for the amazing bounty of our country," I felt like I might be getting closer to my true vocation.

Food writing was not going to pay the bills, though, and I was burning through my savings doing research (eating) for my stories. I started answering Help Wanted ads in *La Nación.* Eventually, I found a job, managing projects at a satellite telecommunications company with an office in the Microcentro, though I knew nothing about satellites or telecommunications. At night, to the amusement of my colleagues, all of whom were Argentine and none of whom danced tango, I went to the *milonga*. "What are you doing there?" they asked me. "You think you're going to be a tango star? Or marry a *milonguero*? *¡Muy buena suerte!*"

Still, a few of my co-workers were intrigued when I told them I was going to Sunderland, a mythical *milonga* in a neighborhood clubhouse in Villa Urquiza, on the northern edge of Buenos Aires, where elite *tangueros* went in packs, danced exclusively with people they knew, and frowned on women who showed up alone, or even in pairs.

Sunderland was the "world's greatest tango club," according to my tango teachers: It was the *milonga* that had kept tango alive when it was threatened with extinction at different points in the twentieth century—during the military junta in the 1950s, upon the arrival of rock 'n' roll, throughout the Beatles craze in the 1960s, and then again during the military dictatorship in the late 1970s and early 1980s, when the generals in charge outlawed gatherings of three or more people in public.

Sunderland was where young dancers would go to learn the traditional codes of tango from the old *milongueros,* and it was the tango club that provoked the most fear in dancers who performed the late-night solo, an honor reserved for professional or semiprofessional couples who would dance two or three songs to entertain the *milonga's* notoriously critical audience. Sunderland was where Robert Duvall went to dance tango when he visited Buenos Aires, where he was just another dancer. In other words, if the tango was a confessional act and the *milonga* a church, then Sunderland was the Vatican (even if the dance floor doubled as a basketball court during the week).

At two a.m., my tango classmates and I turned our chairs toward the dance floor as Joaquín Aragón led his partner to center court to perform the late-night solo. It was our first time at Sunderland, and we had danced little that night, nor had we expected to—Joaquín, the newly crowned World Champion of Salon Tango, was the reason we were here. Dressed in a pale gray suit, he had swept his thin hair over a hairline that looked as though it were just beginning to recede. His goatee seemed like a vain attempt to bring harmony to a face that would never be handsome. But his cinnamon-colored skin was smooth, and he was tall—at over six feet, practically a giant in Argentina—and had the lean muscles of a dancer.

Joaquín held Sonya, his partner, a black-haired bombshell in a white lace dress with a thigh-high slit, in a motionless embrace in the middle of the floor, waiting for the music to start. Their glamour looked out of place at center court, beneath fluorescent lights and rusting fans, against a backdrop of banners in primary colors advertising shoe repairs, life insurance, laundry service, fish markets, and lottery bingo.

The music started, but Joaquín and Sonya didn't move. Ten seconds passed, twenty, thirty, and just when the audience began to whisper, and I started to wonder if they were going to cling to each other like that for the whole song, they glided into a long, slow side step.

Joaquín drew out every pause in the song—a lush, violin-laden tango waltz—holding Sonya like she was something precious and rare. She moved with her eyes closed, as if in a trance. He turned, once, twice, three times, on one leg, centered on some invisible floor-to-ceiling pole. Sonya ran her instep up and down his calf, drawing figure eights and tiny spirals on the floor with her feet. None of it looked rehearsed. There were claps and whistles and murmurs of *¡Esaaaaaaaaaaaa!*

The room exploded when the music stopped, the roar of the crowd ricocheting off the gym walls, as people stood up to applaud, shouting *¡Ooooooooootra, campeones! ¡Ooootra!* until the music started again, and Joaquín led Sonya into another tango, playful and buoyant this time, dancing on the off beat, trading off the lead. The room exploded again when the song ended. The hair on my arms stood up. Joaquín and Sonya bowed to every corner of the audience, holding hands, beaming, hurrying off the floor as the commotion finally began to recede. A man shook Joaquín's hand, thumping him on the back, telling him he was dancing better every day. A woman who could have been his grandmother took his face in her hands, kissed him on the lips, and said, *"Gracias, gracias, gracias por tu tango."* I waited until the crowd dispersed, until Joaquín settled into his seat, lit a cigarette. When I introduced myself, his eyes moved from the dance floor to my face to my feet.

"I like your dress, Luisa Lane," he said, exhaling smoke through the corner of his mouth, looking from me to the other side of the room, at a redhead in a royal-blue skirt. He nodded at her—this nod was the *cabeceo,* the silent invitation to dance that spared men the risk of crossing the room to ask a woman to dance, only to have her say no. If a man gave a woman the *cabeceo,* all she had to do was avert her eyes to refuse his invitation, and no one would be the wiser. If she did want to dance with him, she nodded back, almost imperceptibly, held his gaze, and rose to meet him on the dance floor—exactly what the redhead was doing.

My face went hot, and I glanced down at the black and white folds of my dress, which, hours earlier, I'd had to hold my breath to zip. (By this time, my tango classmates had introduced me to the magic of ice-cream delivery in Buenos Aires: half a kilo of dulce de leche ice cream—or dulce de leche with chocolate chips and rum—kept cold with dry ice and brought to my front door, cost about five dollars, even at three a.m.). Then I asked Joaquín, more quickly than I wanted to, because he was standing up now, "Could I interview you sometime?" I cleared my throat. "I'm a journalist," I said. *Sort of a journalist,* I thought.

"Sure." He grinned, reached into his pocket, pulled out a card, dropped it next to the ashtray where his cigarette was still burning, and said, "Excuse me," as he slipped into the swarm of people joining their partners on the dance floor. The redhead was at the far corner of the floor, waiting for him. They embraced without a word. I read the card. First line: Joaquín Aragón. Second line: Tango. Third line: his cell phone number. That was it.

"Each tango has its own soul," said Joaquín. "Its own life, its own force, its own . . . *¿Cómo se dice?* Uniqueness. It's not *the* tango. It's *a* tango. You can be dancing with the same person to the same song in the same place, but it's a different day. You're different. She's different. The moisture on the floor is different." He took a short drag on his cigarette. "Tangos are like little beings that last three minutes. Each one has its own soul."

A week had gone by since I'd seen Joaquín dance at Sunderland. I was interviewing him for a story I had no immediate plans to write, at the no-name café-*kiosco* next door to the Tango Escuela Carlos Copello, where Joaquín was the head teacher.

"I started dancing when I was six, as a hobby," he said, as I scribbled in my notebook. "When I was seventeen, I saw a movie I really liked. When I left the theater I was so excited. Maybe you know it? It was called *Dirty Dancing*—"

His cell phone rang. His ringtone was the "Mahna Mahna" song from *The Muppet Show*. I held back a smile, took a bite of *alfajor*—the cookie was dry, a thin layer of dulce de leche between two pieces of shortbread—and reread my questions as I shifted around in my plastic chair, next to a rack of candy bars covered in dust, wondering whom he was talking to.

Joaquín arranged his night with the person on the phone, taking his voice an octave lower: *"¿A las ocho? Bien. Y después vemos. Besoooo. Chauuuuu."* I tried not to listen, tried not to look at his lips—so full and so shapely they seemed to belong on a woman's face—and tried, instead, to focus on his teeth, broken and brown from what I guessed were years of drinking coffee, sipping *mate,* and chain-smoking.

"Sorry," he said, closing his cell phone, ordering a second *café cortado.*

"I wouldn't have guessed you were a Muppets fan."

"Claro que sí." He smiled, pulling another Marlboro out of his front pocket.

"Who's your favorite Muppet?"

"Who's yours?" he said.

"You first."

"Gonzo."

"Why Gonzo?" I said.

"Because he has no fear." He lit the Marlboro and took two puffs, breathing out the smoke through his nostrils. "Who's your favorite?"

"Animal."

"But he's crazy!"

"And Gonzo isn't?"

Joaquín laughed, a deep belly laugh that made the cashier look up from her magazine. "Ay, yay, yay." He leaned back in his chair, crossing his legs, watching me flip through the pages in my notebook. *"Bueno,"* he said. "What were we talking about before?"

"You were saying something about *Dirty Dancing* . . ."

"¡Ah! Sí." He propped his cigarette on the Budweiser ashtray. "Now when I watch that movie I don't know what I liked about it, but it made me believe, I don't know, it made me realize I could live from doing something I really like to do. In that moment, I told myself, 'I'm going to be a professional dancer.' And that's what happened."

"How did it happen?"

"I worked. I got up at six in the morning, went to school, took classical dance classes, contemporary, any kind of dance class I could find. I spent more money on classes than food. And then, *bueno,* I realized I couldn't grow anymore in Rosario—that's where I was born—and I came to Buenos Aires."

"How old were you?"

"Twenty-three." He took another puff on his cigarette, waiting for me to finish my notes before he went on. "That was ten years ago. I was working at the Ballet Folklórico Nacional, and one night we went to see the show *Tango × 2.* And I felt the same thing I felt when I watched *Dirty Dancing.* And I said to myself, 'I want to dance tango. I want to be a tango dancer.'" He stubbed out his cigarette in the center of the ashtray. "That's how it happened."

He paused, gazing up at the smoke stains on the ceiling. "I still don't know what I want to be," he said, "but for now I'm a tango dancer."

I stopped writing. "What do you mean, you still don't know what you want to be?"

"It's a feeling I have." He made an expansive gesture toward the candy bars. "There's something else. Something more."

"Hmm." I tapped my pen on my lip, looking down at my notes, wondering how I was ever going to make sense of my messy shorthand. "I think I know what you mean."

. . .

We agreed to meet for our first private tango lesson in a second-floor studio above the Tango Escuela Carlos Copello, where someone had nailed posters from tango festivals past over the peeling paint on the wood-paneled walls. I stared at the posters—Joaquín and his partner Sonya were in most of them, she in a red strapless minidress, glossy black hair down to her waist, he in a plum-colored suit, with shoes dyed to match.

"You ride the music, like you would ride a wild horse," said Joaquín, snapping to the beat of the tango on the boom box as he sauntered over to the window, pulled a metal thermos out of a leather shoulder bag, and poured hot water into a *mate* gourd with a silver rim. "You can listen to the same tango a hundred times, and dance it in a totally different way each time." He took the *bombilla* in his mouth and, as was the custom, sipped until he made a slurping sound, which was the cue to pass the *mate* to the next person. "That's why I say it's like riding a wild horse. Because you never know what's going to happen. You ride the music, and it takes you where you need to go. If you pay attention to the music, it tells you where you need to go."

He refilled the *mate* and handed it to me. I sipped the bitter liquid to the bottom—I had learned, from my co-workers at the satellite company, that refusing an offer of *mate* was akin to refusing an offer of friendship—and passed the gourd back to Joaquín. I had no idea what he was talking about, riding the music.

He set the *mate* on the windowsill. "Close your eyes." He took my hand, leading me to the middle of the room, and I tried to tune out the sounds of Avenida Corrientes—cars honking, mopeds buzzing, bus gears grinding—outside the thin walls. "Now," he said, "imagine you're at the airport, meeting someone you love after a long, long trip. Don't think about tango. Just hold me. *¡Eso es!* Now relax your arms a little. Give me your hand. No, don't lose the feeling. Remember, we're at the airport. *¡Sí!* That's it. Wait a second."

He reached out to press a button on the boom box. A slow tango I didn't recognize started to play.

"The tango has its own energy, its own current," he said. "Relax. Try to let yourself flow with the current."

We danced for a few minutes, not saying anything. There was something in his embrace, a containment I hadn't sensed with anyone I'd danced with so far—as if he were taking me in, telling me something terribly personal, but, at the same time, as intently as he was holding me, I still had room to move, to find my own way into the music. I tried to be pliant and light in his arms, to flow the way I imagined he wanted me to flow. But when the song ended, his eyes were frustrated.

"Are you afraid of falling?" he said.

"What?"

He let go of me, resting his hands on his hips. "Do you not trust me?"

"What?" I glanced down at a knot in one of the wooden slats on the floor. "No, that's not it."

He went to the window and picked up his *mate*.

I looked up. The image of Sonya doing the splits in her red dress in the poster from the Genoa Tango Festival caught my eye again. "No matter how many times you tell me to relax, I *can't* relax," I said. "I don't know what you're going to do. And if I don't know what you're going to do, I don't know what I'm going to do—"

"Ah." His face softened. He set the *mate* back on the windowsill.

"I don't want to make a mistake, you know?"

He walked up behind me, resting his hands on my shoulders. "Human beings are such amazing creatures."

"What do you mean?"

"We always end up doing exactly what it is we're trying to avoid."

My shoulders stiffened. "I don't understand."

"You know the story of Oedipus, how his father banished him from his house because he was so afraid of him?"

I nodded.

"Then Oedipus came back, fell in love with his mother, and ended up killing his father. *Exactly* what his father was afraid of," he said. "That's just what you're doing. Manifesting what you're most afraid of. What's so bad about not knowing where you're going?"

I felt like he had slapped me: trying so hard not to make a mistake was the greatest mistake, and I knew I wasn't just doing it on the dance floor. But how could I trust where he was going if I had no idea where that was?

"The language of the body never lies, especially in an embrace," said Joaquín, starting the music again. "You know what a person feels when she dances, no matter what words she uses."

4

It was as if I were awake in dream, or intruding on some glamorous underworld, as I descended the stairs to La Viruta, the tango club in the basement of the Armenian Cultural Association: it was four a.m., the lights were blue, the tourists were gone, and the floor belonged to dance teachers, old *milongueros,* well-known *tangueras,* and the truly obsessed.

Earlier that day, after another lesson—was it our third, or our fourth?—Joaquín, who was now officially my new tango teacher, had sent me a text message: "I'm going to La Viruta tonight. Are you coming?!" His timing was good—I'd been looking for an excuse to put off writing an article I had due, about an eighty-year-old wine-maker in Mendoza who still used a wood basket press to crush his grapes. I attempted a disco nap. I tried on outfit after outfit, flinging rejected skirts on the bed, half watching an episode of *No Reservations* on the Travel Channel—Anthony Bourdain was in Bangkok, asking a tuk tuk driver to take him somewhere good to eat—and thinking about what Joaquín had taught me, or was trying to teach me, that afternoon: *"Contención,"* he said, as we danced to a tango called "Poema." *"Contención* is when you give yourself to another person and accept what the other person is giving you at the same time."

Hours later, standing on my tiptoes, I tried to look nonchalant as I scanned the dance floor and the chairs that surrounded it, searching for Joaquín in the dim blue light. My stomach flipped when I spotted him, in the same pale gray suit he'd worn for his solo at Sunderland, dark hair slicked back, sitting at a table in the back of the room, near the bar. He put down his beer when he saw me, stood up partway, gave me a customary kiss on the cheek, pulled out the empty plastic chair next to his, handed me a bonbon in a red and yellow wrapper, and said, *"Hola, Layne! Permiso, pero . . . ,"* before he rose to meet a brunette in crisscrossed spaghetti straps on the other side of the dance floor.

I unwrapped the bonbon—waxy chocolate and powdery peanut butter that disintegrated as soon as it hit my tongue—not sure why he'd given it to me, and for the next two hours, I watched him dance with the most beautiful women at the *milonga,* wondering why he'd invited me. When he wasn't dancing, he was wandering around the room, shaking hands, kissing cheeks, making small talk with other *tangueros,* returning to our table for quick sips of beer and momentary puffs on his Marlboro.

"I can't stand to sit when it's so crowded," he said. "I feel trapped."

"Entiendo," I said. I understand. Did I? Joaquín strolled across the floor, where a woman with caramel skin in a violet cocktail dress was waiting for him.

I looked over at the *tangueras* at the table next to ours—a pretty brunette and a bottle blonde who might have been in their forties. They had been eyeing me since I'd arrived at the *milonga,* watching me as I watched Joaquín. I was relieved when they invited me to join them. They were killing a bottle of cheap champagne.

"Ay, me muero." Oh, I could die, said the brunette, who was wearing masses of silver bangles that jangled down her forearms whenever she clasped her hands, which was every time the DJ played a tango she liked.

"You know about the men who die on the dance floor?" said the blonde. "It happens a lot. All those cigarettes and whiskey."

"Do you think maybe they *want* to die on the dance floor?" I said.

"Of course they do!" said the brunette.

"¿Bailás?" Joaquín tapped me on the shoulder, surprising me from behind. The *tangueras* looked at each other and smiled.

I followed him to the edge of the floor. He slipped his arm around my back, above my waist, his fingers resting just behind my breast. The music had started, but he held still, and I felt the air shift as other couples danced around us while he searched for my breath, making sure his exhalations matched mine before he began to move, whispering the lyrics in my ear as we circled the floor.

. . .

"¿Te gustaría ir a casa conmigo?" Would you like to go home with me? said Joaquín, a few hours later, when the fluorescent lights came on and the DJ started playing *cumbias. "Así tenés más para escribir, y te vas a entender más de mi esencia."* This way you'll have more to write about, and you'll understand more about my essence. *"¿Tu esencia?"* I smiled, and we laughed, and I followed him up the stairs, out of the basement, into the gauzy light of daybreak, telling myself that going home with him was more inevitable than it was unwise.

We climbed into the taxi and he held my hand, greeting the driver, who was wearing a pink polo shirt, by his first name, Pablo.

"You know everyone," I said.

"It takes very little effort to know people," he answered.

The clouds were turning purple behind the jacaranda trees on Calle Armenia. The city felt languid, as if it were easing itself into the humid morning, as we drove. I could smell the smoke from Joaquín's Marlboros, from everyone's Marlboros, in my hair.

"Che, Pablo, stop here, would you?" Joaquín said. "I want to buy some *facturas."* He pointed to a bakery where the light shone golden behind the frosted windows. Pablo paused the taxi meter.

"Qué buen tipo." What a good guy, said Pablo, after Joaquín hopped out of the taxi, an unlit cigarette dangling from his lips. "And what about you?" Pablo turned around and glanced at the satin shoe bag on my lap. His large brown eyes, framed with short, straight lashes, looked younger than the rest of his face. "How's your tango?"

I traced my finger over a gash in the back of the passenger seat. "I think I'm in my tango adolescence."

Pablo smiled. "What do you mean?"

"For example, I can't say, 'I don't know anything' or 'I just started learning' to the guys at the *milonga* anymore . . . But I still make a lot of mistakes." I looked out the window. Joaquín was coming out of the bakery, carrying a paper-wrapped tray of pastries tied in twine.

"Bueno," said Pablo, "but don't forget, *linda"*—he faced forward again, taking hold of the gearshift—"sometimes you have to suffer for your tango."

Joaquín threw his cigarette in the gutter, opened the taxi door, and handed me the pastries. *"Vamos a casa,"* he said to Pablo. "I want you to meet Sofía," he said to me.

"Who is Sofía?"

"My dog."

I laughed.

"A casa entonces," said Pablo. Home then.

Sofía bounded down the stairs as soon as she heard the front door squeak open. *"¡Hola, mi amor!"* Joaquín stroked the bridge of her nose and scratched behind her ears. *"¡Hola, princesa!"*

The black Labrador wagged her tail, licked his fingers, and leaned her gleaming body against his legs as soon as we reached the top of the stairs. I held the packet of pastries above my head and offered her the top of my other hand, *"Hola, Sofía,"* I whispered. *"Hola."* She sniffed my palm for a second, tail still wagging, lifted her nose toward the pastries, and went back to licking Joaquín's fingers.

"She's beautiful," I said, running my fingers along her back. "How old is she?"

"She's three." He knelt down, letting her lick his face. *"Sí, mi amor, ya sé."* Yes, my love, I know. *"Bueno, Sofía, bueno. ¡Vamos!"*

They raced down the stairs like old playmates. I set my shoes and the pastries on a beanbag chair and walked around the living room, studying the photos on the sea-green walls. There was a woman who had to be Joaquín's mother, a checkered apron around her apple-shaped middle, small eyes and full lips, the same as his, frowning in black-and-white, and there was Joaquín, in rubber sandals, showing off a homemade fishing pole. His hair was curly, and he was missing two front teeth.

"I was cute when I was little," he said, wiping his feet at the top of the stairs, letting go of Sofía's collar. "I'm not so cute anymore." I laughed. Sofía shook herself and lay down beside the beanbag. "I'll make the *mate,"* Joaquín said, walking into the kitchen as if we ate breakfast together every day. "You can take the pastries to the *terraza."*

. . .

Before Sofía, when he wasn't dancing, Joaquín told me he liked to walk the streets of Buenos Aires at night. "I wanted Sofía because I wanted to see if I could care for someone," he said, passing me the *mate*. I brushed the *medialuna* crumbs off my fingertips before I took it.

"But I feel guilty leaving her alone, when I'm at the *milonga*," he continued, petting the paw Sofía laid in his lap. He wasn't eating. We were sitting at a wrought-iron table that took up most of his *terraza*, where the cement was veined with cracks. "I don't know how I would be if I had a family. It worries me."

"You can't know," I said, taking short sips of *mate*, feeling the heat of the metal straw on my lips more than I was tasting the bittersweet liquid. "Isn't that like telling me you know how you're going to dance the next tango?"

He lowered his head, still rubbing Sofía's paw. The neighbor's flowered bedsheets fluttered on a clothesline a few feet away.

"Sos tan delicada," he said. *"Tan culta, tan femenina."* He looked up at me. *"Me encanta."*

I blushed. I felt like a slice of meatloaf next to the dazzling women he had danced with at the *milonga. Delicada? Culta? Femenina?* As soon as he said them, I knew I would carry the words with me for days, weeks maybe. I also knew that we, or this, whatever it was, would not, could not, last. But I couldn't let go of my desire to feel what might happen in the meantime.

A breeze blew the twine from the packet of pastries off the table. Sofía pounced on it and started chewing. Joaquín pressed his fingers on her jaw, forcing her mouth open. "Give me that, Sofía, it's not for you." The string fell from her tongue into his hand. "Come on," he said to both of us, "let's go inside."

"How did you learn to seduce with the tango?" I asked him. We were lying on our backs on the shag rug in the living room, with Sofía between us, listening to Brazilian boleros.

"Ah," said Joaquín, "I seduce when I dance tango? Ha, ha, ha. Ho, ho, ho." He rolled onto his side, propping his head on his elbow.

"When? When I'm dancing with you? Or when I'm dancing with someone else?"

"In general."

"I don't know. I didn't know I seduced, I mean my intention isn't to seduce."

"It's not?"

"No." He worked his hand under Sofía's collar, rubbing her neck. "I know it's a seductive dance. But in general what I try to do when I dance is open myself up to the other person. I guess that's seductive."

"Well, yes."

He lay down on his back again, folding his hands over his chest. "When a person shows himself exactly as he is," he said, "when someone is transparent, I guess it's something you don't see very often these days, and that's why it's seductive. People don't know who they are. They're always trying to show other people what they think they want to see. So when someone can be open—I don't know. I think more than seduction, it's a connection I'm able to make. Now, yes"—he cleared his throat—"I know sometimes there are things a person can do when they dance, to seduce another person—"

"Which are?"

Sofía rolled over, paws in the air.

"Which are intentions, breaths, embraces, pauses, tension in your arms—but I don't try to seduce the girl. No, no, no! I try to connect with her through the embrace. If I like a girl, I'll dance differently, but I won't dance differently so she'll like it."

"OK," I said, petting Sofía's belly, "but—"

"When you try to get something from the other person, *that's* seduction. I don't want to get something from the other person. What I do is open myself up to what I feel, or to what the other person is making me feel. *Es eso.*" That's it.

"*¿Nada más?*" Nothing else?

"*Nada más.*"

Sofía raised her head. Joaquín trailed his fingers along her jaw until she yawned.

"But you know what?" he said. "I'm not interested in friendships with women."

"Oh?"

"Women always want to be friends with me," he said. "Then within a month or two they fall in love with me. It happens every time. I'm totally sick of it."

"So," I said, "I am one of many."

"Yes."

I laughed. In that moment, his honesty only made him more attractive. I reached over Sofía, took his hand, started massaging it. "Relax your fingers." He closed his eyes. "I learned this in Thailand. Did you know there are a hundred sixty-four strokes in Thai massage? I forgot most of them."

Joaquín kept his eyes closed. When I let go of his hand, he watched Sofía lick my fingers.

"Don't worry, Sofía," he said, "you'll always be the queen of the house." She wagged her tail. He patted her stomach. "She accepts you into our tribe," he said. "I'm the alpha male, and she's the alpha female, but she's letting you in. Her licking you is accepting you." He kissed me, tasting more like *mate* than Marlboros. "I like you."

"I like you, too," I said.

When I left his apartment, he was sleeping, facedown on the dirty sheets. I kissed him in the middle of his back, taking a mental photograph: cinnamon skin, long hair strewn over his face, his body spanning the length of his twin bed in the sunlight peeking through the torn window shade.

5

"You look tired," said Liliana, flicking her wavy blond hair over her shoulder as she helped herself to a slice of pizza. We were meeting at least once a week now, Liliana and I, if not at a tango concert, then at Guerrín, a seventy-five-year-old pizzeria on Avenida Corrientes where the mozzarella dripped off the spongy crust like honey.

"I feel like a vampire," I said, staring at the drops of grease in the pool of cheese on our *muzzarella chica*. These days I was struggling to keep my eyes open at the office, where I felt like a charlatan to begin with: I was working as a project manager, responsible for coordinating satellite installations on three continents, though I had no understanding of the engineering behind the operations I was orchestrating, even as I assured clients in Geneva that we were resolving power outages in the Philippines, or begged our logistics manager to rush a satellite dish to Kampala. Life, real life, began after midnight, when I would meet Joaquín at the *milonga*. We would stay until four, five, six in the morning, and I would take a taxi back to my apartment as the sun was coming up. I had never taken, nor had I ever seen, so many taxis in my life. Liliana told me there were thirty-eight thousand of them in Buenos Aires—three times the number in New York, I learned later—and relatively few *porteños* rode in them regularly, except for the ones who danced tango, since the *subte* stopped running at eleven p.m., late-night buses were hard to predict, and the best *milongas* didn't peak until after two in the morning.

"He's turning you into a *perra milonguera*," said Liliana.

"A *milonga* bitch?"

"That's what Mariano calls me." Mariano was her beau. "When

we talk about *perras milongueras,* we're talking about really sexy, really sensual women who go out dancing all night long."

"You think so?" I smiled.

"Mmm hmm." She nodded, pushing a slice of pizza onto my plate. "But remember, *nena*"—her eyes were concerned, as they had been, weeks ago, when I'd told her about Joaquín—"if you go out with a man who goes to the *milonga,* he'll still want to be with other women. This is the rule. Not the exception. Now"—she pointed at the pizza—"eat."

I met Joaquín at La Viruta later that night. It was after two a.m., and Lalo, the *milonga* organizer, was celebrating his birthday, cutting a sheet cake and passing out pieces of it on Styrofoam plates to everyone in the room.

When the DJ played "Poema," I looked for Joaquín. He was standing at the bar, engrossed in a conversation with a green-eyed girl in an emerald dress, and as he led her onto the floor, his hand on her bare back, bowing his head to whisper in her ear, I sensed his fascination with her—in his eyes, even in the half-light, I thought I could see adulation, even a willingness to submit—and just then, sitting at the table with a giant piece of Lalo's meringue-frosted dulce de leche birthday cake, which was so sweet it made my molars throb, I realized, though I knew that I was one of many, that he lived his life in song sets, that he was addicted to the night and the *milonga* and the theater that went with it, that I was not prepared for this moment, not yet.

"The tango makes me feel free," I remembered him saying, during our faux interview. How long ago was that? I had no sense of time anymore. "The tango, the *milonga,* the embrace: to feel another person's body that isn't a friend, a relative, someone you love—not your mother, not your father, not your girlfriend—a stranger's body, a complete stranger. To suddenly feel that body, those tiny bones, the way her chest molds to yours—it's instant communion. It makes you feel like you can connect to the entire world. At least for three minutes."

The *tanda* ended, and Joaquín held on to the woman in the emerald dress until the next song set started. I'd never seen him dance more than one *tanda*—a set of three or four songs that lasted about twelve minutes—with the same woman, much less without a pause in between. In the language of tango, at least according to Liliana, two *tandas* in a row was code for "I'd like to take you home."

I jabbed the plastic fork into the remains of my cake and changed out of my tango shoes. Why was I getting so upset? Liliana had warned me, and Joaquín had always told me the truth: "Sometimes I'm really attracted to a girl, so I dance with her. Sometimes I dance with an old lady, who isn't attractive, who's fat, but I love the way she moves. I look for sensations. All of them. Laughing, having fun, vibrating—emotionally, I mean. I never stop searching for sensations . . ." *Neither do I,* I thought as I watched him dance (and dance and dance) with the woman in the emerald dress, feeling as though something were slicing me in half.

In the taxi, on the way home, the driver, whose black hair was just beginning to go gray, tried to fix me up with his son.

"Don't get mixed up with those guys at the *milonga,*" he said, eyeing the satin shoe bag in my lap. "Believe me, they'll eat you alive."

I hadn't told him anything, but I guessed he had seen his share of red-eyed, puffy-faced women leave the *milonga* alone. "You're not a dancer, are you?" I shook my head. "You're a writer? *¡Ay, qué linda!* Have you read Manuel Puig? *The Kiss of the Spider Woman*?" I shook my head again. "*That's* a book you have to read. What about Cortázar?"

"Not yet," I said. "I've been meaning to, but—"

"*Rayuela,*" he said. "You have to read *Rayuela.* Everyone is always talking about Borges. Borges, Borges, Borges. He never even won the Nobel. But *Rayuela,* for me, is the best novel of the twentieth century. Cortázar is a *maestro.* Very experimental, but good."

I pushed my tango shoes off my lap, took out my notebook, and wrote down *Rayuela.*

"It's difficult for a man who wants to be with a writer, isn't it?" he said.

I nodded, absentmindedly. Joaquín had probably noticed that I'd left La Viruta by now. Or maybe not. The taxista made a slow turn onto Avenida Santa Fe. It was four a.m., but the flower kiosks were still open, with carnations and lilies and blue roses for sale.

When we stopped in front of my building, he said, "You're too smart for my son, but you're going to have a good life. What's your name? Tell me. Someday I'll be able to say I gave you a ride."

I stayed awake that night watching old episodes of *No Reservations* on YouTube, trying to forget the *milonga* and imagine I was on the road with Anthony Bourdain. How I envied the traveling chef: swooning over suckling pig in Puerto Rico, scorching his lips on fish head curry in Malaysia, picking capers on Pantelleria, and expounding on every dish with the flying eloquence of Hunter S. Thompson. *He's living the dream,* I thought, as the first streaks of morning light filtered through the blinds. *And what are you doing?*

6

I could hear the music coming from the ballroom on the second floor when I walked into La Confitería Ideal. The lament grew louder and louder as I climbed the marble staircase, which wrapped around the wrought-iron cage of an elevator that was out of order.

When I reached the top of the stairs, I spotted Liliana and her big blond hair. Her black silk blouse slipped off her shoulder as she waved me over to her table, next to a rose-colored marble column, just a step from the dance floor. It was a little after two p.m. The Saturday-afternoon *milonga* had barely started. I held my breath—the smell of incense and cat pee was stronger than ever, one muskiness overlapping the other in a tango parlor that seemed to embody the lost decadence of the city itself.

"La Ideal," as Liliana and other regulars called it, contained all the grandeur of Buenos Aires's Belle Epoque: crystal chandeliers from France, stained glass from Italy, hand-carved oak paneling from Slovenia. But its fortunes had declined along with Argentina's—a few months after I went there for the first time, a chandelier fell from the ceiling, in the middle of a tango class, onto the head of a seventy-six-year-old man. (He survived his severe cuts, and La Ideal closed, temporarily, for slapdash repairs.) But despite its dangers, its awful perfume, and the iffy quality of the dancing—tourists who had never tangoed before liked to come here, too—I loved the bygone beauty of this place. So did Liliana.

"*¿Cómo te va, nena?*" she said, leaning across the table to kiss me on the cheek. "You look terrible."

"I know." I ran my fingers under my eyes, as if I could erase the circles that had been there for days, resisting the urge to look at myself in the distorted mirrors on the wall. Things had started to unravel with Joaquín after I left him at La Viruta. I didn't hear from him until three days later. And then I didn't hear from him at all.

"I can't stay long," I said. I shouldn't have been here in the first place. I had been disastrously unproductive at the satellite company that week—"*¿Qué te pasa?*" my usually forgiving boss said. What's wrong with you? *"Nada,"* I told him. Nothing. I promised to finish a rollout report for all our African and Asian sites by Monday.

Liliana rested one of her French-manicured hands on my wrist. "When was the last time you heard from him?"

"A week ago," I said. "He was supposed to call so we could go dancing." I bit the inside of my cheek. "But then nothing." I hated the idea that Joaquín and I had only gone far enough for things to fizzle, that we hadn't even cared enough to argue before the end.

Liliana was surveying the tables on the other side of the floor. "You have to keep dancing, you know." A man in a tweed jacket was staring at her, nodding, eager to dance, but she avoided his eyes, and turned to me. "You cannot let him take your tango away from you."

I looked over at the table next to ours. A man in a tan blazer was pulling a pair of dancing shoes out of a plastic grocery bag. "I don't know where he stops and tango starts," I said. "Tango . . . Buenos Aires . . . Joaquín . . ." I counted the words on my fingers, and folded my hand into a fist.

"*¡Mozo!*" said Liliana. I blinked back tears. A waiter in a polyester vest rushed over to our table. "Two glasses of *champán,* please," said Liliana. "And two *empanadas de carne.*" The waiter bowed his head and beelined it to the bar, ignoring the raised hands in his path.

"First of all," Liliana said, taking my hand in both of hers, "you have to understand that this is a rite of passage. Everyone who gets serious about tango has some kind of affair, sooner or later."

"I know." The *tanda* ended, and the dancers dispersed, stepping off the floor, finding their seats again. I glanced down at the tablecloth, noticing a cigarette burn in the linen. "But it just wasn't enough time."

Liliana sighed, letting go of my hand. A new song, a tango waltz, was just starting, and Mariano, her beau, was walking toward our table, smiling at her. They'd been dating almost four years, she and Mariano—an exceptional feat for a nonprofessional tango couple.

Mariano was wiry and compact, shorter than she was, and slightly bowlegged—in his body, Liliana liked to say, were traces of the knife-fighting *compadritos* (tough guys) who ruled the street corners on the outskirts of Buenos Aires, where tango was born, at the turn of the twentieth century. But Mariano looked nothing like a *compadrito* when he danced: there was refinement in his gait, a kind of majesty in his posture, and he was always mindful of where he was on the floor, never bumping into other couples, no matter how fast he was moving or how crowded the *milonga* happened to be.

"*¿Bailás?*" said Mariano, who was smiling at me now.

I looked at Liliana.

"Dance with Mariano."

"But—"

"*Vamos,*" said Mariano.

"Go," said Liliana.

My legs wobbled as I followed Mariano to the corner of the floor. I had never danced with him before. He was well-known in the tango clubs, one of the more respected social dancers in the city. If I danced well with him, I would be getting invitations to tango for the rest of the afternoon. If I screwed up, I would be sitting.

Mariano started dancing double-time to the waltz, turning faster and faster as the song went on. I did my best to keep up with him, but I was forgetting to spot my turns, getting dizzier and dizzier as the tango progressed, and before long, I stepped on the wrong side of my long, spindly heel, and it collapsed under me, and I started to fall. *Oh, no. No, no, no . . .* I let go of Mariano when I realized I couldn't right myself. He jumped backward, his face contracting in horror, trying to dodge the pencil-thin heels on my tango shoes as they stabbed the air. Down, down, down I went, landing right on my derriere, too shocked to feel any pain. *Please let this be a dream,* I thought, as an old couple sashayed around me, in a perfect waltzing 1–2–3. Somewhere among the tables next to the dance floor, I heard a woman giggle. Mariano yanked me to my feet.

"I'm so sorry," I said, my face aflame, a bruise beginning to form on my backside.

"Don't worry," he said, avoiding my eyes. "Maybe you need a rest." He led me back to the table next to the rose-colored column, holding my triceps with his fingertips, like a dirty rag. Liliana was gone, on the other side of the dance floor, absorbed in a beautiful tango waltz with a beautiful dancer half her age, but the *champán* was on the table, and so were the empanadas, exhaling microwave steam and a faint cumin smell. I wanted them. But I didn't want anyone at La Ideal to remember my face.

Mariano excused himself and headed for the bathroom. I changed out of my tango shoes—the bronze paint on the right heel was chipped now, exposing the black lacquer underneath. I tried to catch Liliana's eye, but she was still dancing, and she didn't see me. I would call her later.

I hurried away from La Ideal, searching for a taxi. A fall rainstorm was wreaking havoc on the streets of Buenos Aires, and an out-of-season *sudestada,* the strong, icy wind that carried the cold northward from Antarctica, was adding to the usual traffic chaos on Avenida 9 de Julio. A blast of wind rushed over the sidewalk, dismembering the spokes in my two-peso umbrella, turning it inside out. *Really?* I wanted to shake my fist at the sky. *You're doing this* now? My stomach let out a growl that was almost a roar, reminding me of the empanadas I had just left behind. For the first time in weeks, I was starving.

I stuffed the umbrella in a trash can, waving at taxi after taxi. They drove on, ignoring me, their LIBRE lights off, as the water rose to their hubcaps.

I had never had trouble finding a taxi in Buenos Aires. On any given day, at any given moment, on practically any street, I barely had to raise my arm, and a cab would stop for me. Not today. Today, the *sudestada* had caught the city by surprise, and there wasn't a free taxi in sight. Meanwhile, the pangs in my gut were getting sharper, and my blood sugar was sinking into the danger zone of dizziness and trembling hands and irrational thoughts. I scanned the snack bars on the *avenida*—no *milanesa,* no *sandwich de miga,* no *medialuna* looked the least bit appetizing, and I did not want to eat for the sake of refueling. I had been doing this for weeks now, eating but not tasting—microwaved empanadas, sad pizza, leftover pastries—with Joaquín. He ate to function, for purely physiological reasons. I ate for joy, whenever possible, to nourish what I considered to be a spiritual need. But being with him was not, had not been, about food.

I hurried past the Hotel Panamericano, and its famous and famously expensive restaurant, Tomo I, ignoring the menu posted outside the brass door. I was in no mood to be tempted by Patagonian lamb I couldn't afford. Why, oh, why, had I let myself get so swept up in tango? I hugged my stomach, remembering Joaquín's prophecy from our first lesson, about always ending up in the place we fear most. Yes, indeed: I had forced myself to go to the *milonga*—trying to elude despair—and had only compounded my misery.

Now the bruise was smarting on my backside, and I was getting soaked to the skin. A taxi stopped at a signal a few blocks away. Its LIBRE light was on, its red glow radiating in the gray afternoon. *See me,* I thought, raising my hand, wiping the raindrops off my forehead. *See me.* He was too far away to see me. I stood on my tiptoes, waving my arm. The taxista's headlights flickered. The signal turned green.

I felt a manic flash of joy when I realized he was fighting through four lanes of traffic to pick me up.

And somewhere in that manic flash of joy, watching the taxista maneuver his way toward me in his bumblebee-colored Fiat, I had an idea, an idea that had been percolating in the back of my mind for a while, an idea I hadn't been brave enough to enact until now. It was a crazy idea, driven by hunger, and the feeling that I had nothing left to lose.

I dug around in my purse for my faux wedding ring, a paper-thin gold band that had belonged to my grandma, which I wore from time to time to ward off men. My hand shook as I slipped it on. The taxi stopped. I opened the door, tossed my tango shoes in the back seat, and climbed in. *"Buenas tardes,"* I said, wishing I had thought to wring out my hair as the water trickled down my back, onto the seat.

The taxista turned around. His brown eyes were almond-shaped, rimmed with faint wrinkles, flecked with gold. *"Buenas tardes."* He smiled, open-mouthed, as if he were on the verge of laughter. "Where do you want to go?"

I twisted Grandma's ring with my thumb. "I have sort of a weird request." I was trying to prepare him for my question. I was trying to prepare myself, too.

"Yes?"

I looked at the clock on the dashboard: it was after three o'clock already—lunch was almost over.

"Señorita," said the taxista, still smiling, "where would you like to go?"

I leaned forward, between the front seats, shifting my weight to the unbruised side of my butt, and said, "Could you take me to your favorite restaurant?"

The taxista braked in the middle of the *avenida*. Cars honked and swerved around us, but he didn't seem to care. He switched off the CB radio and turned to stare at me, his eyes confused.

"I'm hungry," I said, talking fast, "and I don't have a lot of money, and I was hoping you might know a good place that's not too far away."

"Eh?" He knit his eyebrows, deepening the crease in the center of his forehead. He hadn't turned on the taxi meter yet.

"Maybe a place you would go with your family?" I said. "For example."

"What kind of food are you looking for?" He took his foot off the brake.

"Nothing fancy." I pressed my palms against the hollow in my stomach. "You know, typical stuff, empanadas, steak . . ."

"Steak?" He smiled. "What about Siga la Vaca?"

"Siga la Vaca?" I had heard the name somewhere. "Don't a lot of tourists go there?"

He steered to the right, coasting next to the gutter, "You're right. Everyone knows that place. Let me think . . ." He still hadn't started the meter. "A good steak, a good steak . . ."

I started to wonder if this was such a good idea. How many times had Liliana warned me about the taxistas in Buenos Aires? "You look Argentine and you speak the language, but you still have an accent, and they're going to know you're not from here if you say more than two sentences. And once they pick up on that, they'll drive you in circles."

But the taxistas had never driven me in circles, as far as I knew. I thought about all the rides to and from the *milonga,* and all those early-morning trips from Joaquín's. How I would walk away surprised (at the taxista who told me there was no theory greater than practice) or wiser to my surroundings (after listening to the taxista explain the lyrics of "Cambalache," the tango that railed against the realities of Argentina's so-called Infamous Decade in the 1930s), or duly warned (after the ride with Pablo, who said, "You have to suffer for your tango"—how right he was!). The taxistas of Buenos Aires had well-formed opinions about everything from Maradona and God to love and potholes. Was it so far-fetched to think they might know where to find something good to eat?

"Ah!" said the taxista. "There's a place, maybe fifteen blocks from here, I can't remember the name. But it's one of the best steak houses in the city, *segúndo me.*"

"Really?"

"You will like it," he said, turning on the taxi meter.

My stomach was grumbling loudly enough for him to hear. *"Bueno."* I smiled at him in the rearview mirror. *"Vamos."*

"Are you going to take me with you?"

I twisted my faux wedding ring, my face going warm. "Sure." What else could I say?

The taxista grinned at my reddening face. A few blocks later, his cell phone rang. I sat back and pretended I wasn't listening.

"Hola, mi amor. Can I call you back in five minutes? I'm busy right now . . ." He made a measured right turn. *"Sí, ya sé,* but I'm driving . . . *Bueno, ya sé.* Five minutes, OK? *Beso. Chau, mi amor. Chau, chau.*"

The rain was slackening, no longer coming down in apocalyptic surges. We crossed Avenida Córdoba, heading south. "I know it's around here somewhere," said the taxista, sitting up straighter on his beaded back rest. "Aha!" He pointed through the rain-speckled windshield to a crowded storefront behind a pair of sycamore trees. "There it is!"

I looked out the window. Men in suits were huddling under the dripping awning, smoking cigarettes. I couldn't tell if they were going in or coming out.

"It looks popular," I said.

"You see? I wouldn't lead you astray. Here, take my card," He reached into his back pocket and pulled out a strip of paper, creased at the corners, that read TAXI ENRIQUE.

"Here's my cell phone number. Call me if you need anything. I mean it! Good luck!"

I grabbed my tango shoes and hopped out of the cab. Oh, was I hungry, and, oh, did I like the look of the place: an unassuming glass and metal façade with a blue and white sign barely visible under the trees. I waved goodbye to Enrique, slipped his card in my purse, moved past the men in suits, and walked into Parrilla Peña.

The first thing I saw when I opened the door was the grill—a six-foot barbecue laden with slabs of beef, racks of ribs, whole chickens, blackening bell peppers, sausages, and sweetbreads. The smell of smoke and steak was everywhere. My mouth watered. My stomach rumbled. I wanted it all.

Heads turned as I pulled my soggy clothes away from my skin and searched the dining room for an empty seat. Men in dress shirts and dark sweaters were spreading blood sausage on white rolls and slicing into steaks that dwarfed their plates. Wine bottles rested in wall-mounted racks. Ham shanks hung from the ceiling. A waiter in a white chef's jacket approached me. "Do you mind sharing a table with those guys?" he said, pointing to a four-top where two men on the far side of fifty were sitting across from each other, gesticulating over plates piled high with rib bones.

"Not at all."

The men went silent, smoothing their sweaters over their bellies and looking me up and down, damp and disheveled as I was, while I scooted into a chair next to them. I left the menu on the table and asked them what they recommended. The ribs here were the best in Buenos Aires, they said. Grilled provolone was excellent, too.

The waiter in the chef's jacket came to take my order. "You're eating alone?"

I nodded.

"Let's see." He crossed his arms, fixing his eyes on something on the ceiling. "You could get half a tenderloin, a single rack of ribs, skirt steak . . ."

"Half a tenderloin," said the man in the V-neck sweater. "That's what you want."

"Half a tenderloin," I said. "And grilled provolone."

"That's too much for one person," said the waiter.

"Maybe I could take it home, if I can't finish it?"

"Sure, she can take it home," said the man in the V-neck sweater.

The waiter nodded once and retreated. My tablemates restarted their conversation—something about an apartment in Palermo one of them wanted to sell. I flipped through the menu. There was every cut of meat and every sort of offal imaginable, from T-bone and sirloin and crosscut ribs to *chorizo criollo* and chitlins and tripe. There were house-made pastas, plates of local cheese and roasted vegetables, salads, *milanesas* (breaded veal cutlets), empanadas. No dish cost more than forty pesos (thirteen to fourteen dollars).

I closed the menu when the waiter brought the provolone, smoke rising from the grill marks, olive oil shimmering on top. The two men watched me take my first bite. Cheese, barbecue smoke, and oregano commingled. I shut my eyes. I felt like I was satisfying a hunger I had had for a long, long time.

"You're eating the best *provoleta* in the city," said the man in the V-neck sweater. I nodded, agreeing with so much gusto one of my bobby pins fell out. He and his friend laughed and went back to talking real estate.

A few minutes later, the waiter brought a steak half the size of my head. I pushed the provolone to the side and sliced off a steaming piece of meat. I hadn't told him how I wanted it cooked. Apparently I hadn't had to: The *asadero* had grilled the beef to a rosy medium-rare. Its juices trickled to the edge of the plate. The only seasoning was a little salt, and that was all the steak needed. It almost made me forget that I had just bitten the dust on the dance floor at La Ideal.

My tablemates paid their bill, raising their eyebrows as they watched me work my way to the end of the steak. "Now that you're all taken care of, you don't mind if we leave, do you?"

"Of course not."

"Here, let me give you my number," said the man in the V-neck sweater. I pulled out my notebook. "Feel free to call me if you need anything," he said.

The waiter cleared and reset their places, and a bald man in a slate-colored suit walked into the dining room, glanced at my faux wedding ring, and squeezed into the chair next to mine. Just as I was about to ask for my check, the waiter brought him a plate of fried green pancakes.

"What are those?" I said.

"Spinach cakes," said the bald man. His brown eyes were almost black, and his smile was kind, if a little forlorn. I guessed he was in his late forties. "They only make them on Fridays. Want to try some?"

"Oh, no, that's OK."

"No, here, I insist." He cut off half a spinach cake and set it on the edge of my empty steak plate. I offered him some *provoleta*.

"If it weren't for this place, I'd be sick and starving," he told me. "I'm a bachelor, and I don't know how to cook, so I'm here every day."

The bachelor called the waiter over and asked him to explain the Argentine way of cutting steaks, complete with a diagram of a cow. He told me about his favorite dishes (skirt steak, kidneys, sweetbreads) and the daily specials (hamburgers on Thursday, fish on Fridays). He ordered tiramisu for us to share, explaining that Parrilla Peña's version was the best in Buenos Aires. "They use real mascarpone," he said. "*Not* Philadelphia!"

He pointed out the round-faced man behind the cash register while we waited for dessert.

"That's one of the owners. He's a really good guy. Unlike most Argentines, he's committed to good service and good quality at a good price. I consider him a real patriot. Most people in this country try to take you for all you've got, but not him."

"Is he always here?" I said.

"Every day."

The waiter brought our tiramisu. I waited for the bachelor to taste it before I took a spoonful. *"Maravilloso,"* I said, and it was—cocoa and coffee and ladyfingers coming together in a rich, carefully composed harmony.

The bachelor beamed. Then he asked for his check, stood up, buttoned his blazer, and handed me his card. He was a lawyer, he said, and his office was a few blocks away. "Please call me if you need anything at all. It was a genuine pleasure."

We exchanged a traditional right-cheek kiss, and he left, saying goodbye to the owner and the *asadero* on his way out. I ordered three empanadas to go. When I went to the counter to pay for them, the owner handed the bag to me.

"These are on the house." He smiled. "I hope we see you again."

"You will," I said, rubbing my belly as I walked out the door, onto Rodriguez Peña Street, carrying empanadas and tango shoes, unable to shake the feeling that I was in the middle of a very good dream. In this dream, I had not fallen on the dance floor at a legendary tango parlor, and I was not waiting for a phone call from a wandering *milonguero*. In this dream, a stranger delivered me to a steak I would never forget, and randomness was beautiful—far more beautiful than anything I could engineer.

I dug through my purse and pulled out Taxi Enrique's card, holding on to it like a lucky charm as I strolled through Barrio Norte, over cracks in the sidewalk and yellowing sycamore leaves, past dripping balconies and umbrella vendors, through the last of the rain.

7

"Sos una loca suelta." You're a crazy on the loose, said Liliana, when I told her about the ride with taxista Enrique, and the perfect steak at Parrilla Peña, as we sipped *cafés con leche* at Café la Paz and gazed out the window at the men selling lottery tickets and cigarette lighters and *garrapiñada* (cocoa-covered peanuts) on Avenida Corrientes. A man in a fleece coat walked by, nibbling an *alfajor* cookie in a lavender wrapper, checking us out through the glass in that brazen, proprietary way of men in Buenos Aires.

Liliana stood up, ignoring the man in the fleece coat, tossing the end of her tasseled scarf over her shoulder. She was in a hurry to get to the *milonga,* and she was not happy I wasn't joining her. Mariano had filled her in on the details of my fall at La Ideal, which she'd seen but hadn't believed. Neither my fall nor the implosion of things with Joaquín was a good enough reason, in her eyes, to stop dancing tango.

"I'm not going to stop," I told her. "I just need to pause for a bit." In the afterglow of the trip to Parrilla Peña, munching on the *empanadas de carne* the owner had given me, I felt as if I had tapped into something unusual, and serendipitous, as if the city were re-introducing itself, hinting at possibilities I hadn't been aware of. What if I hopped into a random cab every week and asked the taxista to take me to his favorite place to eat? I asked Liliana what she thought of the idea. She tore off the end of a *medialuna* and waved it in my face. "Remember what I told you! Taxistas are the biggest cheats in Buenos Aires—"

"What about Enrique? I don't know how long it would've taken me to find that *parrilla* on my own—"

Liliana was still waving the *medialuna* around. "They'll drive you in circles, or rob you, or rape you . . ." She shook her head, dropped the pastry, gathered her shoes and purse, and hurried out of the café, frizzy blond hair trailing her like a comet's tail. I watched her disappear into the crowd on Avenida Corrientes, not wanting to believe her.

I attempted a second taxi adventure a few days later, in spite of Liliana's objections but uneasy in light of them. By now I'd had time to imagine everything that could go wrong—the scenarios she described were not out of the question—and I was afraid. And when I hailed a taxi at Plaza Salguero and asked the driver, *por favor,* if he could take me to his favorite restaurant, he rolled his eyes and looked at me as if to say, "Some of us have to work for a living."

"I'm a taxi driver!" he said, raising his voice over the pizzicato chatter of the soccer commentators on the radio. "I eat every meal at home. If you give me an address, I'll take you wherever you want to go."

"No, *señor.*" I leaned forward, poking my face between the front seats, spotting the Boca Juniors flag hanging on the rearview mirror. Boca was the soccer equivalent of the New York Yankees in Argentina. They had lost badly in a game against their biggest rivals, River Plate, the day before, and Boca fans were now in deep, collective mourning. "I'd like to go to *your* favorite restaurant," I said to the taxista, "if you have one."

He sighed and pulled over, idling under the rosewood trees across from the high-class shops and the high-rise apartments bordering the plaza. "I don't have the faintest idea about restaurants around here."

He reached under the driver's seat and pulled out a binder, propping it on the steering wheel and flipping through pages sheathed in crinkled plastic until he found a list of places to eat. I looked over his shoulder at the restaurant cheat sheet. Every place on the list was in the foreigners' ghetto around Puerto Madero, where the only locals I had ever seen were businessmen feeding overpriced steak to visitors who sounded Texan.

"What do you want?" the taxista asked. "A nice restaurant?"

"No, nothing too nice—"

"Buffet? All-you-can-eat?"

"I don't think so—"

"Well, what then?"

I bit my lip. This wasn't working.

"You know what? I'm sorry for bothering you. Maybe I should look for someplace on my own? I—"

The taxista snapped the binder shut. "OK."

I climbed out of the cab and walked along Avenida Las Heras, doing my best to ignore the pastries at a French bakery that probably looked better than they tasted, trying to push away the thought that my plan was going to fail. The chemistry in the taxi was off somehow, and it wasn't just because the taxista was grieving over Boca Juniors.

Maybe this is a frivolous idea. I had read somewhere that there were taxistas in Buenos Aires who couldn't even afford a hot dog. Maybe Liliana was right. Maybe the ride with Enrique had been a fluke. Maybe so, but I was hungry. I ducked into the *subte*. Maybe I could find a taxi in a more down-to-earth barrio. I was looking for good food, but I was also looking for cheap food, or what I was coming to think of as democratic food: accessible to everyone, often, but not always, portable (like tacos and empanadas), delicious enough to draw people from all social strata, but not part of a chain. As far as I could tell, Plaza Salguero was no place for democratic food.

About twenty minutes later, I was standing on Avenida 9 de Julio, inhaling the midday fumes as buses wheezed past, and mopeds played chase with Fiats and Renaults. I started to raise my hand, listening to the rumble of the drums of the *piqueteros* on Diagonal Norte growing louder, and more insistent, when a taxi stopped in front of me. I could hear the techno music through the rolled-up windows. I opened the door and climbed in, feeling the bass vibrating through my sandals, and glanced at the taxista in profile. His eyelashes were so long that they brushed against the lenses of his sunglasses. I looked at him in the rearview mirror: Roman nose, flaring cheekbones, dimpled chin. He may have been the most beautiful man I had seen in a city full of beautiful men.

He turned down the techno and smiled—there was a thin gap

between his front teeth, and even this was flattering, in the manner of a model's signature quirk—and asked me where I wanted to go. I willed myself to stop turning red. The last thing I wanted was an *aventura* with another Argentine.

"If you had to leave Buenos Aires tomorrow," I said, fumbling around in my purse for my notebook as he pulled away from the curb, "where would you eat today?"

He grinned at me in the rearview mirror. "Are you going to invite me to eat with you?"

"What?"

"Are you going to invite me to lunch?"

I was blushing in earnest now. "Sure . . . We could eat lunch . . ."

"No kisses?" He was still grinning, and barely accelerating, letting the taxi fall behind the flow of traffic on the *avenida*. A bus veered around us, belching a dark cloud of diesel.

"No kisses."

"Not even a kiss on the cheek?"

"Mira," I said, thinking there were few things in this world more dangerous than a man who was well aware of how good-looking he was, except maybe an Argentine man who was well aware of how good-looking he was. "This is how it's going to be. You take me to your favorite restaurant. We have lunch. I take the bus home. You drive away in your taxi. And that's it."

"So it has to be on your terms?"

"Yep."

"Then I don't accept."

I laughed, surprised and flattered and confused by the idea that the taxista with the perfect face wanted me, even as I reminded myself that flirtation was a fact of life in Buenos Aires. If I wanted to keep from repeating my mistake with Joaquín, I had to start handling seduction the way Liliana dealt with sweet talk from her tango partners at the *milonga:* "Lie to me," she would say. "I like it."

We were on Avenida Córdoba now. My stomach was making sounds of protest. The taxista paid no mind to the red lights, honking his horn to announce our presence as we cruised through the intersections.

"*¿Sabes qué?*" he said. "One time I picked up this redhead, near the casino. She was about forty. *Belleza.* We got to talking, so I invited her for coffee. We ended up at my house, in the shower, didn't come out until dinner the next day. I took her to La Taberna de Roberto—"

"Oh, yeah!" I said. "I know that place. The food is good!"

But he didn't want to talk about food: He turned off the radio and began to tell me all about his other conquests as we drove. He had met most of his girlfriends, and other men's girlfriends, in his cab. The saltier his stories got, the hungrier I became, and as the minutes passed, and my stomach continued to growl, I wished he would try to seduce me some other way. *Lie to me,* I thought. *I need it.*

We crossed Avenida Rivadavia—the street, according to Borges, that divided Buenos Aires into north and south—still undecided on a destination. The asphalt ended and the cab bounced over the cobblestones. The vertigo I felt now resembled the vertigo I felt at the beginning of a tango: I didn't know where I was going, or how I was getting there, and I was leaving it all up to a stranger.

"Have you ever had a one-night stand?" said the taxista.

"I'm not going to tell you that."

"Oh, come on! That's not fair."

"I'm guessing you've had a few?"

"Of course."

"So your taxi is literally *tu vehículo al amor.*" Your vehicle to love.

"Love?" he frowned. "No, no, no. Passion, maybe. But not love."

We were in Boedo now, on the south side of Buenos Aires, where the city felt older, where stone buildings from the turn of the twentieth century had been left to languish in their own rubble. It was siesta time. Metal blinds were down, curtains closed. *Where are we going?* My hands started to shake—I was well into the desperation phase of hunger—and I thought about Joaquín: *If you pay attention to the music, it tells you where you need to go—*

"Do you like pizza?" asked the taxista.

"Yes, I love pizza. Yes."

At last he stopped, on the corner of Avenida Boedo and Juan de Garay. Next door to a wholesale leather store, on the bottom floor of a modern, whitewashed, three-story apartment building, was a pizzeria called San Antonio. The street-facing windows were trimmed in the light blue of the Argentine flag. On the glass doors were stencils of a halo-topped, pot-bellied, pizza-bearing saint who reminded me of Friar Tuck.

"Are you sure you don't want me to come with you?" the taxista said.

I wasn't sure.

"At least let me kiss you." He took off his sunglasses. His eyes were hazel, a lighter shade than Joaquín's. "By the way, I'm Hernán."

And if I did kiss him? I could already hear him describing me to his next conquest. ("One time I picked up this crazy gringa. You wouldn't believe the way she ate . . . !") Plus, I would have to wait who knows how long before I could taste San Antonio's pizza, and I really couldn't wait any longer. My hunger had reached that terrible point when I felt close to crying, or fainting, or both.

"You don't want to kiss me," I told Hernán. "I'm too much trouble for you." I handed him ten pesos and climbed out of the taxi.

"Wait!" he called. "What about your phone number?"

I shook my head, staring at him as he leaned out the passenger-side window, doing my best to memorize the sculpture of his face before I turned around and walked into the pizzeria, where the air smelled like roasting onions and rising dough.

I slid into the only free seat—it looked like the whole barrio was here, and I was the only person eating alone. I studied the crooked white letters on the black menu board above the bar, where two men stood eating, bald spots gleaming under the fluorescent lights.

A waiter in a thin white dress shirt was sharing a joke with the retirees drinking beer at the table next to mine. He glanced at me, reading the hunger on my face, took my order, not writing it down, and came back a few minutes later with a piece of *fugazzetta*—a mass of melted mozzarella and a pile of sliced onions on an inch-thick crust—and a slice of *fainá*. Individually, neither was anything special. But together, the *fugazzetta* (a Buenos Aires staple invented in the late nineteenth century, when local pizza makers added heaps of mozzarella to the focaccia their Genovese ancestors had brought across the Atlantic) and *fainá* (garbanzo bean flour and olive oil baked into a dense slice) made an ideal starch-on-starch combination. Chickpeas checked the richness of the cheese. Onions, oven-roasted and paper-thin, added a sharp, oregano-laced sweetness.

I watched the neighborhood come and go as I ate. The retirees nursed their beers, studied the soccer scores in *Clarín,* and pretended not to notice me. Young couples fed toddlers who couldn't sit still. Teenagers in Catholic school uniforms schlepped stacks of twine-bound boxes of pizza to go. A *pizzaiolo* in a paper hat pulled a cast-iron sheet pan from the oven, dropped it on the tile countertop with a *thwack,* and sliced a fresh batch of *fugazzetta* into squares. I noticed a plaque between a pair of thirsty philodendrons that said the pizzeria had been operating for more than sixty years.

I was almost finished eating when the waiter in the white dress shirt came over to check on me.

"And? How do you like your *fugazzetta?*"

"It's perfect." I said, smiling at him, and at the mound of mozzarella and the tangle of onions on my plate, glad I had a few bites left.

8

"¿De qué te reís?" What are you laughing at? asked the man with the brass-handled cane who passed me on the street as I walked away from Pizzeria San Antonio, scribbling in my notebook, heading in what I believed was the general direction of Avenida Santa Fe. *"De tantas cosas,"* I wanted to answer him. At so many things: Hernán; the waiter in the thin white dress shirt who'd stood next to my table, making sure I finished my *fugazzetta;* the ice-cream poster at the *kiosco* on the corner that bordered on soft porn. But more than anything I was laughing because I was overjoyed—there was no other word—to have my appetite back.

I had created a blog, and named it *Taxi Gourmet,* where I had started to document the taxi adventures—for myself, for my family and my friends. I wanted to pay homage to the particular magic of Buenos Aires. *What other city could have given birth to the taxi adventures?* I thought, looking back at the man with the brass-handled cane, who was smiling at me as though trying to decide whether I was loony or whether I might be onto something. To write about the taxistas and their food was to remind myself why I was here. The blog gave my writing a structure it hadn't had before: even if my audience was small, and virtual, it was still an audience, and I imagined they expected at least one story a week.

I wrote about the trip to Parrilla Peña with taxista Enrique, about Hernán and San Antonio, growing a little more confident after each adventure: There was the ride to Barrio Norte with a taxista named Abel, who drove with a postcard of the Virgin of Luján pasted to his windshield, who dropped me off at a pasta parlor called Pippo and (wisely) suggested I order vermicelli with olive oil and marinara sauce. There was the trip to Las Cañitas with Juan Pablo, the red-haired taxista who led me to Panadería Santa Teresita, where Abuela Beatríz made *struffoli* (honey-covered fritters flavored with anise) by hand. And I would never forget the drive to Montserrat with a lingerie salesman turned taxista who delivered me to a gas station café where a woman named Marta was serving breaded hake fish and mashed sweet potatoes that practically lulled me into a state of grace.

Before long, people I didn't know began to comment on my posts. And after I published the story of the taxista who dropped me off at a steak house called Chiquilín—named for a tango called "Chiquilín de Bachín," about a homeless boy who sold flowers in the theater district—I got an email from a musician named Hugo, a *bandoneón* student in Vermont who referred to himself as a "displaced Argentinean": I really enjoyed your wonderful article about "Chiquilín de Bachín," he wrote, and I am also very grateful to notice your compassionate perception of life in Buenos Aires. He was grateful, too, he said, that he could share my post with his musician friends. Now I can offer them the perspective of a "gringa" *(lo digo con cariño!)* that can speak more directly to them . . .

I read and reread Hugo's message, moved, and a little incredulous, that an Argentine—and a tango musician at that—liked what I was doing. I felt like I had found a groove, a purpose, an inspiration for my food quests, knowing I was going to publish something about them in cyberspace, imagining strangers were reading what I was writing.

But fortune favors the bold, and the idealistic, for only so long: A few days after Hugo's message arrived, I got into a cab with a taxista who had no enthusiasm for my quest. "Just give me an address," he shouted over the reggaeton music that rattled the windows of his newish-looking Fiat. "I'll take you wherever you want!"

QUIERO SACU-DIR-TE CO-MO TERREMO-TO . . .

I want to shake you like an earthquake?

"Actually," I said, trying to keep a straight face, "I'd like to go someplace *you* like to eat."

"Bueno." The taxista started the meter, looking more indifferent

than stumped, and turned up the music louder still, answering my questions in monosyllables as we plunged into the potholes on Avenida San Martín and rushed toward the jaywalkers on Avenida Nazca, sending them sprinting to opposite sides of the sidewalk. After a while, after I began to suspect we were driving in circles—*didn't we pass that Korean restaurant already?*—the taxista stopped on Plaza Flores, in front of a cafeteria that spanned half a city block.

I peered into the restaurant. A thin-haired man in a flannel shirt was sitting alone, bent over his plate, next to the smudged windows facing the plaza.

"This is your favorite place to eat?" I hollered over the music, which was sounding more and more like an invitation to a sado-masochistic sex party *("Pantera ATRAPAME . . . Acorralame y luego matame"; "Trap me, pantheress . . . Corral me and then kill me")*. On the way to the restaurant, all I could think about was escaping the cab. Now that we were here, at Pueyrredón Restaurante, I didn't want to get out, in spite of the music.

"I was here last week," said the taxista. He turned up the stereo one more time. The windows banged against their frames, threatening to shatter.

I opened the Fiat door, light as cardboard, stepped over a pile of plastic bottles in the gutter, reached through the passenger-side window, and handed him twenty pesos, about double what I had been paying for cab fare on my taxi adventures until now. "What is it you like to eat at this place?" I asked him. "Do you have a favorite dish?"

"It's buffet," said the taxista. *"Tenedor libre."*

The waiter at Pueyrredón Restaurante was a tall man with copper skin who moved with exaggerated efficiency. "You know how it works here?" he said, handing me a menu that looked more like a notebook, spiral-bound with lots of laminated pages.

"No."

"It's all you can eat," he said, in a tone that suggested I should be grateful for my good fortune, "for thirty-three pesos. You tell me what you want, and I'll bring you as many dishes as you like. Plus you get a drink."

I flipped through the menu pages, ears ringing from reggaeton, looking for the lesser-evil candidate among ten cuts of steak, seven varieties of *milanesas,* ham rolls with eggs and olives, and pasta with four-cheese, béchamel, or pink sauce. In the end I chose *revuelto gramajo:* a greasy mishmash of French fries, julienned ham, formerly frozen peas, chopped tomato, and scrambled eggs that tasted better than I thought it would, though I could get through only half of it. The copper-skinned waiter reappeared as soon as I put down my fork, frowning at all the food I'd left on my plate.

"The portion was huge," I said, grabbing my spoon and pushing some stray French fries into the pile of leftovers, trying to make it appear smaller than it was. "I can't eat any more."

The waiter left the plate on the table, surveying the dining room, pausing on a group of older ladies in pastels who were in the middle of dessert. "You're not from the neighborhood, are you?" he said.

"No." I laughed.

"Where are you from, then? California?" He attempted a smile, which looked out of place on his gaunt face. "Ah, but California must be beautiful," he said. "You know, Argentina would be as well off as you if it weren't for the corruption." He stopped smiling. "I mean, look around. You throw a seed anywhere in this country, and it grows. But we need stricter laws. We should be like the United States—we need the death penalty, so people understand they can't break the law."

Before I could challenge his logic, he hurried over to the ladies in pastels, replacing a spoon one of them had dropped on the floor. He returned to my table with a dessert menu.

"Things were better when the military was in power," he said, positioning the menu in front of me as though it were a contract I was supposed to sign.

"*¿Cómo?*"

"Eighty percent of what the military did was good," he said. "If they hadn't laid down the law, we'd be like Colombia right now."

Maybe I wasn't understanding him correctly.

"Twenty percent of what they did during the dictatorship was bad," he went on. "And people don't want to forgive them for that twenty percent."

I kept quiet, sifting through my indignation, searching for a response. All my Argentine friends, including Joaquín, who was a toddler at the time, knew someone, or knew someone who knew someone, who had been "disappeared" during the Dirty War—from 1976 to 1983, when the military junta executed over thirty thousand suspected rebels—but no one would talk about it. I didn't have intimate knowledge of the dictatorship, but I had read sickening things—among others, about the *vuelos de la muerte,* on which dissidents were sedated, stripped naked, and pushed from helicopters into the Río de la Plata to drown.

"Stronger laws don't always change the way people behave," I said to the waiter. The *revuelto gramajo* was settling into an unpleasant mass in my stomach.

"Señorita," he said, shaking his head, "you have no idea what you're talking about." He snapped up the dessert menu—the ladies in pastels wanted more tea—and brought my bill a few minutes later, saying nothing, avoiding my eyes. I had heard there were people who longed to return to the illusory stability of the dictatorship, but I had never met anyone who expressed this longing. I walked out of the restaurant, sour and queasy after the terrible oddity of that meal, and the taxi ride that preceded it, and for days after the trip to Pueyrredón Restaurante, I plodded down Avenida Santa Fe, raising my hand, then lowering it before a taxi got too close to see me.

9

I didn't know how to write about the trip to Pueyrredón Restaurante. I wasn't sure if I should write about it at all. Until now, every taxi adventure had had at least one bright spot—if it wasn't the food, then it was the conversation with the taxista—but there was nothing redeeming about this particular adventure. If anything, it had a sinister tinge.

A week later, riding the *subte* to the offices of the satellite company, I still hadn't posted anything on my blog, nor had I attempted another taxi adventure. Weren't there easier, more sensible ways to find something good to eat? I hugged my purse and shut my eyes, wishing I could skip the morning conference call with an unhappy customer in South Africa who was threatening to downgrade his bandwidth.

I opened my eyes when a little girl in a lime-green dress set a packet of glitter-coated pencils in my lap, and on the lap of each person in the subway car. *"Dos pesos,"* she said, shifting the handles of a black plastic bag from one wrist to the other. *"A sólo dos pesos."* Two pesos was about sixty-five cents. Some people ignored the pencils, letting them sit on their laps untouched. Others turned the packets over in their hands, inspecting them as if they were pieces of jewelry. A few passed the pencils back to her, not looking at the little girl, whose eyes were fixed on the floor. I unzipped my purse. She was in front of me in an instant, spreading her plastic-shoed feet far apart so she wouldn't fall when the train slowed down. I looked in my wallet—the only cash I had was a fifty-peso bill. She wouldn't have change for that, I was sure. (Like a lot of people in the city, she had to do business in spite of the Great Buenos Aires Coin Shortage, which, according to Liliana, was brought into being by a change mafia that collected coins and small bills and sold them at the Retiro bus station for a fee. End result? No one liked to give out change, especially to gringas running around with big bills.) *"Lo siento,"* I said to the little girl, zipping up my purse. I'm sorry. She snatched the packet off my lap, collected the rest of the pencils, and slipped out the *subte*'s double doors as soon as they slid open.

By the end of the day, I hadn't been able to break my fifty-peso bill, and I decided I had to be frank—*just tell the story!*—with whoever was still reading my blog: I finally wrote about the journey with the reggaeton-loving taxista who'd driven me in circles, and the waiter at Pueyrredón Restaurante who was nostalgic for the dictatorship. No one made any comments.

"How much longer you gonna stay down there, kid?" said Dad, on the phone on Sunday.

"I don't know." I was beginning to wonder whether I belonged in Buenos Aires, or at least whether it made sense to stay much longer: The Dirección Nacional de Migraciones had denied my application for long-term residency. (There was no legal residency category for freelancers, much less freelance writers, in Argentina, and I was just a consultant at the satellite company, and didn't want to involve them in my immigration issues.) Liliana offered to adopt me, so I could stay—as moved by her offer as I was, I thought it was too much to ask. Instead, I had been hopping the border—to Uruguay, to Chile, to Brazil—every three months to renew my tourist visa, and I'd accumulated so many stamps in my passport I had to ask the embassy for extra pages. Now, when I looked up at the sky and noticed the planes taking off to the north, I caught myself wondering when I would be on one of them.

"How long have you been down there now?" said Mom.

"Two years." Going on three. What had I done in all that time? Learned to tango—passably, though I hadn't been to the *milonga* in months. Had a fling—was that the word for it?—with Joaquín, and only heard from him now via mass emails about his tango workshops, or his performances. Dated a guitarist from Patagonia who'd never eaten an orange in his life, and an Australian on the verge of becoming a writer who introduced me to the greatness of William Trevor and Richard Yates. Published a handful of food articles. Arranged satellite dish installations in countries I would probably never visit. Started a blog, and a series of taxi adventures, I wasn't sure I should continue. (After the ill-fated run to Pueyrredón Restaurante, I eventually persuaded myself to try another taxi adventure— and ended up at a *parrilla* across the street from the city's only casino, where the *chinchulines,* chitlins, tasted like rancid vegetable shortening mixed with cigarette ashes.)

"You want me to read you your horoscope?" said Mom.

"Sure." This was how we usually ended our weekly phone call.

"Now where did I put it?"

"I don't know, sweetie," said Dad.

"I know you don't know." I could picture her shuffling through the stack of newspaper clippings next to the phone in the kitchen. "I know I put it here . . . Here!" She started reading with a newscaster's inflection: "The lunar eclipse in your sign is putting you on the spot—"

"Eclipse?" I said.

"Can you see it from down there, kid?" said Dad.

"I don't think so." I peeked out the window. Between the apartment towers, the night sky was overcast.

Mom cleared her throat and started reading from the top: "The lunar eclipse in your sign is putting you on the spot. You are going through something intense and awkward. It has *some*thing to do with the realization that your life is starting to change. It's tempting to back away from this and just carry on as normal—"

"Uh-huh," I said.

"*In*wardly, though, you know that you can't. An era"—she paused—"has come to an end. A new phase of the future simply *has* to begin." She switched back to her own voice. "How do you like that, honey?"

10

I wasn't thinking about my horoscope as I stood near the curb on Avenida Gallardo, shielding my eyes from the midday sun, jutting out my hip and raising my hand high, doing my best impression of a self-possessed *porteña*.

"I can't take you anywhere," said the taxista who stopped for me. His hair was silver, his Bart Simpson T-shirt too big in the shoulders.

"Oh," I said. "OK." I stepped away from the passenger-side window, back onto the curb, a little unsteady on my platform sandals.

"No, *señorita* . . ." The taxista shook his head. "Wait," he said. "I can't take you anywhere, because my favorite restaurant is there!"

He pointed across the intersection, to a sign crowned with three laughing, life-sized plastic pigs. LOS CHANCHITOS, the sign read. The Little Porkers.

"Get in," he said, grinning. "I'll drive you."

I could have easily walked. The taxista was going to have to wrestle his cab through some crazy lunchtime traffic to make it across the street, but I got in anyway, and as he shifted into first gear, I noticed a pair of sky-blue baby shoes dangling from the rearview mirror.

"It is our responsibility as Argentines to make foreigners feel welcome," he said, making a U-turn in many parts and finally braking in front of the restaurant. "Go," he said, waving away the pesos I offered him. "And have a wonderful lunch."

I wished Liliana were here. Maybe she would have said it was luck. (She hadn't been surprised when I'd told her about the trip to Pueyrredón Restaurante.) But when the silver-haired taxista refused to let me pay him before he shooed me out of his cab and into the Little Porkers, where the pancetta-wrapped pepper steak was so tender I could cut it with a butter knife, it felt like more than luck.

. . .

I decided to quit working full-time for the satellite company. I came to Buenos Aires to write, I told my boss, not long after the trip to the Little Porkers, and I had finally figured out what it was I wanted to write about. "And what is that?" he wanted to know. Food? Yes. But more than anything, the question about restaurants was a way in to a larger conversation with the taxistas. My boss looked at me as if I'd told him I was planning to swim to Uruguay. Then he offered me a telecommuting job, in the Customer Care division, calling up the satellite company's clients in Europe and Africa and the Philippines once per quarter, summarizing their satisfactions and/or their complaints, and sharing them with the CEO. I took the job, because I needed to pay the bills, and because it was flexible: now I could arrange my formal work around the taxi adventures and my blog, instead of the other way around.

The freedom was worth the pay cut. I had no idea who was reading my blog—I deliberately kept my distance from internet analytics and bounces and clicks and page views—but more and more people outside my circle were emailing me about *Taxi Gourmet:* émigrés like Hugo, who liked my gringa's take on Buenos Aires, *porteños* who told me they had never heard of many of the restaurants I was writing about (and wanted to try them), undergraduates from the U.S. who had been urged to exercise extreme caution with the taxistas in Buenos Aires during their semesters abroad. I answered them all, savoring what felt at last like a sense of purpose—*I'm not writing in the dark!*—and before long, perfect strangers started asking to join me on my food quests.

"Do you ever get nervous?" said Sandra, a pretty, short-haired journalism student from Texas who'd introduced herself via email a few days earlier, as we approached a taxi parked under the sycamore trees in Plaza del Congreso. She was the first person I was bringing on a taxi adventure: Though I wasn't sure about the chemistry, I liked the idea of having someone else see what I was seeing. And I wanted people to know I wasn't making up the stories on the blog.

"I always get nervous," I said, glancing at the taxista through the windshield. He was bald, but he looked young, maybe around Sandra's age. "The doubt is always there. But I like to think I'm getting better at telling the difference between instinct and anxiety."

The taxista scanned the midday traffic on Avenida Rivadavia like a farmer surveying the sky. He told us he was a sculptor. I asked him if it was difficult, doing his art and driving the taxi. "The rich man isn't the one who has the most," he answered, as the sun shone through the windshield, onto his olive skin, which had the smooth polish of a rock in a mountain stream. "He's the one who needs the least." He drove as though immune to the frenetic maneuvers of the other cars on the road, dropping us off at a cantina in Balvanera where the door was painted black and the air smelled like the barbecue never stopped. There was a line of taxicabs parked outside, and a crowd of men on the sidewalk, elbowing their way toward an open window where a man in a red apron was handing out sandwiches.

"I was here yesterday," said the taxista, rubbing his stomach. "I had a *sanduche de vacío . . .*" He swallowed. "See? My mouth is watering just thinking about it! But I can't eat here today."

"Why not?" said Sandra.

"I'm on a diet."

"A diet?"

"Look at my belly."

I leaned forward, between the seats. The taxista lifted his hand off his stomach so I could get a good view of his middle. "I don't see a belly."

"Well, it's there. And summer is coming. Later I'll have a yogurt."

"Aren't you hungry?" I said.

"No." He ran his hand along the garland of silk flowers draped over the rearview mirror. "I just take my mind somewhere else."

When we said goodbye to him, I wasn't quite ready for the ride to be over. I felt the way I used to feel when the music stopped after an especially good tango. *Tangos are like little beings that last three minutes,* I remembered Joaquín telling me, as we watched the taxista drive away.

Heads turned when Sandra and I walked into El Litoral, where all the customers were men, sitting at tables covered in kelly-green vinyl, or standing at the counter, which was crammed with Tupperware containers of lemon slices and chimichurri and *salsa criolla*. How, I wondered, as we traded bites of a *sanduche de vacío*—a crunchy-outside, soft-inside roll with slice after slice after slice of beautifully marbled flank steak—could the taxista take his mind off a sandwich like this? And why, I wanted to know, as we took leisurely forkfuls of *queso y dulce* (soft cheese and sweet potato paste), did the connection in the taxi feel so much like a tango? Because it didn't last?

When lunch was over, Sandra and I promised to keep in touch, and I walked back to the apartment on Avenida Santa Fe, notebook in hand, thinking of ways to describe this latest incarnation of steak, stopping in the middle of the sidewalk every few steps, jotting down ideas as they came to me. As usual, I couldn't write fast enough.

However, also as usual, when it came time to transform my notes into an article for my blog, I struggled for hours to find the story, to translate moments that felt miraculous without sounding corny or overwrought. For all that struggle, I stayed on the surface when I wrote about the sculptor, as I did in my other blog posts, reporting the highlights of the conversation in the cab and appraising El Litoral, and the taxista's *sanduche de vacío,* as matter-of-factly as I could.

Still, something was happening to me below the fun-loving surface of my project. Somehow, in the taxi, I could be open. Fluid—more fluid than I felt anywhere else. Even though I was afraid, even though I was in a stranger's space, even if I didn't know where we were going. And even when the path seemed to lead to an odd place, or no place, I did get nervous, but I was no longer paralyzed, as I'd been so often at the *milonga*. In the taxi, I was beginning to feel like the tango dancer I could never be.

II

It was close to noon, and I was still in my pajamas, listening to the tango station (a city-sponsored radio station, La 2x4, 92.7 FM, that played tango music and tango commentary twenty-four hours a day, seven days a week) on low volume as I sat at the kitchen table that doubled as my desk, going through the fourth or fifth draft of my post about the taxi ride to El Litoral. This was the trouble with having your own blog, I decided, biting into a *medialuna,* this "freedom" to revise and republish every entry ad infinitum—what a fine curse, this freedom, for a perfectionist like me, I was thinking, when my computer pinged, letting me know I had a new email. I wiped the crumbs off my fingers and clicked over to my inbox, raising my eyebrows when I saw the subject line: **Washington Post.**

> Hi Ms. Mosler,
>
> I'm a reporter at the *Post,* based in Rio de Janeiro, but I'm in Buenos Aires for the next few days . . . I enjoy your blog and thought your search for good food with a taxi driver might make a good subject for a story. . . . Maybe I could tag along on your next outing?

" 'Tag along'?" I closed the email. I opened it again, rubbing my eyes. The *Washington Post!* I turned off the radio and reread the message, aloud this time. How had he found me? *Of course you can tag along* . . . When should I answer him? I started to type a response, writing sentences, deleting sentences, weighing every word. I made myself wait ten minutes before I sent it: I would love to have you on my next adventure, I wrote, knowing I sounded eager, but not too eager, I hoped. Maybe we could meet at Las Violetas, on the corner of Rivadavia and Medrano?

I chose Las Violetas, a café in the Almagro barrio, for its history—and for the story of its rebirth. Liliana told me the place had closed in the late 1990s, after anchoring the neighborhood for more than a century, and reopened in 2001, thanks to locals who convinced investors to save it from ruin. Las Violetas was where Osvaldo Pugliese, my favorite tango composer, used to eat cake. It was also the place where the grandmothers of the Plaza de Mayo held meetings, disguised as birthday parties, to make plans to find their missing grandchildren, the sons and daughters of "subversives" who were "disappeared" during the Dirty War. Almost a decade after its grand reopening—after all the Italian marble and art nouveau stained glass and gold-leaf ceilings had been restored—there was still a triumphant buzz in the air at Las Violetas. I couldn't think of a better place to start a taxi adventure, particularly this one.

I got to Las Violetas early, more than half an hour before I was supposed to meet the reporter, and drank an expensive glass of orange juice, hoping low blood sugar was the reason my hands were shaking. In the forty-eight hours between his email and the moment he walked into the café, a colossal pimple had taken root next to my nose, and I had come up with a series of worst-case scenarios: What if the taxista spoke in monosyllables? What if he drove us in circles, like the one who had brought me to Pueyrredón Restaurante? What if he insisted on taking us to Siga la Vaca? What if he only ate at home? What if the whole adventure was just plain dull? I hadn't factored in developing an instant crush on Joshua, the reporter, who looked like a Rio de Janeiro–relaxed version of Clark Kent, with wind-blown, ash-brown hair, a five o'clock shadow, and black-rimmed glasses. He carried an army surplus canvas bag and wore his clothes as if he had better things to do than roll up his sleeves evenly.

It was summer. The night was hot and humid—eighty-five degrees, with a *sensación térmica* of ninety-two, according to the weather report on the tango station. Even the asphalt on Avenida

Rivadavia shimmered as though it were perspiring. I was sweating in my sleeveless top, trying to act as if hailing a cab with a good-looking foreign correspondent were a natural, everyday occurrence. I moved to Joshua's left, so he couldn't see my pimple in profile. He looked at his watch with a deliberate sort of nonchalance, possibly aware of the effect he was having on me.

"Just do what you usually do," he said, taking a step back so I could survey the street.

I checked the time on my cell phone—it was almost ten o'clock at night. Dinner time in Buenos Aires. I moved closer to the curb, closed my eyes, and raised my hand. A taxi pulled over a few seconds later. *Wait,* I thought, *I'm not ready!* I felt like someone was pushing me onstage before I'd had time to learn my lines.

"After you," I said, opening the cab door with feigned confidence, climbing into the back seat after Joshua, trying to forget about the volcano on my face and to focus on the taxista. The first thing I noticed about him was his mustache—gray and bushy and combed straight down over his upper lip, like Einstein's.

"I have sort of a strange request," I said, thinking it was a good sign that the belly under the taxista's short-sleeved dress shirt grazed the bottom of the steering wheel. "Could you take us to a good place to eat?" I paused, meeting his sleepy-looking eyes in the rearview mirror. "A place where you would eat with your family, or your friends?"

The taxista pursed his lips under his mustache. "I know such places, but it has to be nearby? Or where?"

I didn't want to give him too many parameters: "It could be nearby. But it doesn't have to be." I was trying to be breezy, to stay cool, even though my heart was picking up speed, even though it made me uneasy that the taxista, unlike the taxistas on my adventures of late, didn't seem to have any initial ideas about where to go. *Bailar la pausa,* I thought, sliding closer to the edge of the back seat. Dance the pause. It was one of the last lessons Joaquín tried to teach me, a lesson that somehow made more sense in the taxi than at the *milonga: Be open, in between movements,* I remembered him telling me. *Especially between movements . . .*

A bus whizzed past as we pulled away from the curb, and we

coasted along the *avenida* in the dark, drifting into a conversation that had nothing to do with food. The taxista told us his family fled to Argentina in 1952 to escape the Franco dictatorship in Spain. He had lived fifty-seven of his fifty-nine years in Buenos Aires, he said, but he was born in Galicia, on the northwest coast of Spain, and we should know that he would die a Spaniard.

I looked over at Joshua. His expression was polite and neutral—a reporter's poker face—as he jotted microscopic words on his notepad.

"Argentina is different from every other country in Latin America," the taxista continued. "Did you know this is the only country in South America with three Nobel Prize winners in science?" He raised three fingers to the rearview mirror. "If you work hard here, you can get somewhere. And the only thing a Galician like me knows how to do is work."

I laughed and looked over at Joshua again. He glanced at his watch one more time.

The more excited the taxista became, the slower he drove. When we passed Saverio, a hundred-year-old ice-cream parlor another taxi driver had shown me a few months earlier, I realized we were in Caballito, the middle-class barrio in the geographical center of Buenos Aires. My mouth watered at the memory of Saverio's *ristretto granizado* (espresso ice cream with bittersweet chocolate chips). Joshua scratched his head with his pen.

The taxista opened his wallet and pulled out a picture. "Just look at her!" he said, holding up a wrinkled snapshot of a little girl with curly auburn hair who looked about three. "This is Lola," he said. "My granddaughter." He passed the photo to me, so I could admire it more closely, but before I could say anything about it, he launched into a story about the failure of his garage door factory in the 1980s. "Inflation," he sniffed. "What are you going to do?" This was when he started driving the taxi, he told us. He put all three of his daughters through university on a cab driver's salary, and all three were very, very successful.

"You must be very proud." I smiled. I was still holding Lola's picture. "She's a doll!" I said. I showed the picture to Joshua, who nodded, cool and polite as ever. If Lola, who really was a doll, couldn't soften his reserve, maybe nothing could. I handed the photo back to the taxista, who kissed it.

"I am proud," the taxista said. "But you know what I'm most proud of? The fact that they're good people."

Joshua lowered his notepad and looked at his watch again. I wasn't sure how much time had passed since we had hailed the cab on Rivadavia and Medrano. In any case, whatever grace, whatever ease, whatever confidence in fate I'd acquired over the course of the taxi adventures was vanishing in the reporter's presence. Had I been alone, I liked to think I wouldn't have been worrying so much about where we were going—we still had no idea—or how hungry I was.

The taxista stopped at last, on the corner of Avenida Pedro Goyena and Avenida Moreno, across the street from a restaurant called Tía Susanita, where a dozen people were lined up under the turquoise neon sign.

"Why is it good?" said the taxista, nodding out the window, combing his mustache with his thumb. "Because so many people are waiting." I trusted him. And I was so caught up in his charm, I didn't ask him any of the questions I had learned, after almost two years of vetting food recommendations from cab drivers, to ask. I didn't ask him how he had found the place, or about the last time he had eaten there.

Joshua snapped a few pictures and asked the taxista to spell his name, almost cracking a smile as we said _gracias,_ and good luck and goodbye, and walked into the restaurant.

I tried to look past the white tablecloths—taxistas were not in the habit of dropping me off at white-tablecloth restaurants, and I hoped this was not a bad omen. I glanced at the young couples holding hands, the old couples ignoring each other, at a black-haired infant squishing mashed potatoes in her tiny fists, but their faces offered no clues about what they thought of Tía Susanita's food. I noticed a waiter in a bow tie carrying a salad with fresh basil. A good sign, I told Joshua: I wasn't used to seeing fresh herbs in Buenos Aires. This was also a city where people on the bus moved away from me on days when I ate even a single clove of garlic. When I opened the leather-bound menu, I spotted smoked trout, and oysters—and I realized I had also forgotten to ask the taxista about his favorite thing to eat here.

"It looks promising," I said, studying the menu, trying to relax into the smell of fried calamari that was wafting through the dining room, trying not to let Joshua see how disconcerting it was to sit across from him, hands folded in front of my pimple, about to share a meal.

He left his menu on the table, brushed his bangs out from behind his glasses, and told me I should choose everything we would order.

"Is there anything you don't eat?"

"Order whatever you think is best."

Oh, dear.

The menu was heavy on seafood. But Buenos Aires, as I had learned on a few expensive attempts to find good fish here, was not really a seafood town. Sure, the city borders the Río de la Plata, the giant river estuary that forms part of the border between Argentina and Uruguay, but fish lovers knew that the Uruguay side of the Río, where the water was cleaner, was generally a better place to eat seafood. I hoped for the sake of my stomach and Joshua's—he must have been as hungry as I was by now—that Tía Susanita would be a Buenos Aires exception, and that the seafood here would be good.

"She ordered fried calamari," he wrote, in the article that came out five days later, "as well as an appetizer of sautéed mushrooms with prosciutto and egg, of which she said, 'I wouldn't order it again.' None of it, nor the decor of odd oil paintings of boats and violins, was particularly impressive . . ."

"How could I have made such a rookie mistake?" I said. "Why didn't I make sure we ate somewhere the taxista had been already? I'm such an idiot!"

"But you're on the front page!" said Mom. I pulled the headphones away from my ears—she had a voice that belonged in the theater or in a pulpit, especially when she got excited.

"Not the front page, Mom, the front-page *section*—"

"And your quotes are great. Aren't they great, Leroy?"

"Great, kid!" said Dad.

"And the photo isn't bad. He did you a *huge* favor. Did you say he was cute?"

"Yes, Mom, very cute. But he's not interested in me."

"How do you know?"

"I just know." Joshua had been courteous, and nothing more, when he answered my email thanking him for joining me on the taxi adventure. "Plus, he might get transferred to Afghanistan."

"Oh!" said Mom. "Oh, well. But what's this about New York?"

Joshua had caught me off guard when he asked me where I was planning to take *Taxi Gourmet* in the future. I wasn't sure where the adventures were leading, but part of me hoped they were leading somewhere beyond steak: I was running out of adjectives for the *bifes* that the taxistas almost always wanted me to try. Not to mention I had now accumulated seventeen TOURISTA 90 DÍAS stamps in my passport—at any moment, the Dirección Nacional de Migraciones might decide to stop believing I was a tourist, and refuse to let me reenter the country the next time I came back from a border hop to Uruguay.

New York was the first place that came to mind when I thought about where to go next. For one thing, I spoke the language; for another, there was a critical mass of cabs—and I knew of no other city, not even London, where taxis were so much a part of the iconography. I began to consider it more seriously when someone who read my blog sent me a *National Geographic Traveler* article about a group of Nepali Sherpas who were driving yellow cabs in New York. ("The taxi drivers say the mountains and the traffic both require Zen-like patience, so it's not that difficult a transition.") At Tía Susanita, after a few bites of mushrooms that tasted as though they had been sautéed in old oil, I told Joshua about the cab-driving Sherpas, and how I was starting to fantasize about finding them and asking them about their favorite places to eat momos (Nepali-Tibetan dumplings). By the time we got to the main course—a desiccated piece of trout under a pile of mealy mussels—I confessed that New York, more than Hong Kong or Rome or Mexico City (street tacos notwithstanding), was where I wanted to try the taxi adventures next.

"The cab drivers are from everywhere," I told Mom and Dad, paraphrasing what Joshua had written in the article. "New York probably has the most well-developed taxi culture on the planet. And the food! The food is going to be incredible."

"What about tango?" said Mom. "Do they have tango in New York?"

"Of course they do." A picture of a *milonga* somewhere in Central Park began to take shape in my mind. "But it's probably not the same."

12

The cats in the Jardín Botánico darted out of our path as Liliana and I walked past ferns and bromeliads. I was telling her about the lady who'd sat next to me on the *subte* the day before.

"When I got out my book," I said, "she asked me what I was reading. It was *The Book of Laughter and Forgetting*—"

Liliana pulled her shawl tighter around her shoulders.

"She asked me if I liked Kundera," I went on. "And when I told her I did, she said I had to read *The Joke*—that was his first novel, and *Slowness*. And then she gets off the train. 'Sorry! I have to go,' she says. 'I have to make lentil stew!' Can you believe it?"

Liliana shrugged. "There are better writers," she said. "Kundera just keeps writing the same book over and over again."

"*Bueno,*" I said, "*puede ser.*" OK, maybe so. "But I still can't get over how much people here love to read. I think I've learned more about literature from Argentines than I did in school."

"*Bueno, puede ser.*" She shrugged again. "But we still can't check books out of the library. You know why? Because no one ever returns them."

She glanced at a *palo borracho* tree, whose branches were covered with mud-colored spikes, and walked toward a wooden bench where the *Espectáculos* section of *La Nación* lay draped over an armrest. We sat, and I continued to talk, trying to defuse the tension in our silence.

I told her about the taxistas I had been meeting since the ride-along with the reporter from the *Post*. "The last one, Jorge, he had a Smurf suctioned to his windshield. His favorite is ham and pepper pizza at La Continental," I said. "And before that I met Esteban—he wears rhinestone earrings." I pulled on my earlobe. Liliana smiled, trying to mirror my enthusiasm. "You'll appreciate this," I said. "He was going to therapy, but then he started gardening instead. He says gardening works as well as therapy, but it's cheaper. Isn't that perfect? Anyway, he told me the empanadas at Punto y Banca are good. So I tried them—actually only the fried ones are good—"

"Entonces te vas de Buenos Aires," she said. So you are leaving Buenos Aires. Something twisted around in my stomach. Liliana tugged on the ends of her shawl. "Are you sure you want to go?"

I crossed my arms over my middle, listening to the traffic hum behind the trees. A flock of pigeons landed a few feet away, pecking at the remains of a *medialuna,* reducing it to crumbs.

"Are you going to tell Joaquín?"

I rested my elbows on my knees and studied the pigeons. Joaquín was on tour with his new dance partner in Australia, according to the mass email he'd sent two weeks earlier. Liliana knew I still thought about him, even after all this time.

But over time, after I started the taxi adventures, my feelings for him had begun to shift: he was less a perennial *milonguero* than an old soul, and a gifted teacher. And I could see, though sometimes it stung to see, that he had passed on to me the metaphors at the heart of my project: *Dance the pause, ride the music, what's so bad about not knowing where you're going?* It was thanks to him, and all those afternoons at the Tango Escuela Carlos Copello, and all those nights-into-mornings at the *milonga,* that I could somehow contend with the uncertainty of hailing a cab and leaving my destination up to someone I'd never met before.

Still, I wasn't going to tell him I was leaving.

That night I dragged myself to La Viruta at three a.m. to dance tango, hoping and dreading I might run into Joaquín, though I knew he was an ocean away. Changing into my tango shoes, I thought about Liliana: "You can dance tango in any city in the world," she had said, as we were leaving the Jardín Botánico, "but you will find *nothing* like the *milongas* in Buenos Aires. Those people in New York, they dance to 'La Última Curda' "—the darkest of dark tangos, an ode to alcohol, death, and oblivion—"with a smile on their faces!" Liliana had never danced tango in New York, but it didn't matter. I suspected she was right.

Joaquín was not at La Viruta, but a forty-something man with a corkscrew ponytail and a leather hip pack was. When I stepped onto the floor with him, he held me so tightly I could barely move my legs, and when he noticed I was lost, unable to find his lead—it had been many months since my last tango, and it showed—he started to tell me what to do: "Don't rush. Do an *ocho*. Yes! Now do a turn."

After one song, he pulled a cell phone out of his hip pack. "I have to make a call," he said, and walked off the floor. I was devastated. At the *milonga,* it was tradition to dance a *tanda* (song set) until the end, with all your heart, regardless of how your partner looked or smelled. "You should only interrupt a *tanda,*" Liliana had taught me, "under the most dire of circumstances. Like if they're drunk, or having a heart attack."

I left La Viruta then, though I had made it a rule never to leave a *milonga* after a bad *tanda,* and jumped into a taxi, forgetting that I had only a fifty-peso bill. When we arrived at my apartment building, the *taxista* couldn't give me change.

I offered him the three pesos I found in the bottom of my purse, but it was a six-peso ride, and he said no, we had to go look for change, and that I should have told him from the beginning I only had a fifty-peso bill.

It was almost five o'clock in the morning. Where were we going to find change? "This is *your* business," I said. I had no more patience with the Great Buenos Aires Coin Shortage. "It's *your* job to have change."

"You're in *my* country now," said the *taxista,* his full lips suddenly thin, receding in anger. "You have to respect the rules of my business. Not your rules—*my* rules."

My face burned. I was, I knew, on the verge of committing a red-card offense. I got out of the cab and slammed the door, biting my cheeks until I tasted metal, flinging the three pesos onto the passenger seat, walking away.

"*¡Estafadora!*" the *taxista* yelled after me. Swindler! "*¡Estafadora de mierda!*"

I shook my head and thought: A city tells you when it's time to go.

I attempted a taxi adventure a few days later. I could leave the *milonga* after a bad *tanda,* but I couldn't leave Buenos Aires after a bad taxi ride, and when I climbed into the cab on Calle Arenales, the first thing I noticed was that the taxista was all gray—gray sweatshirt, gray acid-washed jeans, short, thick, wavy gray hair. The second thing I noticed, after we had driven two blocks, was that the taxista was a woman.

"People prefer women drivers," she said, in a bored, brittle voice that made me wonder how often she had to put up with the astonishment of her passengers. "We don't complain like the men do, and we're a lot calmer."

I had been hoping to meet a woman behind the wheel since I'd started the taxi adventures two years earlier, but in all that time I hadn't run into a single lady cab driver, and at some point had abandoned that hope. Female taxistas had become a myth to me, an unlikely phenomenon in a city notorious for its machismo. Yes, Argentina elected a female president in 2007, but Cristina Fernández de Kirchner's arrival in office had done little to change people's attitudes about the role of women here. Yes, Argentina was a matriarchal society—where else in the world did supermarkets have priority cash registers for pregnant ladies?—but it was still a place where girls learned ballet while boys played soccer. If driving a taxi in Buenos Aires was brave, driving a taxi as a woman in Buenos Aires was heroic.

"Men get in and don't say anything," the taxista said. "But I catch a lot of them looking at my feet. They want to see how I drive. But that doesn't bother me as much as the women sometimes. Once a lady got in and said, 'Do you have kids? How can you drive a taxi if you have kids at home?'" She rolled her eyes. "I told her it might be better if she took another taxi."

We pulled up to a red light on Calle Paraguay, and a boy with hollow cheeks and a dirty squeegee approached the cab, fixing his eyes on the taxista, weighing whether she might give him something in exchange for washing her windows. She nodded, and he cleaned the windshield with quick, uneven strokes, standing on his tiptoes. As the light was changing, she rolled down the window and handed him a two-peso bill. Water streaked down the windshield in dirty rivulets as she accelerated. "With taxi driving, you either love it or you hate it," she said. "There's no in-between."

"*¿Y usted?*" I said. "Do you love it, or do you hate it?"

"Do you think I'd be sitting here if I hated it?"

She was fierce, which I liked, though it flustered me a little, and I wondered if she was this way to begin with, or if driving the taxi had hardened her: practically every Buenos Aires taxista I'd met so far had been robbed, or threatened with a weapon, at least once.

"Where do you want to go?" she said.

"Uuuhm." I cleared my throat. "Sorry. It would be great," I said, "if you could take me to your favorite place to eat . . ."

"What?"

She braked behind an idling bus.

"Maybe a place you like to eat with your family."

She reached into the pocket in the driver's side door and pulled out a pack of Lucky Strikes. "You mind if I smoke?"

"No. Go ahead."

I followed her gaze to a woman sitting cross-legged on the sidewalk next to the bus stop, surrounded by rows of animal-print cell phone covers. How many did she sell in a day? I wondered. We crossed Avenida Córdoba.

"Spiagge di Napoli," said the taxista, a cigarette twitching between her lips, unlit.

"*¿Cómo?*"

"Spiagge di Napoli. I take my granddaughter there sometimes."

"Oh, I've heard of that place!"

"Of course you've heard of it," she said. "It's good!" She cocked her head toward the side mirror. Another cab was moving into her blind spot. "I used to go there with my daughter."

"*¿Ah, sí?*" I wanted to keep the conversation going, so I asked the question I always asked when people told me they had children. "How old is your daughter?"

The taxista pulled the cigarette out of her mouth. "She died."

I closed my eyes. "I'm so sorry."

"Five years ago."

"I'm—"

"You didn't know."

I folded my hands and looked down at my lap. We didn't say anything for a few blocks. We crossed Avenida Rivadavia. The traffic petered out and leaves from diseased-looking sycamore trees were clogging the gutters.

"I even take my great-granddaughter sometimes," said the taxista. "She's two."

"To Spiagge di Napoli?"

"*Sí.*" She tucked the cigarette behind her ear. "She drives me crazy. Jazmín is her name." She shook her head, as though she were exasperated, but not entirely. "I also have two granddaughters. Teenagers. They live with me."

We braked in front of a Coca-Cola awning and she turned off the meter, switching on her hazard lights after I handed her my pesos. "By the way," she said, putting the taxi in Park, "I'm Mabel." I was surprised when she got out of the cab with me.

"Come on," she said, waving me over to the curb. She was so tiny that, if I squinted, I would have thought she was in elementary school. "I'll introduce you to the manager."

Mabel held open the door to Spiagge di Napoli, a glass door trimmed with lace curtains. People stared as we entered the dining room. This was the first time a taxista had come into a restaurant with me. I followed her as though she were leading me down the red carpet, smiling a lot at no one in particular.

"Please give her a nice table," Mabel said to a man with a menu under his arm who was standing beneath a dangling salami, "and take good care of her."

The man led us to a table in the corner, below a wooden shelf that was buckling under the weight of wine bottles. "You should order *rabas,*" Mabel said, "and *sorrentinos.* That's what my daughter liked."

I wanted to hug her, but I thanked her instead, though it didn't feel like enough. "*Que la disfrutes,*" she said. Enjoy it. She walked out the door, hands in her pockets, without looking back.

.   .   .

Four generations of family pictures hung on the walls at Spiagge di Napoli, along with a sign that read SALÓN PARA FAMILIAS. Every table was covered with a red-checkered cloth, and almost every table in the hundred-or-so-seat dining room was occupied by Argentines aged, as far as I could tell, from seven to seventy.

"Pastas are our specialty," said a waiter in a button-down vest, handing me a menu bound in vinyl. "They're all house-made." And they had been making them since 1926, according to the cover page on the menu.

The waiter brought Mabel's *rabas* (squid rings fried to a perfect crisp in a light, tempura-like batter) and *sorrentinos* (round pillows of pasta stuffed with mozzarella and fresh basil and topped with puttanesca sauce) minutes after I ordered them. They had cooked the pasta al dente, taking care not to drown it in the capers and garlic and anchovies in the sauce, and as I was eating it, and already wishing I had time to come back for it, a woman in a full-length black fur coat and dark glasses hobbled into the restaurant, auburn hair done up in a beehive, like a tower of spun sugar. The waiter in the button-down vest rushed to her side, and she held his arm as he led her to a table next to the dessert refrigerator.

A city tells you when it's time to go, I thought, watching the woman greet every member of the staff by name as she made her grand entrance—but that doesn't mean it won't remind you why you fell for it in the first place.

When Liliana and I made our entrance at the *milonga* at Salón Canning a few hours later, couples in close embraces—men in dark suits, women in shiny, back-baring dresses—were moving counterclockwise around the dance floor, and waiters were dashing to and fro, balancing *champán* bottles on small trays, while the disco ball seemed to be holding its glitter in check in the dim light. *Why,* I thought, as I looked around the room, *am I leaving this beautiful place?*

I didn't want to dance. I kept my eyes on the ballroom floor, watching Liliana move through tango after tango. She hardly sat down between *tandas*. Men kissed her hand when they escorted her back to her chair, but she was up in an instant when the music started again. I had felt her embrace, whenever she hugged me hello and goodbye, and I could understand why they wanted to dance with her: she was beautiful, and blond, but she was not the most beautiful, nor the only blonde. She was a good dancer, but not the best dancer. What they found in her arms was uncensored warmth. They wanted to dance with her because she was, as she herself once explained it, *una persona que es fiel a lo que se siente*—a person who is faithful to what she feels.

"*¿Bailás?*"

Julio, who was maybe in his early seventies, who wore the same fading navy-blue suit to every *milonga* in town, was bending down behind my chair, whispering in my ear. He always asked me to dance, except when I had been with Joaquín, and I liked dancing with him, too, even though his hands shook, even though all we really ever did was walk to the music. He was an architect, he said, the first time—and every time—we danced together, and he had divorced his wife, he reminded me with pride, because she refused to tolerate his tango addiction.

"*¿Y?*" said Julio. "*Qué hace tu tanguero?*" And? What's your tango dancer up to? It didn't matter how long ago Joaquín and I had stopped seeing each other. Julio always asked about him.

"I don't know." I did know, though. It was Sunday. If he hadn't been on tour, Joaquín would have been dancing, and holding court, at a *milonga* called Porteño y Bailarín.

The first song in a set of Di Sarli tangos, full of sweeping violins and light touches on the piano, was just starting. Julio took my hand, and I rested my head on his shoulder. His suit smelled like dust and champagne.

I closed my eyes and kept them closed as Julio and I moved in a gentle orbit around the floor, complicit in our slow progress.

"Your posture is better," he said before the last song in the *tabla*. "I remember when I first saw you. Was it at La Ideal?" I nodded. "Your posture! It was terrible! Now you're straighter." He pressed his palm on the middle of my spine. *"Más abierta."* More open. *"Pero mucho más abierta."*

He led me toward the center of the floor. "This is not just for the dance floor, Luisa Lane. This is for your life." We started to walk to the music again. *"¿Pero vos ya sabés eso, no cierto?"* You already know that, don't you?

I left Salón Canning after the tango with Julio. Liliana nodded at me from the floor, she understood, and so did the taxista with the plastic statue of St. Christopher—the patron saint of travelers, the only patron saint I knew—mounted on the dashboard. After I told him my address, we didn't speak, which was unusual, but the silence was not uncomfortable—it was as if we were making a mutual decision to be quiet, and as we played leapfrog with the after-hours buses on Avenida Santa Fe, listening to Cyndi Lauper, I wanted to drive all night, and not think about New York.

PART II

New York City

"And now, Joey, I'm going to tell you a little more about my lonely nights in New York, how I walk up and down Broadway, turning in and out of the side streets, looking into windows and doorways, wondering always when the miracle will happen, and if."

—Henry Miller, *Aller Retour New York*

13

"You picked a hell of a city," said the taxi driver, squinting at me in the rearview mirror as he followed the racetrack curves of the service road that led from JFK to the expressway. His hay-colored hair was cowlicked and greasy, and there were patches of perspiration on his T-shirt. "You been to New York before?"

"Just for three days," I said. I opened the window, turning my face into the wind. It was June, and the air in the cab felt as sticky as jam. "But I spent one of them in bed with food poisoning."

"Eeesh!"

"Bad clams in Little Italy," I said, looking down at the wrinkled scrap of paper where I had written my new address.

"What?"

"Bad clams in Little Italy!" I leaned forward, almost shouting, so he could hear me through the opening in the Plexiglas partition that divided the front seat from the back.

"Eeesh!" he said again. "Well, I'm not surprised. There's some bad restaurants in Little Italy." He glanced over his shoulder, pulling into the fast lane. "Where you comin' from anyway?"

"California, originally," I said, curling and uncurling a corner of the paper between my fingers. "But I've been living in Argentina—"

"Argentina!" The taxi driver whistled. "The Peronists really did a number on that country, didn't they?"

"That's what my friends like to say." I raised an eyebrow. "Have you been to Argentina?"

He shook his head. "I'm from New Orleans," he said. "And I like to read."

"Touché." I smiled. *Here is New York,* I thought—so plugged into the rest of the world, maybe I could escape return culture shock. "How come you don't have an accent?"

"I've lived in New York City for twenty-five years. That'll take away your accent."

He pulled off the expressway. The sun was going down behind a diner called Neptune. A few doors away, the letters in the middle of a neon sign at a twenty-four-hour bodega were burned out.

"This is the first time I've taken a cab in New York," I said, trying to smooth out the scrap of paper with my new address, which was barely legible now.

"Ha!" said the taxi driver. "I hope I'm making a good impression."

It was almost dark when he dropped me off, in front of a flat-roofed, three-story, soot-covered brick apartment building indistinguishable from its neighbors. I rang the doorbell, peering through the glass door with the steel bars, trying to catch my breath. There was no disorientation, I decided, like the disorientation of reducing your possessions to a suitcase and a carry-on and showing up in a new place where your life had no pattern, no rhythm, no roots, no relationship to any other person's life. And there was no way around it, this disorientation—no way to skip over it or rush past it. The only way was through.

I rang the bell again, listening to the drone of the traffic on what I guessed was the Triborough Bridge, wishing I could stop the sweat from dripping down my armpits. Was I in the right place? I'd rented the room sight unseen, in Astoria, Queens, just across the East River from Manhattan: "The apt has a living room, bathroom, kitchen and hallway with two storage spaces," said the Craigslist ad. I would be sharing the place with a jazz cellist named Jefferson, whom I'd only met over email. Why wasn't he answering the door? I checked the slip of paper with my new address again. My sixth address in four years, having moved from furnished apartment to furnished apartment, wanting to feel out different neighborhoods in Buenos Aires. How embarrassing to be so unsettled, I thought, staring down at the weeds pushing through the concrete under my suitcase, to be searching (still!) for the thread in the labyrinth.

Maybe the thread was here. I thought back to that first trip to New York, during that awful semester of graduate school in New Jersey: how in awe I'd been, despite the bad clams, buying mangos at a cart on Broadway, listening to the bucket drummers in Times Square, laughing at a leather belt vendor's sign on Canal Street (KEEP YOUR PANTS UP: $3). It was a magnificent city, massive in all directions, proud to stand at its full height, like a tall person with perfect posture. A kind of feverish energy rose up through the sidewalks. Even the smells—hot dogs, urine, kebabs, cumin, perfume expensive and cheap—seemed to move at a wild charge. And the implicit message from the New Yorkers I talked with was this: to live here was an accomplishment, a right to be earned.

"Magnetic" was how I'd described it to Mom and Dad, vowing to come back someday.

I never imagined how spectacularly alone (I had no friends in the city), how underemployed (an online editing job I'd found, along with the Customer Care gig with the Argentine satellite company, were barely going to pay the bills), and how uneasy I would feel, now that I was here, waiting for a stranger to come to the door, in Queens.

"Most cab drivers live in Queens," said a pair of New Yorkers I had met in Buenos Aires, who'd contacted me through my blog. She was a *New Yorker* cartoonist with Botticelli skin. He wrote screenplays. They had been living in Greenpoint, Brooklyn, for a decade. "Queens still has those little ethnic food neighborhoods you don't find in Manhattan anymore," I remembered them telling me. "Queens is where you should live."

I almost cried with relief when Jefferson, a balding, big-bellied man in a linen kaftan who was at least six-foot-three, finally answered the bell: "Layne?" I couldn't tell if it was my sweat or his when we shook hands. He grabbed my suitcase and carried it up the three filthy flights of stairs, which we climbed in silence, our feet landing on the depressions in the middle of the steps. The higher we went, the dimmer the fluorescent lights got. When he opened the door to the apartment, the hot, heavy air smelled like raw onions, and as he led me to my room—where the ceiling was cracked and water-logged, and an Ikea desk and a futon bed with a thin, stained mattress took up most of the space on the listing hardwood floor—all I felt was dread.

"Right," said Jefferson. "Well. Here you are." Then he went into his room and closed the door.

Jefferson was gone when I got out of bed the next morning. "Oh, man" was all I could say when I looked at the apartment in the light of day. The living room, empty except for a yellow plaid sofa and a black leather armchair that had faded to gray, was covered in what looked like several years of dust. Paint was peeling off the bathroom ceiling like dead skin after a sunburn. Ivy plants were marinating in bowls of rancid water on the windowsill in the kitchen, where layers of grit and cooking oil coated the stove and the range hood. There was a roach motel in every corner of every room.

"Oh, man," I said again, dusting, sneezing, starting to unpack. I pulled out *Here Is New York,* E. B. White's love-struck, late-1940s ode to New York City, written "in a stifling hotel room in 90-degree heat, halfway down an air shaft, in midtown." His conditions, I reminded myself, sounded a little worse, or at least more claustrophobic, than mine, and his were the words I'd clung to on that first sleepless night in Queens:

> There are roughly three New Yorks. There is, first, the New York of the man or woman who was born here, who takes the city for granted and accepts its size and its turbulence as natural and inevitable. Second, there is the New York of the commuter—the city that is devoured by locusts each day and spat out each night. Third, there is the New York of the person who was born somewhere else and came to New York in quest of something. Of these three trembling cities the greatest is the last.

I finished unpacking, my stomach growling as I wrote up a grim report for the Argentine satellite company about our biggest client, in Rome: *Satisfaction at an all-time low. Meeting with CEO in March has not yielded the results they were hoping for with respect to spare parts distribution and*— I stared at the flashing cursor, thinking back to Ruth Reichl's descriptions of Chinese food in Flushing, which had driven me crazy when I'd read them in Buenos Aires, where I couldn't find anything close to smoked fish with star anise or drunken crabs or turnip cakes or handmade Shanghai soup dumplings. Now all of this was within reach. I closed my laptop and slipped *Here Is New York* and my notebook and a packet of almonds, left over from the plane, into my purse.

I tried to stay upbeat on the subway, to retreat into fantasies about Chinese food as the 7 train traveled farther from the silvery promise of Manhattan and deeper into the sprawling drabness of the horizontal city (didn't Kerouac say there was something brown and holy about the East?). Every time we stopped at a station, the terrible industrial screech of the train yanked me out of my reverie. So did the expressions on the faces of my fellow passengers. A filmmaker I'd met in Buenos Aires told me once that you could get a sense of a city, of its truth and its mood, if you studied people's faces when they didn't realize they were being observed. On the 7, eyes that weren't closed were full of fatigue or fury, mouths turned down, foreheads gathered in pensive lines.

It was drizzling when I got to Flushing, and the wind was blowing the drops sideways. I had dressed for yesterday's heat, and my arms were bare, and I was sorry I'd forgotten my jacket as I stood at the intersection of Main Street and Roosevelt Avenue, staring at storefronts with signs in English and Mandarin (or was it Korean? Or both?), ravenous, wondering which way to go.

Where are all the cabs? I thought, lowering my head under the drizzle. When I'd come to New York the first time, it seemed like every other car was a yellow taxi—I didn't see any now. I wandered around for twenty minutes, past the Fancy Wave Salon and the QQ Fruit and Flower Shop, salivating as I caught whiffs of ginger and garlic and simmering pork, looking for a taxi and refusing to buy an umbrella. I was about to give up when I spotted four gypsy cabs parked outside the New World Mall.

I didn't want to take a gypsy cab. Gypsy cabs, or livery cabs, or black cars, according to the *New Yorker* cartoonist with the Botticelli skin, were technically not allowed to pick up passengers on the street, and they didn't have meters. "Ride in them at your own risk," she told me. "For what you want to do, you should definitely take yellow cabs."

Now was not a moment to be choosy, though. I walked up to the first gypsy cab in line, a black Buick with a dent in the front fender. The driver rolled down the window. He was a slip of a South Asian man, shriveled and mustachioed. "My favorite restaurant is home," he said. "And when I don't eat there, it's McDonald's."

I tried to convince myself to approach the gypsy cab behind him, to assume that fluid, open-hearted, ready-for-anything posture that I'd learned in the tango. But I couldn't get past the sour, fishy smell in the gutter outside the New World Mall, or the frustration of being hungry and lost in my own country. The last gypsy cab in line honked at me as I walked away from the taxi stand, really laying on the horn, and I stumbled, startled, into the shopping bags of two ladies who expressed their outrage in a tonal language I didn't need to speak to understand.

"Hey," said Jefferson, my roommate, who was hunched over the stove, steaming dumplings in a pasta cooker, when I walked in the door. Jefferson, who was born in Trinidad and grew up in London, had been living in New York for ten years. He'd come here to study music, and now he was a professional jazz cellist. When he wasn't teaching jazz theory at City College, he played in different bands at clubs all over the city, and he went on tour every summer. New York was a dream city for a musician, he told me. He'd just recorded his fifth CD.

"Hey." I gave him a halfhearted wave and slumped against the kitchen door frame.

"How's the taxi thing going?" He turned off the stove, lifted the basket out of the pasta cooker, poured the dumplings into a stainless-steel bowl, and doused them with Bragg's Amino Acids.

I held back a sigh. The taxi thing was not going well. I'd been in New York City for nine days, spent more than seventy dollars on cab rides, and the only restaurant lead I had so far was McDonald's. Mom and Dad were wondering why I wasn't updating my blog. "I can't write about a place," I told them, "if it's not recommended by a cab driver." And now that I was in New York, I couldn't afford to eat out for the sake of eating out: I had to save all my disposable income for the taxi adventures.

"Think you'll keep trying, then?" said Jefferson. He opened the refrigerator and pulled out a Tetra Pak of coconut water.

"Of course I will," I said, trying to keep the edge out of my voice. I had already arranged my life in Queens around the taxi adventures, doing the online editing work and the Customer Care calls for the Argentine satellite company in between.

"I'm sure you'll get it sorted," said Jefferson. He slid past me, the bowl of dumplings in one hand, coconut water in the other, heading for his room. How could he be sure? I retreated to my room, too. I didn't want to think about *Taxi Gourmet*. I tried to piece together another (alarming) report for the satellite company instead— *Equipment that was supposed to be sent to Kenya was sent to Rome and is still in customs*—but I ended up pulling down the shades and watching YouTube videos of Joaquín performing with his new partner. He and Sonya had stopped dancing together professionally after she had an affair with one of their students and got pregnant. His new partner, a pale brunette with a round face and a stagey smile, was younger— she strutted where Sonya used to float. But Joaquín held her—they were dancing to a song called "Esta Noche la Luna" at a tango festival in Seoul—as if he didn't want her to get away.

"Why do you wanna know where I eat?" said the taxi driver, turning his unshaven face away from the opening in the Plexiglas partition.

"I'm a journalist," I said, feeling around in my purse, looking for my notebook. "And I—" The N train roared overhead, on the elevated tracks above 31st Street in Astoria, drowning out the rest of my words—but the taxi driver had heard enough.

"No, no, no." He waved his hand at me like he was waving away a fly. "No journalists."

"No"—I left my hand in my purse, holding on to my notebook—

"wait." The heat in New York had turned tropical again, and I was sweating through my jeans, onto the vinyl in the cab's back seat. "It's not like that," I said. "I have this blog and I write about taxi drivers and where they like to eat—"

The cabby was shaking his head. "I don't *have* a favorite restaurant." I looked at him in the rearview mirror. His eyebrows were so bushy they looked like twin mustaches.

"Are you sure?" I scooted to the edge of the back seat, closer to the opening in the partition. "Not even—"

"Lady," he said, "I need to work." He gave me another fly-swatting wave. "If you don't wanna go anywhere, maybe you should get out."

I got out, clutching my purse, almost throwing it in the gutter. I had spent the morning preparing for the taxi adventure as if I were preparing for an expedition, boiling eggs in case I got hungry, packing my purse so my notebook and camera would be within easy reach, trying not to think about the fact that it had been weeks since my last blog post, trying to visualize positive outcomes, in which I had a fascinating conversation with the taxi driver, who would lead me to a basement in Sunnyside or Jackson Heights where laugh-lined grandmothers would be frying pupusas or rolling out chapati.

Instead, I had spent the past hour and a half trudging up and down the streets of Astoria, searching for a yellow cab, trying not to get desperate as I cracked my boiled eggs against low brick fences and tossed the peels in the squares of dirt under the trees on the sidewalk. The cabby with the mustache eyebrows was the first yellow-taxi driver I had seen all afternoon.

What am I doing here? I thought, not for the first time, walking in the shade of the subway tracks on 31st Street, kicking an empty Dunkin' Donuts cup to the curb as I watched the cabby drive away. I recalled the flood of taxis on Avenida 9 de Julio, and the taxistas, who always seemed glad to talk to me, and their *choripanes* and their empanadas and their steaks—I'd never eaten so much steak, or so much good steak, in my life—and I wondered if I had just moved ten thousand miles for nothing.

A man in a Yankees cap was grilling souvlaki at a pushcart when I got to the corner of 31st Street and 31st Avenue, his chicken and lamb skewers sending oregano-scented smoke into the sky. Every time I left the apartment, there seemed to be some fabulous smell in the Astoria air—falafel or ćevapčići or focaccia—that I couldn't afford to taste, because I couldn't write about it, because a taxi driver hadn't led me to it. I was determined to remain faithful to my project. But now, for the first time, I was beginning to curse it: How was it possible to be so unsatisfied in a city full of so much wonderful food? I took another whiff of souvlaki smoke, looking up and down 31st Street—still no yellow cabs.

"Where are all the cab drivers in Queens?" I asked Jefferson when I got back to the apartment. We were in the kitchen, and I was opening a can of garbanzo beans. Besides hard-boiled eggs, garbanzo beans and rice were the only things I'd been cooking since I'd landed in New York—they were cheap and fast and filling, and I could make them without coming into too much contact with the grime on the counters and the stove.

"Cabs in Queens?" Jefferson pulled a bag of dumplings out of the freezer and dumped a dozen or so into the pasta cooker. "I never take cabs here. Only in Manhattan."

"Manhattan?" I poured the garbanzos into a strainer and rinsed them under the faucet, thinking back to what the cartoonist with the Botticelli skin had told me: Most cab drivers lived in Queens. But that didn't mean they *drove* in Queens. I turned down the flame on the rice. It was so obvious I blushed.

The next day, I got on the N train to Manhattan, sitting across from an ad for a book called *Unleash Your Inner Vixen: How to Find, Seduce, and Keep the Man You Want,* wavering somewhere between pessimism and anxiety, breathing the shallow, shaky breaths I recognized from my time on the line at Vertigineuse. This was how I used to breathe, standing before my *mise en place* when the restaurant opened, knowing full well how ill-equipped I was for the chaos that was about to ensue.

Would this be my fifth attempt at a taxi adventure in New York? My sixth? I closed my eyes, listening to the singsong voice of the lady announcing the stops on the subway—"This is a Manhattan-bound *N* train. The next stop is . . ."—each time we pulled into a station. There was something congratulatory in her tone, as if she were praising everyone on board for traveling around the big city.

The train slowed into a turn, brakes squeaking as it struggled to round the curve just before Queensboro Plaza. I opened my eyes. There were droves of yellow taxis on the streets below, piling up at the foot of the Queensboro Bridge, and there was the Manhattan skyline, all that mighty geometry, more intimidating than inspiring.

I tried to stay out of everyone's way when I got off the subway at Union Square, watching people stream toward the turnstiles like ants in a well-run colony, stopping to listen to a man in an alpaca poncho who was playing a pretty convincing version of "My Heart Will Go On" on a pan flute. I wandered from exit to exit, pausing in front of the signs, trying to guess which one might be closest to a taxi stand.

When I surfaced on University Place, people were crowding around a street acrobat in jade-green spandex, who backflipped and twisted as if he were beyond the pull of gravity. Yellow cabs were everywhere, speeding across 14th Street, breezing down Broadway, edging through clumps of pedestrians, back seats empty, on-duty lights on. *This is the place,* I thought, though it was starting to rain.

I walked toward Filene's Basement and hailed a cab. The driver was punching something into his cell phone when I climbed in. "I have sort of a weird request," I said.

He didn't answer.

The cars behind us started to honk. "Sorry," he said, slipping the phone into his shirt pocket. "Where you goin'?" His blue eyes were puffy, rimmed with red, and he was wearing a Knicks cap.

"Um . . ." I moved to the middle of the back seat, positioning myself to project my voice through the Plexiglas partition. I was beginning to hate the partition. The taxis in Buenos Aires didn't have them. "I was wondering . . ." I was shouting. I had to shout in the cabs here, and it didn't feel natural. "Say you had twenty-four hours left in New York—"

The cabby started the meter.

"—where would you want to eat?"

He wrinkled his nose.

I smiled at his profile, at the stubble on his double chin.

He turned on the windshield wipers. "You want a restaurant?"

"Mmm hmm." I pulled my notebook out of my purse.

"OK. How about Tavern on the Green?"

I lowered my pen. "Have you ever eaten at Tavern on the Green?"

The windshield wipers skipped across the glass.

"No. I haven't."

This isn't new, I thought. There were taxistas in Buenos Aires who tried to take me to touristy places, too. "I just moved here," I said. "And I don't know much about the food in New York." I poked my nose through the opening in the partition. "I'd really like to go someplace *you* like to eat. Maybe, how about, where do you like to eat when you're on duty?"

"Oh!" he said. "That's easy!"

I sat up straighter, turning to a fresh page in my notebook. Maybe he would take me to his favorite chicken and rice cart. Maybe he knew something about pizza, or Szechuan noodles. Or was he a pastrami man? My mouth began to water.

"I eat at Subway," he said, slowing down for a jaywalker in a sweatsuit who was taking his time crossing the street. The taxi driver honked. The jaywalker flipped him off. The taxi driver ignored him. "And sometimes I eat at McDonald's," he said. "They have salads now, ya know."

"Oh . . ."

"I have high cholesterol, see. And I gotta go where I can park. And use the bathroom."

"Do you like anywhere besides Subway and McDonald's?"

The taxi driver swerved around a steam hole. "What's wrong with Subway and McDonald's?"

"Nothing," I said.

His eyes narrowed.

"Nothing," I said again. "I just—I'm looking for . . ." What *was* I looking for? Democratic food suddenly seemed like a snobby goal: *What's wrong with Subway, if that's where the cabby likes to eat?* Except

I knew I couldn't write about a Subway Club. I couldn't put any passion behind it, not after spending day after day fantasizing about the flavors behind the luscious smells of Queens.

"You know what?" I closed my notebook. "I think I better get out."

"Whatever," said the taxi driver. He pulled over and stopped the meter.

I ducked under an awning to wait out the rain, flipping through my notebook, stopping at an entry I'd written a few weeks earlier, before I'd left Buenos Aires:

> *New York scares me shitless. Huge, impossible.*
> *How will I survive? Have to brace for a butt-kicking . . .*
> *No!*
> *New York could be my Ithaca.*
> *New York will be magic . . .*

New York will be magic. It wasn't a belief, it was a command, rooted in fear and false hope. I glanced up from my notebook. The rain was tapering off, but the sidewalk was still jammed with open umbrellas.

I turned to one of the last entries I'd written in Buenos Aires, after my last tango with Julio, the elderly architect with the quivering hands who liked to walk to, more than dance to, the music, who'd said *"Los angeles no tienen peso"* ("Angels are weightless") when I'd stepped on his foot: *There is no embrace in the world,* I'd written that night, *at least that I've felt—that can match the warmth of an Argentine's . . .*

Had it been a mistake to leave Buenos Aires? Or did I have to look at the city from a distance to see it clearly? No, that was too simple. I thought about Joaquín, about one of the tango lessons toward the end, in that mirrorless, poster-filled room at the Tango Escuela Carlos Copello.

Every step is different, he said, stopping in mid-turn, letting the music, a slow Osvaldo Fresedo tango, play on the boom box. *You know how the great singers put a different feeling behind every note? Tango is like that. Each step has a different feeling, a different intention, behind it. You can't do this automatically! You can't do the same step, even if you've heard the song before . . .*

There it was: I had to adjust my steps. What had worked so well with the free-spirited taxistas of Buenos Aires was obviously not going to sway the no-nonsense cabbies in New York. I needed a new way to approach the drivers here. By the time I stepped out into the drizzle, I had an idea.

14

I waited on the curb across the street from Bloomingdale's, watching the yellow cabs stop and go as they struggled to get up to speed in the midday traffic on Lexington Avenue. Whether or not I could make the taxi adventures work in this town, a few things were becoming clear: (1) I had to give the cabby a destination, even if it wasn't where I wanted to go; (2) asking a taxi driver about his food as soon as I got into the cab was not going to work; and (3) everyone in New York City, from the hot dog vendor to the hedge fund manager, had an agenda—and they assumed I did, too. Taxi drivers were no exception.

I stepped off the curb, into the street, half raising my hand. The taxi driver who stopped for me gave me a bewildered smile when I motioned for him to roll down the passenger-side window.

"Could you take me to Union Square?" I said, resting my forearms on the bottom of the window frame, standing between the taxi and a line of parked cars.

"Sure." He was a slim African man with a plumpish face, wearing a polo shirt with red and navy-blue stripes. I guessed he was in his mid-thirties. He nodded toward the back seat.

"There's just one thing," I said. Cars were lining up behind the cab, honking their horns. "I'm a journalist," I went on, talking faster, "and I'm writing about taxi drivers, and I was wondering if it would be OK if I asked you some questions while we go?"

There was a flicker of confusion in his eyes. The honking was getting louder. The cabby stuck his hand out the driver's side window, motioning for the cars to go around him. "Sure you can ask me questions," he said. "Get in."

"Super." I climbed into the back seat. The radio was tuned to classical piano. The cabby turned it down. I dug around in my purse, looking for my notebook, my hands a little shaky. I was hungry, and hesitant: the yellow cabs in New York still felt like unfriendly territory. I tried to read the name on the taxi license in the Plexiglas holder behind the driver's head. "Your name is Godfred?"

"Yes."

"How long have you been driving a taxi?" I thought I would start with easy questions, questions people probably asked him every day.

"Five years."

"Have you always lived in New York?"

He pulled around a pair of double-parked delivery trucks, steering with one hand. "I've lived here eight years. I was born in Ghana, but then I lived in Germany for some years, and I also learned French." He had a faint British accent, and he paused between his words, as if choosing them carefully.

"How many languages do you speak?"

"Besides English?" He ran his hand over his head, which was shaved so closely I could see his scalp under the coiled roots of his hair. "French, and a little German. Plus Akan and Ashanti. Those are dialects in Ghana."

"Five languages?"

He nodded, slowing down as we passed Grand Central Terminal, craning his neck and looking up at the Chrysler Building.

"The skyscrapers," he said. "I love them."

I glanced out the back window of the cab until I couldn't see the Chrysler Building anymore. I loved the skyscrapers, too—the first time I visited New York. Now that I was living here, eating garbanzo beans for breakfast, falling asleep to the rattle and hum of cars and trucks on the Triborough Bridge, sharing a dingy third-floor walk-up in Queens with Jefferson—who remained a stranger, and who for reasons I didn't understand had been acting melancholy, and increasingly reclusive, as the days went by—New York and its marvelous skyscrapers felt more distant, more foreign to me than Buenos Aires ever had.

"Would you say"—I looked at Godfred in the rearview mirror—"that this is home for you?"

"New York is everyone's dream." He smiled as if bearing good news. "My life is here." He turned right at Gramercy Park, where Lexington Avenue ended. "I go back to Ghana, but only to visit," he said. "There's no point in going back."

He made a left onto Park Avenue. My stomach started grumbling.

I hadn't asked him about his food yet. I was waiting for the right moment. But when was the right moment? We were close to Union Square, where he was about to drop me off, and I remembered something Joaquín had said, in a taxi—was it our last taxi ride?—on the way to La Viruta: *I'll tell you the truth*—he was staring straight ahead, talking more to himself than to me—*I'm more myself when I'm improvising at the* milonga *than when I'm dancing onstage* ... And maybe I was more myself when I was improvising in the taxi.

"Hmmm," said Godfred. "I don't know any restaurants around Union Square."

"That's OK. It doesn't have to be around Union Square."

"Hmmmmmmm." He pulled over, putting the cab in Park. I slipped a hand into my purse, searching for one of my hard-boiled eggs.

"Well . . . I know a place in Harlem—"

"Really? What's it like?"

"Do you like Senegalese food?"

"I don't know." I smiled. "But I'd love to try it."

"La Marmite," he said. "That's what it's called. Actually, they make food from all over West Africa. It's on Adam Clayton Powell. And One-twenty-second, I think. I haven't been there in a looooong time." He reached for the meter, getting ready to turn it off.

"Wait." I leaned forward, pulling my hand out of my purse. "Could you take me there?"

"You want to go now?" He looked at the meter, which was at $11, and then he turned around to look at me.

"Yes." I couldn't afford a long cab ride, but I also couldn't afford to miss what felt at last like a chance at something good, maybe even something delicious. And I wanted to keep talking to Godfred.

He smiled, and I couldn't tell whether he was more perplexed or amused. "Oooo-kay," he said, restarting the meter, turning right, then right again, heading uptown on Sixth Avenue. The traffic in midtown was brutal, and our pace was slow. My stomach, sensing we were onto something, began to rumble more insistently.

"How do you like driving a taxi in New York?" I asked him as we rode past the horse-drawn carriages lined up on the south side of Central Park.

"You know, I like it better since I drive *my* taxi."

"This is your taxi?"

"My taxi. My medallion." He beamed, pointing through the windshield at a blue and white badge soldered to the hood. "I just bought it. For four hundred and fifty thousand dollars."

"Four hundred and fifty thousand—?" I tried to whistle. "Whoa, that's a lot of money!"

"Yes," he said. "It's like a house. You make a first payment. A down payment. It took me five years to save this money." We turned onto Broadway. All the yellow taxis in the city, Godfred explained as we continued uptown, were medallion cabs. But the price of a medallion made it impossible for most drivers to own their cabs, so most guys leased their taxis by the day or by the week. Leasing, Godfred said, was like flushing money down the toilet. He knew from the moment he got his taxi license that he wanted to be an owner. "Sometimes I worked eighteen, twenty hours a day."

"Twenty hours?"

He nodded, "Now I have twenty-five years to pay it off. And you know what? The price has already gone up a hundred and thirty thousand since I bought it. By 2020, maybe it will be worth one million dollars!"

"Are you serious?"

He nodded again. "There are only two times in history when the yellow-cab medallion lost value. The first time was during the USA's war with Korea. The second time was after nine-eleven." He paused. "I'll tell you something"—he was looking at me in the rearview mirror—"New York is the best city. They give opportunity to anyone who deserves it. No matter where you're from. But you have to work *hard*."

We passed 110th Street. We were in Harlem now. The farther north we drove, the fewer yellow taxis I saw. Godfred steered around a pond-sized pothole and stopped the cab on Adam Clayton Powell Jr. Boulevard, in front of Restaurant La Marmite Inc. The windows under the awning were dark, the blinds pulled down. My stomach sank when I read the sign in the window: SORRY! WE ARE CLOSED!

"I'm very sorry," said Godfred. "I didn't know."

I tried to smile. "It's not your fault." He really was sorry—the disappointment in his eyes was genuine—but now that there was no food on the immediate horizon, my hunger began to morph into panic.

He drummed his fingers on the steering wheel, gazing through the windshield at the northbound traffic. "Do you want to go to the Bronx?"

"Do you know a good place in the Bronx?"

"Yeah," he said. "That's where I live."

"I'll go anywhere if the food is good."

I'd never been to the Bronx. What little I knew of it, I'd inferred from Sorina, a photographer who was born and raised there, whose parents had immigrated there after escaping the Ceauşescu dictatorship in Romania. Sorina had lived across the hall from me in college and hated California with an East Coast passion: she wore a full-length black trench coat, even when temperatures were in the triple digits, carried a four-and-a-half-inch switchblade wherever she went, and walked with long, ferocious strides that said "Don't even *think* about fucking with me." "Promise me you'll never go to the Bronx," she said to me once, as I rollerbladed past her door in the dorm.

"Do you want to go to the Bronx?" Godfred asked me again, glancing at the taxi meter. We were $34 into our journey.

Why not? I thought. "Let's do it," I said. I'd find a way to afford it.

He shifted the cab out of Park. We followed a bus across the Harlem River, and he turned onto the Grand Concourse—an eight-lane boulevard whose vast sweep reminded me a little of Avenida 9 de Julio in Buenos Aires. But instead of three-star hotels and dated office buildings and the *obelisco* in the middle, the Grand Concourse was lined with Kentucky Fried Chickens and 99-cent stores and houses of porn.

"The Bronx is cool," said Godfred, nodding at a group of African men playing pickup soccer, shirts versus skins, in the park across the street from Yankee Stadium. "You can't bullshit here now. The police took control. There are even white people living here."

We passed apartment buildings that took up entire city blocks. There was a kind of heaviness in the architecture, a beaten-down cast to the buildings, which looked as though they were exhausted from years of weathering East Coast winters. Godfred braked at a red light next to a salon called Faith Unisex, and I watched a trio of teenage girls in skin-tight T-shirts strut down the sidewalk, their faces set in runway pouts. One of them caught me staring and crossed her eyes at me.

Godfred laughed. "See? The Bronx is cool."

I laughed, too, but hunger was making it difficult to form coherent thoughts. I felt around in my purse for the hard-boiled egg again, but I left it alone. I didn't want to make a mess in his cab. Finally, over an hour after we had started our journey on Lexington Avenue, we stopped at 184th Street, and parallel-parked next to a storefront with tinted windows and a sign on a burgundy awning that read PAPAYE RESTAURANT: WE SERVE AFRICAN & CARIBBEAN FOOD. I paid the fare—$52, which hurt a little, though the amount was no surprise, given the distance we'd traveled.

"It's hard to find African restaurants in Manhattan," said Godfred, unfastening his seat belt. "You have to come to the Bronx if you want African food." He climbed out of the taxi and pointed east on 184th Street, at a six-story brick apartment building with an oatmeal-colored façade. "That's where I live."

"Then you must eat here a lot."

"A few times a week," he said, walking with me to the entrance.

Is he going to eat with me? I began to wonder at my good fortune until I caught another glimpse of the tinted windows. They were pitch-black. *Oh, no.* Something did a nosedive in my stomach. Was this place closed, too?

Godfred tried the door, and it swung open. I felt like raising my hands to thank the heavens.

When we walked in, the dining room went silent, except for the sound of Afropop. Every eye traveled in our direction: ladies in multi-colored head wreaths interrupted their chatter, and men who had been fixated on the giant flat-screen TV turned to stare at us—at me, actually.

Godfred walked me to the counter, greeting everyone in our path. The men slapped him on the back as if they were glad he'd made it home. The ladies looked down at their tables, or at the floor. I said hello, too, blushing, nodding, and noticing how immaculate the place was—there wasn't a speck on the walls or on the floor, both of which were covered in white tiles that sparkled as though someone polished them several times a day.

Godfred nodded at the two women behind the counter, who were wearing orange hairnets and wiping the edges of the hotel pans in the steam table. I smiled at them. They didn't smile back.

I scrutinized the pictures of the twenty-one dishes on the menu mounted on the wall behind the counter. What was banku? What was fufu? Was it possible to get okra stew *and* goat? Meanwhile, Godfred was speaking to the ladies behind the counter in what I guessed was Ghanaian dialect.

"I ordered for you," he said. "I hope that's OK."

"Of course. That's great."

The ladies pulled out a pair of CorningWare plates and arranged the food on them with a care that suggested they'd cooked it themselves. Onto the first plate went slices of fresh tomatoes and raw onions, positioned in interlocking rings atop a whole fish with blackened skin. "Tilapia," said Godfred. "Grilled." Onto the second plate they scooped spoonful after spoonful of red-orange rice, making a well in the center for a thick, dark chili sauce. "Jollof rice," said Godfred. "We eat this all over West Africa."

"All of this is for me?" I said, when the ladies handed me the food on a cafeteria tray, its plastic surface barely visible beneath the plates of fish and rice.

They nodded and disappeared into the back kitchen. Godfred picked up my tray and set it on a table with a good view of the flat screen, where two Italian soccer teams were battling it out on mute.

"You're not going to eat anything?" I said.

"I don't have time," he said, pulling out his car keys. "I have to go back to work. Will you be OK?"

"Oh, yeah." I admired the heaps of food in front of me, which looked and smelled like ambrosia after having contemplated the egg in my purse for two hundred blocks. "Thanks for bringing me here," I said. "I never would've found this place on my own."

"I hope you like it," said Godfred, nodding at my tray. He shook hands with a few of his friends again on his way out the door.

I ate slowly, ignoring the soccer game and watching the other customers eat with their hands—ergo the sink in the corner of the dining room—tearing apart softball-sized rounds of what looked like raw biscuit dough, which I later learned was fufu, and dipping it into family-sized bowls of stew. I felt like a fool with my plastic fork, but I knew I'd make a mess if I tried to use my fingers. It was going to take a lot more than using my fingers to fit in here, anyway.

The fish, silky and falling off its bones, tasted of saltwater. And the smoky chili relish elevated the jollof rice—loaded with palm oil and tomatoes and cayenne pepper—to a higher power. There were spices I couldn't put my finger on, too. Eventually—eyes watering, nose running, lips burning—I made it to the bottom of that twelve-dollar mountain of food. How long had it been since I'd tasted something so entirely new? I wanted to laugh out loud. I wanted to tell all my nonexistent New York friends about Godfred and Papaye. I had no idea how I was going to get back to Queens. I put down my plastic fork and smiled.

15

I met Isabel, my first friend in New York, via the random magic of the internet:

> Hi Layne, How are you? I have just left a comment in one
> of your posts at *Taxi Gourmet*. I love your project! I have
> a blog myself, basically about my life in NYC: *Lateral
> Window*. I'm from Brazil and I live in the US for almost
> 5 years—

Isabel and I were having drinks before long, at a place called Brick Café, in Astoria, where she also lived, about ten blocks from me, in a two-bedroom apartment she shared with a stripper who pilfered her mail.

"No matter how long I will be in New York, I will always behave like a tourist," said Isabel, who told me she was born in São João del Rei, a small town in the state of Minas Gerais, where they produced the most, and the best, *cachaça* (sugarcane firewater) in Brazil. She had a spray of freckles across her tiny nose, and the longest eyelashes I had ever seen. "I love Times Square," she said, between ladylike sips of lemonade. "I love the Empire State Building. I love all the little details about the city."

She made me think of Anaïs Nin, when she arrived in New York in 1934: "I'm in love with New York," she wrote to Henry Miller. "When you bring your own riches to it, it's like drinking from a Venetian glass." After two months in the city, my feeling about it was closer to Henry Miller's: "I discount the glittering Babylonian description you give—first effects," he wrote back to Anaïs. "Shake it down. What remains?"

For me, struggle remained. The Customer Care gig for the Argentine satellite company had deteriorated into a sham of a job, featuring conversations like this:

CLIENT IN GENEVA: We need more proactive involvement from you.

ME: Could you tell me what you mean by proactive involvement?

CLIENT IN GENEVA: We've requested bandwidth upgrades at ten sites by the end of the year. Are you planning on visiting those sites?

ME: I can't speak to that directly—

CLIENT IN GENEVA: And how about, don't you have some kind of dedicated project team for upgrades?

ME: Again, I can't speak to that directly. But I understand your concerns, and I'll share them with Emilio . . .

Emilio, whom I called the Tasmanian devil from Colombia, was the satellite company's CEO. I liked him, but his staff didn't always take him, or his lofty promises to clients, seriously.

CLIENT IN GENEVA: (SIGHING)

ME (ATTEMPTING TO SOUND UPBEAT): If you don't hear from Emilio in the next twenty-four hours, please let me know. Are there any other outstanding issues I should let him know about?

The job, senseless as it was, had paid the bills in Buenos Aires, but between this work and my online editing assignments, I was living hand-to-mouth here. The trip to the Bronx with Godfred had given me a taste of how extraordinary the taxi adventures in New York could be. But cabs were more expensive here—everything was more expensive here—so when I wasn't doing the taxi adventures, I was eating a lot of lentils, and garbanzo beans, and trying to stay out of Jefferson's way. He had broken up with his girlfriend, a real estate broker cum performance artist who lived in Park Slope, after which the atmosphere in the apartment went from antisocial to hostile. Now, if Jefferson and I happened to be "home" at the same time, he would take his coconut water and dumplings and Bragg's Amino Acids into his room and close the door.

Isabel had a much tougher row to hoe: she was still finalizing her divorce, from a Peruvian man who had embezzled money from the coffee shop in Astoria they'd opened together. Now she was working under the table as a girl Friday for a powerful Harlem landlord—doing site visits, organizing block parties, corresponding with way-ward tenants. Until she got her green card, she couldn't leave the United States. And her family couldn't visit her here, either: the U.S. embassy had just denied her mother a tourist visa for the fourth time.

"But there's nothing I can do about it," she told me. "I've already cried. If I had the habit of sitting down and stopping my life for any bad stuff that happens to me, I wouldn't be in this country anymore. The truth is," she said, holding her lemonade glass in both (flawlessly manicured) hands, "when you live ten hours by plane away from your family, when you decide that you want to build something from scratch in a country that isn't yours, in a language that you barely speak, among people you don't understand, well, it's kind of tough. But it is a choice, and it was my choice." She smiled, her eyes alight under the curly fringes of her lashes. "I could live here forever."

I nodded, wondering if Isabel loved the city because it had kicked her around, challenging her to love it. Or had she known from the start that New York was home?

"You need help with anything," she said, swirling the ice cubes around the bottom of her glass, "you just tell me."

If it hadn't been for Isabel I might not have met Nidia, my second friend in New York.

I had been surfing the internet, doing research for an article about cabbies in New York I wanted to pitch, when I found this blurb in the *Village Voice:* "If you want a driver worthy of a superhero comic book, you've gotta call Nidia," the *Voice* wrote. "She's one of the very few female drivers in New York, and she has found her niche, safely shuttling women around the city . . . Plus, she'll dish with you about your night and give you candy." In the early 2000s, the *Voice* had singled out Nidia as New York's best cab driver.

Isabel sprang into action as soon as I told her about Nidia, using all her hustle and all her charm—and detective skills she said she didn't know she had—to track down the lady cab driver. When she found nothing on the internet, she looked in the phone book and spotted a woman with Nidia's last name who was living in Astoria. This turned out to be Nidia's daughter, who was happy to give Isabel Nidia's number.

"Sure! When?" said Nidia, when I called to ask if I could interview her, and two days later, we were drinking Greek frappes at Athens Café, across from the sidewalk produce stands on 30th Avenue in Astoria.

"I'm a Nuyorican," said Nidia, stirring a spoonful of sugar into her frappe. "That's a Puerto Rican in New York. But my last name's Pakistani, because my husband's from Pakistan."

She was in her early forties, with *café con leche* skin and biceps that popped out when she bent her arms.

"Man, it is *hot* today!" said Nidia. She had a husky voice, and when she spoke, she bounced from one word to the next as if she didn't have time to pronounce the last syllable. "Usually I'm sleeping right now!"

"Oh, no. I forgot. You drive at night—"

"Yeah." She waved her hand like it didn't matter, and I noticed her ring, which had five small chains that stretched from her middle finger to a silver bracelet on her wrist. If she punched you wearing that ring, your face would split open.

"I worked in a factory before I started driving the cab," she said, sipping her frappe through a straw. "Mmmm, this is good!" She smiled at the drink. "I used to dress dolls. That was a dumb job for me. My hands are way too big!" She put down her glass and held up her palms, wiggling her thick fingers. "Then I drove a tow truck and an eighteen-wheeler."

In 1999, she started driving a cab, a gypsy cab, for Northside Car Service, where she still worked, as one of two female drivers in the forty-person fleet. She had about sixty regular customers, most of whom were women. They called her when they were out at night, or when a yellow cab refused to drive to their neighborhood.

Nidia wiped the sweat off the inside of her elbow. "The taxi's where I belong," she said. She grew up in Williamsburg, she told me, when Williamsburg was dangerous and drugs were all over the place. She knew how to handle herself on the streets. She liked to drive at night. People got in her cab high, or naked, or had sex in the back seat—sometimes all three. They would tell her about their one-night stands, their new loves, their breakups. After the *Voice* voted her New York's best cabby, she became a driver on *Taxicab Confessions,* the HBO series that recorded passengers at night, reeling off racy stories, but she stopped doing it after a while. "People didn't know what they were saying. Most of the time they were drunk. A lot of them were regular clients. It was too embarrassing for them."

She showed me her scars. She had bullet marks, from entry and exit wounds, on her calf. "Not from the taxi," she said. "From a drug deal. I wasn't part of it." She had a bigger scar, from a stab wound that ran the length of her abdomen, from the time she jumped out of her cab to stop a man from beating a woman on the street in midtown Manhattan.

"I cannot stand to see men hitting women." She shook her head. "I cannot *stand* it."

She raised her hand, smiling at the waitress, pointing at our empty glasses and holding up two fingers. The waitress brought us two more frappes. Nidia waited until she was out of earshot before she spoke again.

"When I was thirteen, I got raped," she said. "And then I got pregnant, and then my dad kicked me out of the house."

I put down my pen.

"No, you can write about it if you want. It's OK. My dad hit me sometimes. He wasn't always bad, though. We even used to go fishing together. But when he kicked me out, I had to sleep on the subway. You know those cards the deaf people pass out on the train?"

I nodded.

"That's how I learned sign language."

I pressed my fingers to my temples, searching her eyes—they were what people in Argentina would call *ojos de miel,* honey-colored eyes—for some trace of pain.

"You can write about it if you want," she said again.

"Are you sure?"

"Yeah."

"Can I ask you something?"

"Sure."

"Maybe it's a dumb question. You don't have to answer if you don't want to," I said. "But I don't think most people would be able to get over something like that. How did you do it?" How, I wanted to know, are you fierce and not broken?

"I don't know." Nidia shrugged, looking up at the ceiling. "But if I stopped driving a taxi, I think I'd die."

I started to approach the taxi adventures with a new kind of hope. Some cabbies did give me dud recommendations: burned scallion pancakes at a noodle shop on 49th Street that had grown lazy from its fame, fried plantains resembling Styrofoam at a Haitian place in Hell's Kitchen. But there was also the trip to Sofrito, Nidia's favorite Puerto Rican restaurant, where there was some sort of alchemy in the mofongo, an Afro–Puerto Rican mash of pork and plantains with sweet prawns and a light tomato sauce on top.

A kind of benevolence was in the air, too, on the taxi adventure with Isabel, our first one together: we hailed a Nuyorican film editor who drove his father's cab two nights a week, talked to us for many blocks about the magnificence of bacon, and dropped us off at Ramen Setagaya, in the East Village, where the cooks pulled the noodles by hand. "In what other city," said Isabel, "can you get in a cab with a Nuyorican driver and end up at a ramen bar?"

And then there were the taxi drivers who were beginning to lead me to things like Manchurian chow mein with bird chilies at Tangra Masala (allegedly the city's first Indian-Chinese restaurant, where 108 of the 159 dishes on the menu had chili pepper symbols next to them), and agedashi tofu, in a feather-light panko batter, with soy-vinegar-scallion dip, at Tokyo II Japanese kitchen, across the street from a taxi garage in Long Island City. Flavor was becoming the most seductive thing about New York. The more the taxi drivers showed me, the more I wanted to taste.

"Aaaargh!" said Mom. "It drives me crazy to read your blog. I want that tofu!"

I laughed, turning down the volume on my headset. "I wish you could taste it—"

"Hey, kid," said Dad. He didn't care about tofu. His passion was pot roast. "How's your roommate?"

"Well . . ." I could hear Jefferson through the wall, dragging heavy things across the floor. Maybe he was rearranging the furniture in his room. I had lost count of how many days had gone by since we'd spoken to each other. "I can't really talk about it."

"Well, how's your money situation?" said Dad.

"Just fine! Don't worry."

My money situation had never been worse. But somehow I was scraping together enough for taxi rides to the far reaches of Queens and Brooklyn and the Bronx, where cabbies kept surprising me with things like masala dosas (lentil flour crepes stuffed with potato and pea curry) at Ganapati Canteen, in the basement of a Hindu temple in Flushing. Or salmon soup with fresh dill at Cherry Hill Gourmet Market in Sheepshead Bay, which bore no resemblance to the wretched, oil-clad soups I'd eaten on two trips to Russia. Or cheesecake at De Lillo Pastry Shop, an eighty-five-year-old Italian bakery on Arthur Avenue, where Mohamed, a political exile turned cab driver from Mauritania, liked to buy his pastry.

"I think I need another job," I told Isabel.

"What do you want to do?"

"I don't know."

But I knew I couldn't do anything that might interfere with the taxi adventures.

16

I had fifteen dollars in my wallet when the petite cabby in the purple fedora picked me up near the Queens entrance to the Triborough Bridge. I was a little taken aback to find her in the driver's seat—she was the only lady cab driver I'd encountered, besides Nidia, in five months in New York.

I asked her to take me to Queensboro Plaza. I wanted to attempt a taxi adventure, but I needed to keep the ride short and cheap.

"No problem, honey," she said, starting the taxi meter and flashing me a beauty-queen smile. She was wearing an eggplant-colored sweater that matched her fedora. She looked like she was in her early thirties. "You can ask me any and everything."

She swerved around a van attempting to make a left turn on a round green light. I read the name on the taxi license in the pocket of the Plexiglas divider behind her head: Mary Jo Barnes. She'd been driving for two years, she told me, and she was a native New Yorker. Her parents had emigrated to Jamaica, Queens, from Jamaica in the Caribbean in 1964.

"When was the last time you went to Jamaica?" I asked her, as we sailed under the elevated subway tracks on 31st Street.

"Twelve years ago," she said, accelerating until she was inches from the Audi in front of us. "But I can't do any traveling till I'm out of debt. It's *so* unsexy to come back to bills."

"You're right," I said. "Bills are *not* sexy."

She smiled, riding the Audi's tail until it turned right.

"How often do you drive the taxi?"

"Just during the day. I go to school at night and on the weekends. It kills my social life." She slammed on the brakes behind a Fresh

Direct truck. I braced my arms against the partition and glanced at the seat belt, wondering if she'd take it personally if I put it on. I didn't usually wear a seat belt in a taxi. "I want to be a surgical nurse," said Mary Jo. "The cab is good practice for that, you know?"

"How so?"

"People are hurting," she said. "All over." She turned onto 30th Avenue, unconcerned by the sound of our screeching tires. "But I don't judge my passengers, no-sir-eeee," she went on. "I do pray for them, though. Everybody's got their issues. But dealing with myself is enough. I'm a type A person."

"So am I," I said, clinging to the ledge of the opening in the Plexiglas partition as she skidded to a stop at 21st Street.

"Once I had a job picking up a guy from prison. And I thought, 'Should I be scared?' "

"Were you?"

"When you're walking with God, you shouldn't be scared." The signal turned green, and she turned left, beelining it diagonally across the intersection before any of the cars opposite us could react. "This isn't a job you do for money," she said. "You do it for much, much more."

I peeked out the window as we barreled past auto repair shops and hardware stores and abandoned factories with shattered windows. We were in Long Island City now. It felt like a non sequitur, but if I wanted to find out where Mary Jo liked to eat, I had to ask her now, before she dropped me off at Queensboro Plaza.

"Oh, honey, I *love* to eat!" She flashed her beauty-queen smile again. "I can make a potato salad that'll slap your mama."

"For real?" I laughed. "What's your recipe?"

"Vidalia onions, adobo, red and green peppers, eggs, mustard, relish, ketchup—just a dab, that's the secret ingredient—kosher salt and pepper, white potatoes, Hellmann's, and cayenne. My family?" said Mary Jo, cutting off a bus, ignoring the driver, who shook his fist at her. "We didn't have money, but we were big on food. We don't play. 'Eat up, you growin','' they always said, there's starving people in Africa! I know what it's like to be hungry. But I'm anemic and I have to eat correctly. You know"—she adjusted her fedora—"ninety percent of the food in New York is good. But I like to go places where I can freshen up and eat healthy. If you have a bathroom and the food is good, I'll patronize you all the time. Let me think . . ."

She hit the gas and we flew past a diner with chrome-plated walls. "Bel Aire Diner!" She pointed out the window. "Their western omelet is *good*. And I get *any* omelet at Brown Cup. Now I know what. Do you like Indian food?"

"Oh, yeah!"

"Try Sapphire Indian, on the Upper West Side. I always get shrimp curry and a mango lassi. Have you tried the mushroom burger at Shake Shack?"

"Not yet." I was starting to salivate.

"Dangerous. And Elmo's—that's on Seventh Avenue—they have my favorite French fries. Also dangerous. Cafeteria on Seventh Avenue, too—you *have* to try their crab cakes. Mirandy's on Seventh and Waverly is good for brunch. I always get sugar donuts as a starter. But mostly I try to eat correctly. I go to McDonald's for one reason and one reason only—their bathroom."

"Ha!" I said. "Have you always tried to eat correctly?"

"People of color are very round." She took both hands off the wheel and drew an imaginary belly around her tiny waist. "Four years ago our pastor came up with a diet for us. We had to eat right for forty days. Lots of salads. No chips."

"Did it work?"

"Yes, and no." She grabbed the wheel again. "After that I realized I can never be vegan," she said. "But that's because of curried goat."

Mary Jo's favorite spot for curried goat was a place called the Door, a Jamaican restaurant near JFK airport, not far from where she grew up. "*They* have a serious wickedness to their food," she told me. "And they know how to treat a goat."

"Serious wickedness" was all Isabel needed to hear when I told her about Mary Jo and her goat. Three days after that death-defying taxi ride to Queensboro Plaza, Isabel and I took a long trip on the E train and a short one on the Q111 bus, and showed up at the Door in the middle of Sunday brunch.

No longer able to afford the cab rides from Manhattan to the outer boroughs—where most cabbies lived, and where most of their favorite restaurants seemed to be—I was starting to ask drivers for food recommendations, later finding my way, on the subway and/or the bus, to the places they told me about. I would take long train rides to Queens and Brooklyn and the Bronx, which were more like short trips around the world—to Little Odessa in Brighton Beach, or Naples on Arthur Avenue, or Bogotá in Jackson Heights, or Bukhara in Rego Park, or Calcutta in Sunnyside—feeling as though I were on some sort of culinary scavenger hunt. Like a poem that revealed more at each reading, the outer boroughs were where I was beginning to find so much tempting comestible treasure.

So I had high hopes about the Door, which was packed with an after-church crowd when Isabel and I walked in. I felt underdressed in my flea-market sweater and three-year-old jeans next to all those sharp Sunday suits and chic hats, and the curtains with gold tassels at the entrance to the dining room, and the teal linens draped over the tables.

A waiter in a satin vest showed us to a table with a good view of the all-you-can-eat buffet, and we inhaled the promising smells of stewed chicken and curry as we attacked a basket of what tasted like just-baked cornbread. "Is it OK if we order off the menu?" I asked the waiter.

"Oh," he said, "of course."

He nodded as though he were pleased as he wrote down our order. I showed Isabel the picture I'd taken of Mary Jo in the driver's seat.

"That smile!" said Isabel. "She's beautiful. She drives part-time?"

"Yep," I said. "She's studying to be a nurse." Isabel handed the camera back to me. The waiter brought our soup: chicken and vegetable for me, fish and fresh thyme for Isabel. The broth tasted like slow cooking and patience.

"This," said Isabel, closing her eyes, "is *awe*some."

I moved the camera off the table, looking at the picture of Mary

Jo one more time before I put it back in my purse. She was petite—
but it was power she radiated.

I thought back to my last conversation with Nidia, at Brick Café,
and how she'd asked me, after I'd shown her what I'd written about
her on my blog, if I ever thought about driving a cab. "Me?" I couldn't
imagine doing what Nidia did. "No, no." I shook my head so hard my
bun came loose. "No way."

But my thinking started to change after the ride with Mary Jo.
I wasn't a praying woman like she was, and I wasn't a native New
Yorker who knew the streets like she did, but I couldn't let go of the
idea that if someone like her could drive a cab, I could drive a cab.

The goat curry came. And Isabel's oxtail stew. And fried plantains
and rice and peas. (On the West Coast we'd call them beans. In the
Caribbean they called them peas.)

"What if"—I handed a bite of goat, simmered to tender and
steeped in a mustard-heavy curry paste, to Isabel—"I drove a cab?"

"What?" Isabel ignored the goat and opened her eyes so wide her
lashes hit the tops of her eyebrows.

"What if I drove a cab?" I set the forkful of goat on the rim of her
plate. "You know I need another job."

She grabbed the edges of the table with both hands. "Awesome!"
She grinned, reaching over and clasping my wrist. "Lady, you are
brave!"

"We'll see." I took a breath. "I don't know."

The waiter came back to check on us: "Are you enjoying your
food?"

"Yes!" we both said. He handed us another basket of cornbread.

"You can do it." Isabel passed me a bite of oxtail, which tasted like
it had been stewing in tomato, garlic, and Tabasco for hours. "But
how will you do it?"

"I have no idea."

I wrote Mary Jo an email that night, thanking her for the ride and the
tip about the Door, telling her I was seriously thinking about getting
my yellow-cab license.

I went on your taxi gourmet link, she wrote back the next morning. It was beautiful and delightful as well to have you in my taxi. Yes, the Door is a dangerous ;-) place. I am glad you and your friend tried the curried goat. I tell you the truth, curried goat and Lay's potato chips are going to put me in the grave. hahahaha. Thank you for my five minutes of fame. Let me know about getting your hack license. We will talk.

I thought about it for another forty-eight hours. I needed another job, and even more than that, I was seeing the limits of what I could understand from the back seat—I had a natural tendency to idealize cab drivers, and romanticize cab driving, but there had to be dark sides to the job. How could I expect to learn what they were, as a passenger? And maybe, as a cab driver, I would come to know the city, and its geography, and the people who moved through it at street level. And what if I did some restaurant reconnaissance of my own from the taxi? I liked the idea of sharing the road with Nidia and Mary Jo. It felt crazy, like a lunatic taking over the asylum. And it felt right.

17

"To all outsiders, you *are* New York!" said the man with the crooked bow tie to the cab driver scowling at him in the rearview mirror. The two of them were going nowhere in their cardboard-cutout taxi, in this, the opening scene of "I AM New York: Becoming a Professional Taxi Driver." My taxi school classmates and I covered our mouths, trying not to giggle: this video, which might have been shot thirty years ago on the *Sesame Street* back lot, was the center-piece of the passenger relations portion of the New York City Taxi and For-Hire Vehicle Institute's official training curriculum.

"Turn around. Look at the customer," the man in the bow tie said to the cabby, who looked more constipated than interested. "Ask them their destination. Repeat their destination." *If only passenger relations were all we had to learn,* I thought, as the bow-tied man continued his sermon: "If you make it pleasant for you, it's pleasant for others. It's your style that makes a customer nice or lousy!" Volodya, the man from St. Petersburg who always sat behind me in class and never combed his hair, was paying no attention to "I AM New York." As usual, he was flipping through the pages of his *New York City 5-Borough Street Atlas,* muttering street names as though they were incantations, trying to summon the city's geography into his memory.

"I don't only want to pass taxi test!" said Volodya after class, his blue eyes bright with anxiety. "I don't want to be lost!"

Neither do I, I thought, as I crossed Queens Boulevard to the sub-way station. Volodya's anxiety was my anxiety, too, and when I got on the subway—"This is a Manhattan-bound *Seven* train," said the lady announcer in her upbeat singsong. "The next stop is . . . *Queens-boro Plaza*"—I pulled my *New York City 5-Borough Street Atlas* out of my bag and turned to the first page. Anxiety aside, I loved this map, the way I loved all maps, which to my eye were akin to works of art.

"Can I help you find something?" said the monk sitting across from me, his bald head and bare shoulder looking buffed and lustrous in the afternoon glare. He glanced at The Atlas, spread out on my lap, and extracted an iPhone from the folds of his burgundy habit. "I have GPS," he said, smiling. "See?"

"Thanks," I said, "but no." I smiled back at him. "I have to learn the streets."

"Why?"

The brakes squealed as the train pulled into Queensboro Plaza.

"I'm trying . . ." I felt silly, explaining myself to him, but no one in the subway car was listening to us: their eyes were on a toddler in fuchsia overalls who was pointing an empty squirt gun at a man in a suit working on his laptop. "I want to be a taxi driver," I said.

"A taxi driver?" The monk laughed. The subway stopped and he stood up, slipping the iPhone, encased in a cover that matched the burgundy of his habit, back into the folds of his robe. He glanced at me one more time before he got off the train, still laughing.

So even a monk thought it was funny that I wanted to drive a taxi. *It is funny,* I thought, but when I opened up The Atlas again, the anxiety returned, an anxiety that had emerged, and grown steadily, fertilized by doubt, since the first day of taxi school, when I realized what I needed to learn to pass the test to become a yellow-cab driver: New York City had 6,200 miles of streets, 31 bridges and tunnels, 188 theaters, 28,000 acres of parks, 500 museums and galleries, and who knows how many hotels and hospitals. If I was going to pass the taxi test—an eighty-question multiple-choice exam that "may include questions on geography, map reading, address location, planning routes and Taxi & Limousine Commission Rules and Regulations"—I had less than two months to learn it all.

"Get out!" said Nidia, when I told her I was trying to get my hack license.

"Coolalicious!" said Mary Jo. "If you need any help let me know."

"Why do you wanna drive a taxi?" said Dad, when I finally worked up the nerve to tell my parents, on our Sunday call.

"The best tango dancers have to know how to lead *and* how to follow," I said. They were Joaquín's words, not mine. "If I'm ever going to be a complete dancer, I have to know what the other half of the embrace feels like."

"Huh?"

"I've been a passenger all this time, see," I said, but I wondered, saying it aloud for the first time, if I might be pushing the metaphor too far. "Driving will be like learning to lead."

"But, sweetie," said Dad, "isn't it dangerous?"

"Well, yes and no ..." At this point my fear of getting lost—oh, I knew I was going to get lost—was far greater than any fear I could connect to the actual dangers of taxi driving.

"You've never even driven in New York!" said Mom. "How in the world are you going to drive a *taxi*?"

She had a point. I had been living in New York for less than six months, and I was the newest arrival in my taxi school class. Unlike most of my classmates, I didn't have a clue about freeways or tunnels or one-way streets, because I took the subway everywhere, or walked— which also meant I had no idea how to answer questions like this:

1. The most direct route from the Empire State Building in Manhattan to Citi Field uses:
   a) Clearview Expressway
   b) Long Island Expressway
   c) Major Deegan Expressway
   d) Cross Island Parkway

2. In Brooklyn, which of the following is parallel to Clinton Street?
   a) Atlantic Avenue
   b) Court Street
   c) Flushing Avenue
   d) Fulton Street

(Answers: 1 b; 2 b)

When I wasn't in taxi school—an eighty-hour course at La Guardia Community College, where I shared the classroom with Volodya, four men from Egypt, five from Bangladesh, a DJ from Togo named Sam who told me he liked to eat African food at Accra Restaurant in the Bronx, and a former Bedouin tribesman who gave me a tip about the good lamb at Hadramout, a Yemeni restaurant on Atlantic Avenue in Brooklyn—I was studying The Atlas or walking up and down and across Manhattan, wearing the camel-colored coat I'd inherited from Mom and four pairs of socks that were no match for the crosstown winds and the brutality of the New York winter.

I wandered now so as not to be lost later, trying to memorize bridge and tunnel entrances and Greenwich Village diagonals and Central Park transverses—on foot, since I didn't have a car. I shuffled through the snow in Brooklyn, staring at the street signs on the lettered avenues, taking mental photographs. I rode the subway to the Bronx, and deeper into Queens, searching for the logic behind the layout of each borough. I ignored Staten Island after one of my taxi school instructors, a former computer programmer from Canada who was a refugee from Wall Street, told us he'd only had one fare to Staten Island in twenty years of cab driving.

As determined as I was to know the city, my knowledge felt superficial, poorly digested, like a hamburger wolfed down on the run. I was spending as little time as possible at the apartment, despite the ear-numbing cold on the streets—Jefferson was still in a terrible post-breakup funk, slamming doors and giving me the silent treatment whenever I was there, locking himself in his room, playing the same woebegone sonata over and over on his cello. "He probably just hates all women now," said Isabel. It was the only explanation that made sense to me, but it didn't make living with him any more bearable. When I had to be at the apartment, I listened to tango. Away from Buenos Aires, the melancholy and the longing and the madness in the music made even more sense to me.

The night before the taxi test, I called Mary Jo. "I remember my first passenger on my first day," she said. "Whew, what a mess! I picked up this gentleman on Houston and Avenue Something. He said he just wanted to go to Something Street and Something Avenue. I didn't have a clue."

"Oh, man." It was too easy to imagine myself in a similar predicament.

"And just like they say in taxi school," said Mary Jo, " 'Ask the passenger the best route.' Ooooh, he got so mad, he said, 'No wonder people don't like cab drivers!' Then he got out and slammed the door. He needed a chill pill. What a first day! But, honey bunch, be encouraged. You gotta do *your* thing on the streets."

"How long did it take before you felt like you knew what you were doing?"

"I learn something new every day," she said. It reminded me of what Joaquín used to say when beginners would ask how long it would take to learn the tango: *It takes a lifetime.* "You learn things in the cab that no school can teach you," said Mary Jo.

I was nodding, taking notes.

"You still there?"

"I'm here," I said. "I'm writing stuff down."

"Write this down, honey bunch. You ready?"

"Yep."

"Thank God for grace," she said. " 'Cuz you're gonna need it."

Maybe it was grace—and a love of maps, and a lot of practice tests— that got me through the taxi exam, and I was happy for about five minutes after I passed it, until I realized that there were other obstacles, bigger obstacles, ahead.

"Passing the taxi exam is one thing," my taxi school instructor told me, when I went to pick up my results. "Now you gotta find a garage."

Word on the street was that there were more cab drivers than cabs to drive: forty-eight thousand yellow drivers, and counting, and thirteen thousand yellow taxis, and no more.

"You gonna work steady, or non-steady?" said my instructor.

"Non-steady." In taxi driving lingo, a non-steady hack was a part-time taxi driver. Unlike steady hacks, who committed to driving six or seven days a week, non-steady hacks could set their own schedules.

"Garages like steady hacks better," said my instructor. "And these days, non-steady hacks? There's no guarantee you get a cab. You gotta show up at the garage, two, three in the morning. You gotta be first in line." He clucked his tongue. "But you got a lotta options, young lady! Why don't you lease from an owner?" He pointed at a bulletin board feathered with DRIVERS WANTED flyers. "You can get a better deal from an owner. At a garage you're a serf!"

I scanned the flyers: I could lease a 2009 Ford Crown Victoria for $750 a week from Anwar, or share a taxi with Lulo, driving the day shift part-time, or with someone called AFP, who was looking for a day driver on the weekends, or just call 3479788023 and "start driving by Wednesday." My stomach turned. For some reason, I couldn't picture myself in any of these scenarios.

"You'll find a garage," said Isabel. "I know it. Let me see your license!" We were standing on the corner of University Place and East 14th Street, looking for a cab.

I pulled out my hack license, trimmed in taxicab yellow, with my name in block letters, and handed it to her. "The picture is really bad," I said. I looked like a nose with big hair.

"It doesn't look like you," she said, handing it back to me.

I put my hack license back in my wallet and raised my hand. The cabby who pulled over said yes right away when I asked him if we could ask him some questions on the way to 28th and Lex. He was young—probably in his late twenties—and good-looking, with ash-blond hair and almond-shaped blue eyes.

"I don't look Turkish," he said, when he saw me looking at his hack license. His name was Huseyin. "But I am. There are actually a lot of blonds in Turkey." He steered the cab through the swell of pedestrians crossing Broadway. "I came two years ago to New York, from Hatay. That's in the south of Turkey. I used to be a salesman for Westco. But business got so bad I had to start driving the cab."

"When did you start?"

"Two months ago. My girlfriend doesn't like it. But it's better than delivering baklava."

"Baklava?" I moved closer to the opening in the Plexiglas partition.

"The best baklava in New York. When I first came here, I didn't speak any English, you know? So I worked at the baklava place. Then I met Courtney. She's from Arizona. And now"—he smiled, long dimples denting his cheeks—"I owe her a language."

Isabel and I laughed. "Tell us more about this baklava," she said. I winked at her.

"Güllüoğlu, it's called."

"Guulluu . . . ?"

"Gü-llü-o-ğlu. They make it in Istanbul and fly it to New York. And then a baker cooks it every day fresh."

"Are you kidding?" I said.

"Could you take us there?" said Isabel.

"I thought you were going to Twenty-eighth and Lex."

"We're hungry."

"OK." He chuckled. "Sure. But if you want more than baklava, I know a place . . ."

It was on the Upper East Side, and it was his favorite place in the city for Adana kebab. "You can have baklava for dessert," he said.

He chatted easily with us on the way to the restaurant, cruising north on Third Avenue as if we were on a Sunday drive in the country. He didn't believe me at first when I said I'd just passed the taxi test.

"I can show you my hack license, if you want." I reached for my wallet.

"No, no," he said. "I believe you."

I told him I was looking for a taxi garage.

"Maybe my garage will take you."

I looked at Isabel, my eyes widening. I come from California, where the power of positive thinking is a kind of unofficial religion, but this much serendipity was hard to believe.

"I'll give you the address," said Huseyin. "It's in Brooklyn. Is that OK?"

"I don't think I can be too picky."

Isabel and I were surprised when he parked his cab around the corner from the restaurant, a place called Üsküdar, on East 73rd Street at Second Avenue. We were even more surprised when he walked us inside, introduced us to the manager, and taught us how to say hello in Turkish *(merhaba)*. He didn't have time for Adana kebab. But before he went back to his cab, he invited us to join him and Courtney in Brooklyn for dinner sometime, at a place called A Bay Ridge Shish Kebab, where he was "crazy about the chicken gyro." He also wrote down the address of his taxi garage.

"I'm sure they'll take you," he said.

I thanked him, hoping he was right.

I took the subway to Huseyin's garage the next day. "You ever driven a taxi?" said the manager. He glanced at my hack license and handed it to back me. The armpits on his white shirt were stained yellow, as were his fingertips, from cigarettes.

"No," I said. "Not yet."

His eyes swept over my big red purse, and Mom's camel-colored coat, which was the warmest thing I owned. Hand-stitched, beautifully cut, it looked sharp on the outside. It wasn't until I walked into the taxi garage that I realized the coat probably made me look like a priss. If only he could have seen the disintegrating lining.

"How long have you had your New York driver's license?" said the manager, crossing his arms high on his chest.

I glanced at the two other men in the office, sitting at metal desks, keeping their noses in their papers as if they weren't listening.

"Since October," I said. "Three months." I shifted my purse from one shoulder to the other. "But I've had a California license since 1990."

"You need at least two years of driving experience in New York before you can drive at this garage," said the manager. "Our insurance won't accept your California driving record." He extended his hand toward the door, smiling as though he were relishing the act of kicking me out. "Thank you for stopping by."

I pressed my lips shut and hurried out the door, my breath steaming in the cold as I marched through the parking lot. He hadn't refused me for insurance reasons, I was sure. But what could I do about it?

I tried to calm down as I walked back to Fourth Avenue, sniffing what smelled like a nice combination of garlic and cumin and green onions coming from a halal Chinese restaurant called No Pork. I'd noticed the place on my way to the garage. Its fragrance was tempting, but I kept walking.

It would have been too easy, too poetic, for it to have worked out with Huseyin's garage. His food tips had already worked out so well: Isabel and I would make return trips to Üsküdar for Adana kebab, with ground lamb and minced red peppers, and stuffed grape leaves and spinach tarator (house-made yogurt and walnuts). And Güllüoğlu's baklava—whether pistachio, chestnut, walnut, or sour cherry—was far and away the best I'd ever tasted, with the freshest nuts, and a perfect cross of butter and sugar, and layers of filo that dissolved like snowflakes on my tongue.

Thinking about that baklava brought no consolation as I rode the subway back to Queens. What if no garage would take me? What if they were only looking for steady hacks right now? I thought about all the time and all the money I'd invested to get my yellow-cab license, jumping through bureaucratic hoops and studying maps and walking the streets of four boroughs, plus taxi school, plus an eye exam and a drug test and a new Social Security card and a New York driver's license. What if it was all for nothing? I needed another job—but this was about more than money. I wanted to drive.

"You eva driven a cab?" said the cashier with the spiky gray hair at a taxi garage called Team Systems. "Team!"—this was how they answered the phone—was where I'd taken the defensive driving course that was the first step toward getting my hack license. My taxi school instructor told me to try Team after I got rejected at Huseyin's garage. "They got one of the biggest fleets in the city!" he said. Still, I didn't have high hopes: big fleet or small fleet, there were too many drivers and not enough cabs.

The Team cashier stood in the doorway between the garage and the office, holding my hack license in both hands, squinting at the terrible picture, then at me, through his bifocals.

"No," I said. "I haven't ever driven a cab." *Here we go again,* I thought. I put out my hand to take back my license. "But I got a ninety-six on my exam."

"You're already ova-qualified," he said, holding on to my license, sighing as if all was wrong with the world. He motioned for me to follow him into the office, to a desk in the corner, above which hung a swimsuit calendar from 1999 and a bumper sticker that said NEVER DRIVE FASTER THAN YOUR ANGEL CAN FLY.

"Here." He handed me a stack of forms. "Fill these out and lemme see your driver's license. You had any accidents?"

"Nope."

"I gotta check your record."

I tried to keep my composure as I cleared a space on the paper-strewn desk and filled out the forms: they wanted my name and address and phone number and hack license number and driver's license number and birthday and Social Security number and an emergency contact person. I chose Isabel.

The cashier came back a few minutes later. "Your record's clean," he said. "Give me those." I handed him the forms. "I'm Allen, by the way."

Was that it? Was I in? No insurance issues? No way. It couldn't be that easy. "I'm Layne."

"If you get in an accident, bring the car back to the garage," said Allen.

I was in! "OK." I nodded. "OK, I will." *I promise,* I thought. *Whatever you want.*

"If it's not serious, we'll get you back on the road. If it's bad, you'll have to fill out an accident report with the ladies in the office."

"OK." I looked around the office. I didn't see any ladies. "OK."

"Day shift starts at five a.m. Even if you don't get a car until six, you still gotta bring it back by five p.m." He tapped his finger on his wrist. "Otherwise, you pay a late fee. You know we have a lotta drivers right now. We can't guarantee you a car."

"I know." I couldn't stop nodding. "No problem."

Allen led me out of the office, into the garage section of the garage. Everything—taxis, taxi parts, windows, and walls—was smeared with layers of auto grease. A pair of mechanics in blue jumpsuits were ministering to a yellow cab with its hood up.

Allen turned to me. "You know how to work the meter?"

"Sort of . . ."

"Rabin!"

Rabin, a welterweight with a shaved head and wide-set black-brown eyes, interrupted his conversation with one of the mechanics and jogged over, jeans barely hanging on to his hip bones. He coughed a smoker's cough as he led me out to the parking lot, to one of the taxis next to the gas pumps.

"Get on the driver's side," he said. I climbed in and ran my hands over the steering wheel and tried to find the accelerator. I could barely reach it.

Rabin got in on the passenger side. "You never drove before?"

I shook my head. Something buckled in my stomach.

"I'm training to be a radiologist," he said. "The taxi's temporary." He pointed at the meter. "The meter's easy." He wagged his finger at the bottom button on the far left. "You press one for a fare in any of the five boroughs. That starts and stops the meter. The second button's for when you go to JFK—you know, the forty-five bucks?" I nodded. It was just like they taught us in taxi school. "When you go to Newark, you press three," Rabin continued. "If you go outside the five boroughs, you press four. That'll start doubling the rate. And if you get a flat fare, you know, like to Connecticut or something, you press five."

"OK."

"It's easy." Rabin shrugged. "No problem."

"OK," I said. "Thanks a lot." I followed him back into the garage. It looked easy, but I could already picture myself in a battle with those buttons. I was not good with machines.

Allen was standing in the middle of the garage, hands on hips, belly protruding, tight as a muscle, watching one of the mechanics change a bulb on a smashed brake light. "You know," he said, turning to me, "the taxi driver is the exception in life in every way."

"How so?"

He took off his glasses, breathing on the lenses, wiping them with his shirttail. "It takes a special personality to drive a cab," he said. "To drive in Manhattan, you gotta be on top of your game. You need a *lotta* patience. And a whole lotta juice. Most people, they don't have it." He put his glasses back on. "But some people—some people are born taxi drivers."

Did he think I might be a born taxi driver? I was too afraid to ask.

"Drive safely," he said, pulling my hack license out of his pocket and handing it to me. "And watch out for cops at Thirty-seventh and Lex."

I slipped my license into the window of my wallet. "I will."

18

Eight hours before I was supposed to leave for the garage to start my first taxi driving shift, I was packing everything I thought I would need in my big red purse:

· **Caramel Nips** for nice passengers, inspired by Nidia
· *New York City 5-Borough Street Atlas* We could get a ticket from the Taxi & Limousine Commission, a.k.a. the TLC, if we didn't carry The Atlas in the cab at all times.
· **VanDam Manhattan Pop-Up Map** Mary Jo's tip. Easier to use than The Atlas, and good for quick checks of one-way streets and Greenwich Village diagonals.
· **Receipt book** The taxi meter printed receipts, but the TLC required us to carry paper receipts as backup.
· **Lists** of taxi stands, hospitals, department stores, tourist attractions, transportation terminals, hotels, parks, major museums, Central Park transverses, and entrances to water crossings (i.e., bridges)
· **Manhattan street number decoder** to find cross streets when a passenger only had an address (e.g., 1405 Second Ave)
· **Notebook and many pens**
· **Tape recorder** in case my hands weren't free to take notes
· **Camera**
· **$20 in small bills** + extra money for coffee
· **Pepper spray,** which I hoped I'd never have to use
· **Paper towels and tea tree oil** I wanted my cab to smell great, at least until someone barfed.
· **Swiss Army knife**

- **Water**
- **Taxi driving mix CD** Lead-off track: the *Superman* theme

As hard as I tried to think of everything I would need, I knew
that no amount of Nips, no quantity of maps or street decoders, no
pepper spray or Swiss Army knife, could take away the feeling of
being ill-equipped and unprepared and just plain freaked-out: 96 on
the taxi test would mean nothing once my first passenger gave me an
address. But now, on the eve of my first shift, my anxiety about getting lost was getting mixed up with other, more concrete fears: What
if I crashed the cab? What if I hit someone? What if I got a crazy customer? "Eighty-five percent of people are good," I remembered one
of my taxi school instructors telling us. "Seven point five percent are
not good, and seven point five percent are . . . just so-so."

I made up a mantra as I finished arranging things in my purse:
*I will be safe, my passengers will be safe, my cab will be safe, everyone who
comes near my cab will be safe* . . . I repeated it every time I started to
imagine a gruesome scenario in the taxi.

"You're gonna be fine," said Sarah, my new roommate, leaning
against the door frame, holding a head of broccoli as she watched
me lay out my clothes for the next morning. After New Year's, I'd
moved out of the apartment in Astoria with Jefferson. The place
was only three stops on the N train from Team taxi garage, but in
the aftermath of Jefferson's breakup, the atmosphere in the apartment had become so toxic—he never left his room unless he was
sure I was gone or my door was closed—the silence between us so
total that we negotiated the terms of our roommate separation over
email, sending each other messages from the next room. Less than a
day after I put out an appeal on Facebook—Does anyone know anyone looking for a roommate in New York?—I'd found a cheap place in
Ridgewood with Sarah, an Iyengar yoga teacher I'd met in Argentina,
and Romeo, her techno DJ husband, who were both vegetarians, and
a Chihuahua they called Papichulo. The apartment, on the border
between Brooklyn and Queens, surrounded by 99-cent stores and
Western Union suppliers, was a ninety-minute commute from Team.

I wish you all the best tomorrow, Isabel wrote me as the sun was going down. I know that you are nervous but everything will turn out great! I wish I was the lucky one to get in your cab for the first time! ☺ Break your leg, my friend!!

I went to bed early that night, but I couldn't sleep at all: I tossed and turned for I don't know how long before I gave up and made the mistake of watching *Taxi Driver* for the first time, after which I lay in bed and stayed awake with the image of Robert De Niro as Travis Bickle in his Checker cab, sidling around steam holes in the New York night, picking up perverts and crooked politicians, growing more insane with each passing shift. I wondered whether taxi driving would do to me what it did to him, whether the job would turn my head inside out enough to get a Mohawk and eat Wonder Bread soaked in milk and peach brandy.

When the alarm went off, at 2:30 a.m., instead of the *I will be safe, my passengers will be safe* mantra, I had Travis Bickle's words in my head: "All the animals come out at night. Whores, skunk-pussies, buggers, queens, fairies, dopers, junkies. Sick, venal. Someday a real rain will come and wash all this scum off the streets."

As I boiled water for coffee and gathered my snacks (a fig bar, a hunk of goat cheddar, an apple, a banana, and a hard-boiled egg), I was thinking I should have watched *Women on the Verge of a Nervous Breakdown* instead. The cabby in Almódovar's movie—who drove with tasseled fringe on the windshield, and kept aspirin, Kleenex, trashy magazines, eyedrops, Fanta, and a carefully selected library of Latin music at the ready for his passengers—was the cabby I aspired to be, minus the leopard-print seat covers and the bleached pompadour.

The clouds hid the moon in the four a.m. darkness as I high-stepped through the snow in my winter uniform—long underwear, a pair of sweaters, Mom's coat, four pairs of socks, two pairs of gloves—to the subway station. My fingers were still stinging from the cold when I got on the L train, where a man in a parka was reading the Bible, and a woman who looked like she was wearing all the clothes she owned was sleeping, sprawled out on one of the powder-blue benches, cuddling a plastic bag from Century 21. At the far end of the car sat another woman, maybe in her fifties, wearing fishnet stockings and thigh-high black patent leather boots, blowing her nose. Here was Travis Bickle's New York. My stomach ached like something was trying to hollow it out, despite the fig bar I'd forced down while I was waiting for the train.

Every time the train stopped and the doors opened, the freezing air on the platform surged into the subway car as if seeking someone to punish. I clenched my shoulders and hugged my purse, as if to fend off the cold. At Lorimer Street, a man playing the *Flintstones* theme on a mini-accordion got on with a group of drunk twenty-somethings who groped each other under their long coats as they debated an epic after-party. The woman in the thigh-high boots got off the train, stuffing wadded-up tissues in her pockets. The sleeping woman hoisted herself up. The man with the Bible grew more determined in his reading. I looked at my cell phone. It was almost four o'clock on Sunday morning, or four o'clock on Saturday night—in Buenos Aires, this was when the lights dimmed to blue at La Viruta, when the tourists had gone home, when the teachers and the professional dancers and the truly obsessed took over the floor. It was also the time, according to a few of the taxistas who'd driven me home from the *milonga,* when the veil between this world and the next was at its thinnest.

I transferred to the N train at Union Square, and as I sat alone in the subway car, biting my chapped lips, holding my purse and my snack bag in my lap, I hoped the train would break down, that something would make it impossible to arrive, but when the N surfaced just before Queensboro Plaza and stopped on the elevated tracks at 39th Avenue in Long Island City, across the street from the taxi garage, I grabbed my things and bolted through the sliding doors as though I were eager to get off. From the subway platform, in the icy wind, I could hear the dispatcher calling out the names of the cabbies over a garbled loudspeaker, bidding them to start the day shift.

I stood at the top of the subway stairs and took a picture of the garage. Rows and rows of yellow cabs waited in the parking lot under heavy blankets of snow. Fluorescent lights flickered behind the frosted windows of the office. I watched the night drivers pull in, their brake lights gleaming in the brittle air as they passed through the gate in the chain-link fence, and I remembered Mabel, the first and only lady cab driver I'd met in Buenos Aires, saying you either loved taxi driving or you hated taxi driving, that there was no in-between. I never imagined then that I would be finding this out for myself.

I walked into the parking lot and immediately sensed the curiosity of the night drivers, who looked at me like they were wondering what I was doing there as they lined up to turn in their cabs. I tried not to notice the taxis in the parking lot with the hoods ripped off, the taxis with crushed rear ends, the taxis with the driver's side doors smashed in.

When I pulled open the squeaky door to the office, heads turned away from the foosball table and the TV, which was tuned to a rebroadcast of *Footloose*. The cabbies in the waiting area stared as I traipsed over to the intake window, stood on my tiptoes, and slid my hack license through the opening in the bulletproof glass. It was a little after five a.m.

"Hello." I smiled at the dispatcher. "Am I too late to get a cab?"

His hair was black, frosted with gray, his dress shirt plaid, and his smile, surrounded by laugh lines, so sincere that for a second I forgot about Travis Bickle, and the curiosity on the beat-up faces of the drivers in the waiting area, and the mean cold outside, seeping through the single-paned windows.

"Nah, you're not too late," said the dispatcher, setting my license on the counter next to the microphone. "First day?" I liked his Brooklyn accent.

"Yeah."

"I'm Mike," he said. "Take a seat. We'll call ya in a minute."

I sat on one of the benches against the cinderblock wall. The hollow in my stomach was twisting into a knot. I peeked into my snack bag. I didn't think I could keep down any of the food I'd brought.

"Wanna play?" asked one of the cabbies, pointing to the foosball table. Christmas was three weeks ago, but he was wearing a Christmas sweater, with red and green snowflakes.

"Oh, no," I said. "I'm really bad."

"Really bad?"

I nodded.

He shrugged and sat down next to the other drivers who were waiting for Mike to call their names. Most had their eyes closed. The others were watching the grand dance finale in *Footloose*. Mike turned on the heater, and a gust of hot air whooshed into the waiting room from the mouth of the square pipe next to the TV. Watching Kevin Bacon do backflips made me want to move, too. I'd reached that stage of performance anxiety, just before going on, when the desire to get it over with overpowers the dread of doing it.

"You drive a cab?" said the man sitting to my right.

"It's my first day." I asked him how long he'd been driving.

"Too long!" he said. His nose was crooked, slanting to one side like it had been broken once or twice. He pulled his knit cap over his ears.

"José!" Even through the garbled loudspeaker, you could hear the smile in Mike's voice.

"That's me," said the cabby in the knit cap. "Good luck out there. It's nice to see a lady in here."

"Thanks."

I didn't know whether I liked being an anomaly, but there wasn't much I could do about it. I had done some research on lady cab drivers while I was studying for my hack license: Women had started driving taxis in numbers here during World War II, due to a shortage of male drivers, but in the 1960s and '70s, when violent crimes against New York cabbies reached record highs, all but a few women stopped hacking. The city now wasn't nearly as dangerous as it had been then, but out of forty-eight thousand yellow-cab drivers, at last count, approximately five hundred were female.

"Layne!"

I flinched when I heard my name. Mike slipped my license and a mileage receipt with the medallion number of the taxi I was supposed to drive through the slot in the bulletproof glass. "It's on the pump!" he said.

A man in a fur hat was rushing between the taxis queuing at the gas pumps outside, filling up the night drivers' empty tanks before the cabs got turned over to the day drivers. My cab, or the cab I was leasing for the day, was second in line. My heart was beating like I'd had four cups of coffee.

"Hey, little lady!" said the man in the driver's seat, who was wearing a sweater with rainbow stripes and a matching snow hat. "You gonna drive my cab?"

Well, it wasn't actually *his* cab—he was a steady hack, he told me, and this was the cab he drove six nights a week.

"Yep!" I tried to mirror his enthusiasm. "It's my first day!"

"Your first day? You know how the meter works?"

"I think so . . ."

"Get in."

I climbed into the passenger seat. He counted out five dollars, handed it to the man in the fur hat who was pumping gas, then pulled forward and parked next to a taxi with no bumper.

"I'm Boris," he said, "as in Boris Yeltsin!" And then he guffawed, and I had to laugh, too. Boris was a black man with a full beard who looked nothing like Boris Yeltsin.

Boris described how every button on the taxi meter worked. I didn't tell him Rabin had explained all of this to me a few days earlier, because I wanted to see it one more time anyway. Then he handed me a plastic sleeve, "for your hack license," he said. "The holder's broken, see?" The Plexiglas pocket behind the driver's seat, where we were supposed to display our hack license, was cracked on the bottom, "You don't wanna lose your license!" he said as he hopped out of the cab. "Take good care of my taxi"—he clasped his hands in prayer—"please!"

I promised him I would, and I offered him a Nip. He waved it away with a laugh.

I could smell my own fear as I clutched the steering wheel at ten and two, driving the taxi over the Queensboro Bridge for the first time. I gaped at the half-lit skyline through the windshield, holding my breath against the sour odor of my sweat, listening to the blood churning in my ears. Here, I tried to remind myself, was Whitman's Mannahatta of spires and masts. But all I could think about was the labyrinth beneath the masts, the thousands of miles of one-way, dead-end, no-left-turn streets that I was about to pretend I could navigate.

There was no CD player in the cab, which meant I couldn't listen to the music mix I'd made. There went my vision of driving into Manhattan for the first time with the *Superman* theme playing in the background. I turned on the radio, tuning it to the BBC. I turned it off after a few seconds. The talking was too distracting, and the lanes on the bridge felt too small for the girth of the Crown Victoria. I could only reach the accelerator by sitting up ramrod straight, on the edge of driver's seat, and every time my toe hit the gas, the eight-cylinder engine seemed to roar "Yes!" I'd never driven such a powerful car. I remembered my first car: a 1983 Ford Courier pickup truck I'd painted 1974 Porsche Purple that convulsed when I went over forty-five. The Crown Vic, built for high-speed pursuit, and once the official vehicle of the NYPD, was a beast in comparison. In my first thirty minutes with it, I was afraid to go more than thirty miles an hour.

I pulled off the Queensboro Bridge, turning left on Second Avenue. I must have passed a dozen potential passengers, their hands raised hopefully at first, then flopping angrily to their sides when I didn't stop for them. I hadn't seen them in time, I told myself. I'd cause an accident if I pulled over too fast. In truth I was terrified to pick them up: What if I got lost? What if they were drunk and barfed in my cab?

I drove down Second Avenue and up First Avenue, down Lexington Avenue and up and down Park, tracing the Manhattan grid in the taxi, refusing to stop for anyone, or to take a hand off the wheel. There was something sinister in the darkness and in the silence in the cab. I glanced at the reserve fig bar I'd stuffed in the console, and my stomach grumbled in protest. *Rule number 1,* one of our taxi school instructors had told us: *Never eat in your cab.* This was the one rule I knew I'd eventually break.

I zigzagged through Central Park, driving over all the east–west transverses I'd learned about in taxi school. I looked at the clock on the dashboard: I'd been driving around alone for an hour. *Come on,* I thought, *find a passenger.* I had to find a passenger, unless I wanted to pay the garage a hundred and fifty dollars for the privilege of cruising around New York by myself in a yellow cab for twelve hours.

It was still dark when I drove out of Central Park. I repeated my mantra—*I will be safe, my passengers will be safe, my cab will be safe, everyone who comes near my cab will be safe*—and turned left on Broadway, toward Times Square and the bluish glow in the dark that I could see from half a mile away. When I got to Times Square, it was as bright as noon, and there were tourists wandering around below the *Mamma Mia!* marquee, staring at underwear billboards, lounging on the red glass bleachers on 47th Street, gazing at the fallen New Year's ball. The place was packed with NYPD squad cars. I watched a yellow cab pick up a pair of pierced teenagers in trench coats, and in the midst of all that brilliance, gaudy though it was, I didn't feel quite so alone.

I drove on, downtown, past Madison Square Garden, past Penn Station, past Koreatown and the Flatiron Building. Finally, at 21st and Broadway, I spotted a tall, thin man in a dark blazer with messy, shoulder-length black hair. He was tottering on the sidewalk, his hand high in the air. My first thought was *He looks scary*. My second thought was *That's my passenger!* I pressed hard on the loose brakes, pulled over, unlocked the doors, and turned around to say hello.

"Helloooooo," he said, swinging open the door, unbuttoning his blazer, and sinking into the back seat as though it were a recliner. "Thirty-first an' Madison, please."

"Thirty-first. And Madison?"

"Thirty-first"—he raised his head—"between Madison an' Fifth." His eyes were halfway closed. He wasn't scary. He was drunk.

I pressed button number one to start the meter. It was a simple trip on the Manhattan grid—not more than a few blocks away, but when the man, who was probably in his mid-thirties, sat up and poked his head through the opening in the Plexiglas partition and noticed my ten-and-two grip on the steering wheel, he said, "Are you OK?" He had a five o'clock shadow, and he smelled like whiskey. "You seem a little confused."

"It's my first day." I turned left and left again, trying to remember where Madison Avenue started. "And you're my very first passenger."

"Really?" He grinned.

"Yep."

He poked his head further through the partition, glancing at my big red purse, and at Mom's camel-colored coat, folded up on the passenger seat. "Look at your coat! You don't even have the right coat for a cab driver! Ha ha ha!" He sprawled on the back seat, holding his stomach as he laughed.

I found Park Avenue and turned left, very carefully. I wanted to give my passenger a smooth ride, no matter what. No sudden accelerations, no potholes, no unexpected stops—then maybe there would be no barfing. I stopped at a yellow light. He was still giggling. Thank goodness he was drunk.

I braked as softly as I could when he told me to stop, in front of a steel and glass high-rise on East 31st Street. Before he got out, I asked if I could take his picture. He posed with his fingers in a V-sign. Then he gave me his business card—his name was Iggy, he was a portfolio manager at Credit Suisse—and tipped me a dollar.

A one-dollar tip on a five-dollar fare was just fine with me. I stuffed the cash in my wallet, relieved that I hadn't harmed my first passenger, or the cab, or anyone in our path.

I drove toward Fifth Avenue, glancing at my coat—Iggy was right, it wasn't a taxi driver's coat—and let out a shaky sigh. *You did it!* I thought. *You did it!* But I didn't feel all that triumphant. Was I a cab driver now? I didn't know, but I was feeling a little bolder, and I had a thought: If all the drunk people were as laid-back as Iggy, maybe picking them up wasn't such a bad idea, and maybe they wouldn't care too much if I got lost. I headed to the West Village, where our taxi school teachers had told us to look for passengers at fancy nightspots.

When I noticed a string of yellow cabs parked at Varick and Spring, outside a club called the Greenhouse, where a vertical garden grew on a wall facing the street, I pulled into the taxi queue. The line moved fast as the bouncers hurried beautiful people with wobbly legs into cabs, and before I could count the waiting passengers to see which one would be mine, a man-child with dark blond hair and rosy cheeks climbed into the taxi and said, "Good *eve*-ning. I'd like to go to East Fifth and Second Avenue, please." He spoke too loudly, with an accent that reminded me of the London aristocrats on *Masterpiece Theatre*.

I pulled out of the taxi line, and the Englishman let out a long, vodka-infused sigh, and said, louder still, "You cannot *believe* how many *stew*pid women I talked to in there," and that's when my mental computer crashed. Everything I'd learned from studying for the taxi test, from staring at maps for months—one-way avenues, cross-town streets, where Houston Street was in relation to Canal—vanished from my memory.

"Do you have a preferred route?" I asked him. I left the meter off as we rolled away from the Greenhouse.

"A preferred *route*?" He tossed his head, flipping the bangs out of his eyes. "Right! Well . . ." His smile was goofy. "You'll just want to go up First and turn left on Fifth."

I switched on the meter. I had no idea how to get to First Avenue from where we were. I got us as far as Second Avenue, hitting a dead end at Roosevelt Park, and I had no choice but to turn right, downtown, in the wrong direction.

"Your navigation skills are fairly abysmal," said the Englishman, leaning forward and crossing his arms over the opening in the partition. I glanced over at him. He was nice-looking, in a boy band sort of way.

When I turned back to the road, the light changed from yellow to red, but we were in the middle of the intersection, and it was too late to stop. I slammed on the brakes anyway, looking around for cops. Not seeing any, I hit the gas.

"*Why* are you doing this?" said the Englishman.

"I'm a writer."

"I'm very sorry to see a writer reduced to driving a taxi," he said. "I support the arts, and I *really* think you should be doing something else."

"Maybe you're right." I peered out the window, trying to read the street signs in the dark.

"Why don't we go to breakfast?" he said.

"What?"

"How about breakfast?"

"I can't go to breakfast."

Did we just pass Delancey . . . ?

"Why not?"

"I just started my shift."

"So?"

Houston Street. I had to find Houston, and then I could find First Avenue. Was I even allowed to make a left on First from Houston?

The Englishman sighed another vodka-scented sigh and sat back, looking out the window. "You'll want to make a left at the next light," he said, his voice flattening into a matter-of-fact tone, "When you get to East Fifth . . . Left again . . . Here . . . Brilliant . . . It's just there . . . on the right. Right. Stop here." I turned off the meter.

"How about a little kiss?" he said, leaning toward the partition. "I did help you, after all."

I put the taxi in Park and turned around to look at him. His eyes were red, glassy, awash in alcohol, and he was younger than me. Still, part of me wanted to kiss him. Why not? He supported the arts.

"I'd like to kiss you," I heard myself say, "but I have to work."

"Right." He coughed, to disguise a chuckle. "Well then." He handed me the fare, and a two-dollar tip, which I thought was generous, since I'd probably taken him at least five dollars out of his way. "Good night," he said, giving the back seat a double pat before he opened the cab door. "Or should I say good morning?"

19

"Back for more punishment, huh?" said Mike, the weekend dispatcher, sipping coffee and smiling into his Styrofoam cup. It was four thirty in the morning, Super Bowl Sunday, fifteen degrees Fahrenheit, and I was lining up with the other non-steady hacks at the garage, about to start my third taxi shift.

I tried to return his smile as I pushed my license through the opening in the glass.

"Take a seat," said Mike, setting my license next to the others, arranged like playing cards around the microphone on the countertop.

Four other cabbies were sitting in the Team waiting room, on the bench that ran the length of the wall opposite the dispatcher's window. One of them, a tall man with a silver Afro, slumped against the cinderblocks, eyes closed, arms crossed, snoring softly. The other three were watching *Romancing the Stone* on the TV that sat atop an out-of-order vending machine.

"You wanna make money, you don't drive Sundays," said one of the cabbies, keeping his eyes on the TV as he moved over to make space for me on the bench. His pockmarked cheeks sagged beneath his graying beard.

"Yeah, I know," I said. "But Sunday's all I can drive right now." Actually, Sunday was the only day I felt ready to drive. My first two shifts had been rocky at best: after those first drunken fares, I could barely convince myself to pick anyone up. And when I did stop for a passenger, I got lost every time the trip went off the Manhattan grid, or anywhere in Greenwich Village. I'd also managed to smash into the side mirror of a double-parked Audi in Midtown (whose owner, mercifully, inexplicably, told me to forget about it), and, somewhere near the end of my second shift, I'd almost run over a passenger's foot. On Sundays, our taxi school teachers had told us, besides lighter traffic and laxer no-left-turn laws, most people weren't in a weekday rush. Until I knew my way around the city, and developed a better feel for the Crown Vic, I decided Sundays would be my training days—the equivalent of dancing at what Liliana called the toothless *milongas,* where ancient *tangueros* would forgive me all my missteps.

"She drive a cab?" whispered the man sitting next to the cabby with the pockmarked cheeks. He nodded, still staring at the TV. Michael Douglas was wrestling an alligator that had just swallowed an emerald the size of a softball.

"Hakeem!" said Mike.

The man with the silver Afro rubbed his eyes and stood up, hunching his shoulders, collecting the key to the cab and his hack license from Mike. I glanced at the rest of my colleagues on the bench, who seemed equally exhausted, if not abject, all ashen skin and bloodshot eyes and patchy beards. How many mornings had they spent this way?

The cabby with the pockmarked cheeks closed his eyes. I took out my notebook. *If I idealized cabbies before I started driving . . .*

"Layne!"

My stomach did a cartwheel—*Shit!* I thought. *Already?*—when I heard my name over the loudspeaker.

"It's on the pump!" said Mike, winking at me as he slipped my hack license and my mileage receipt through the opening in the glass.

I swung open the squeaky door and walked outside, studying the faces of the drivers returning their cabs after the Saturday-night shift. Most of them had the triumphant but shattered look of men coming back from battle. "If you can survive Saturday," I remembered Mary Jo telling me, "you can survive anything, honey bunch. Call it a miracle if someone doesn't throw up in your cab."

"Hello, beautiful," said the man in the fur hat who was pumping gas. His breath steamed in the frosty air. "Which cab you drivin' today?"

I showed him my mileage receipt, and he escorted me to the cab with the matching medallion number, which I drove to the far side of the parking lot, where I performed all of the pre-shift rituals I'd learned in taxi school: checking the interior and exterior lights, making sure all the seat belts worked, testing the windshield wipers, adjusting the mirrors, going through the trunk and the back seat for things passengers might have left behind. I also added some rituals of my own: moving the driver's seat as far forward as it would go, dusting off the steering wheel, stacking my CDs in the console, and positioning camera, notebook, tissues, water, and cucumber and cheese slices within easy reach. I gave up on the idea of wiping down the interior of the taxi with tea tree oil—I'd already let fifteen minutes go by. *I will be safe, my passengers will be safe, my cab will be safe . . .*

It was still dark when I pulled out of the Team parking lot. I pressed Play on the CD player, grateful that this cab had a CD player, and out came the foreboding sounds of Astor Piazzolla's "Buenos Aires Zero Hour." The tango was a perfect match for the industrial desolation of Long Island City before dawn. It made me think of Joaquín—he didn't like Piazzolla, he'd told me more than once. He'd sent me an email, a few days ago, Thursday at 09:44:04 a.m. to be precise, not one of those mass emails he sent every few months to announce a tour or a performance or a new series of classes: You won't believe it, he wrote, but I really miss you. I called your cell phone and there's no answer. I'd like to know if you're still in Buenos Aires . . . *Why now?* I memorized the message, but I didn't write back.

I turned off the music and followed the other cabs down 31st Street. Their taillights bled into the crystalline air. We were the only cars on the road. I drove as they drove, slowing down and easing the taxi over the axle-splitting potholes at the entrance to the Queensboro Bridge, trying to adjust my body to the Crown Vic, which was a lot like feeling out a new partner at the beginning of a tango. How sensitive were the brakes? How responsive was the accelerator? Which way did the steering wheel tilt? How far did I sink into the springs in the driver's seat?

In the tango clubs, early on, even at the toothless *milongas,* terrified of making a mistake on the floor, I would refuse to look up, to meet anyone's eyes and risk an invitation to dance. *"¿Y vos?"* And you? said the men who would approach my table, glancing at my tango shoes, *"¿Bailás, o no?"* Do you dance, or not? In the taxi, on those first two shifts, I'd done the same thing, passing so many potential passengers, refusing to stop for anyone who looked the least bit frantic. As long as I was a neophyte, the most frightening passenger was the passenger in a hurry.

Today will be different, I vowed, inhaling the artificial sweetness of the Christmas tree air freshener on the rearview mirror, which was no match for the odors the Saturday-night passengers had left behind. The cab absorbed their cologne, their booze, their cigarette smoke, mixing them with the sweat of the driver before me, and the acrid smell of my own fear. *Hello, Terror. Hello, Disorientation,* I thought, pulling off the Queensboro Bridge and turning left onto Second Avenue, *let's go for a ride.*

The shift played out like a dream sequence, each segment disconnected from and unaware of the last. My first passenger, a man in a magenta blazer with a tuft of curly hair between his chin and lower lip, hailed me at Port Authority. He asked me to take him to Co-op City, in the Bronx. "If you can tell me how to get there, I'll take you," I said. "But you have to give me directions." I didn't want to drive to the Bronx. I'd been back three times since Godfred had introduced me to the (wonders of) Ghanaian food at Papaye, but I didn't know my way around the borough yet, especially not at five a.m. On the other hand, I remembered the vow I'd made in taxi school, inspired, perversely, by Travis Bickle: "Wanna work uptown, nights, South Bronx, Harlem?" the manager of the taxi garage asked him, when he was applying for the job. "I'll work anytime, anywhere," Travis Bickle answered, his gaze even and cool. "Anytime, anywhere."

Anytime, anywhere, I thought, hoping my passenger wasn't smelling my sweat as I drove from the West Side Highway to the Cross Bronx, slowing down on the stretches of the road where the highway lights were broken or burned out. It was still dark outside—I decided I hated driving the taxi in the dark—and I was starting to think ugly thoughts: *What if the cab breaks down? What if I get robbed? Or beat up? Or carjacked?* They were fears rooted in things I'd heard, not things

I'd seen, but I still felt them. In taxi school, I thought I knew where the line was between being street-smart and keeping an open mind. Driving to the Bronx, as the man in the magenta blazer directed me from the expressway to 95 to Co-op City Boulevard to Bellamy Loop, I had no idea where this line was.

We drove past a series of apartment towers so massive I guessed you could see them from space. "See?" he said, when we stopped in front of his building, a thirty-or-so-story high-rise whose severe plainness reminded me of the prefab Soviet superstructures I'd seen on the outskirts of Moscow. "You made it." He handed me the fare, plus a three-dollar tip, and a phone card. "That's for fifteen minutes of free long distance."

"Thanks." My face went hot. Had he guessed what I'd been thinking?

"You can use it to call anywhere in the U.S., anytime. Morning, evenings, weekends, Alaska and Hawaii, too."

"Cool." I turned the phone card over in my hand. "Thanks a lot."

"You're not a New Yorker, are you?" he said, opening the cab door.

"No. Are you?"

"Born and raised in the Bronx." He grinned, buttoning his blazer. "I could never live anywhere else." I watched him cut across the grass to the entrance of his building. "Hey," he said, turning around before he went inside. "You know how to get back to Manhattan?"

A little after seven a.m., the sun rose, and a man in a cashmere coat climbed into the cab with two elementary-school-aged girls.

"Papa, it's a *girl*!" said the older one, who was wearing red ribbons in her pigtails.

"Papa, it's a *giiiirl*!" said the younger one, who was wearing yellow ribbons in hers.

"Yes," said Papa, as we drove north on Lafayette Street under pink and purple clouds, "and she's a very good driver."

Papa was tempting the Fates. I stopped at every yellow light between Astor Place and Grand Central Terminal, terrified that

I would bring harm to the beautiful children, until we finally got to 42nd Street, where Papa and his daughters got out and I said, "Phew!" as a middle-aged woman with a frosted blond bob poked her head in the cab.

"Can you pop the trunk, sir?" she said, not bothering to correct her mistake, not after she got in, not during our silent, eight-minute ride to Javits Convention Center, where she handed me the fare, to the nickel.

Around nine a.m., I headed to Chinatown. I didn't have a fare. I gazed at the bitter melon vendors on the sidewalk, fantasizing about handmade noodles, and spotted some lotus root, which made me think of the Sorceress of Vertigineuse, who used to deep-fry it and use it as a garnish for foie gras with mango butter.

I reached for my snack bag and pulled out a slice of cheese. It had taken less than one shift to realize how unrealistic my idea of doing restaurant reconnaissance from the cab was. In the middle of my first shift, still far short of covering my lease fee, shaking from hunger and a bladder on the brink of explosion, I'd pulled into the BP station on Tenth Avenue and 36th Street, blessed the attendant who gave me the bathroom key, and purchased my first meal as a taxi driver: a spinach and egg flatbread from the Dunkin' Donuts next door.

By ten a.m., I was back in Midtown, still searching for a passenger, and discovering that New York was a city that did in fact sleep: on Sunday mornings, after the clubs closed, before church started.

A little after eleven, from the soft incline of Madison Avenue, I could see five, ten, fifteen blocks ahead, and when the lights changed, people poured into the street, moving in disparate patterns, as though part of a living kaleidoscope.

"It's a miracle that New York works at all," said E. B. White, and there *was* something miraculous about seeing those crowds through the frame of the windshield, about squeezing that boat of a Crown Victoria through the constricted streets of Manhattan, slamming into potholes without the cab falling to pieces, dodging bike messengers with death wishes, and pedestrians who crossed on red lights and gave me dirty looks or flipped me off when I honked at them.

A yellow cabby pulled up beside me and rolled down his window. "You makin' money?" he asked.

"I haven't had a passenger in three hours!"

"It's the Super Bowl." He shook his head. "Everybody's home gettin' ready for the game. Oh, well." He shrugged and sped away, and I felt better. I'd forgotten about the Super Bowl. I didn't even know who was playing.

"Tell me the truth," said the sandy-haired woman with the French twist who hailed me outside Chelsea Market around one p.m., "don't you get scared sometimes?"

"All the time." I took a quick look at her in the rearview mirror. Her brown eyes were clear and round, and she held her head high, with the elegance of a ballerina. "Every time someone hails my cab, I'm afraid I'll get lost."

She laughed. "But you know where you're taking me, right?"

"Oh, yeah," I said. "Don't worry!"

I knew where the Met was, but I couldn't remember how the one-way streets ran around Lincoln Center. I willed the lights to turn red, so I could study the Manhattan pop-up map. I didn't want my passenger to think I was driving her astray.

When we arrived at West 65th Street, the traffic was jammed, and the sandy-haired woman asked me to stop a few blocks away from the Met. She tipped me five dollars on the ten-dollar fare. "Good luck," she said, rearranging her wrap on her shoulders before she got out. "It's nice to see a woman driving."

20

Sarah smiled at me from her yoga mat when I walked into the living room. "Hey," she said, keeping her legs crossed in lotus pose as she reached out to stroke Papichulo's back. "How was your shift?"

I let my backpack slip off my shoulder, envying my roommate her radiance. Sarah always spoke in a soft, encouraging yoga instructor tone, even when she was talking with Romeo, and her big blue eyes blazed with meditative clarity, especially when she was doing Iyengar asanas in our living room, which would have given the place a relaxing aura had it not been for the presence of Papichulo, the Chihuahua, who could probably sense that I didn't consider him a real dog and snarled at me whenever I came anywhere near Sarah. He was barking at me now from his perch at the end of her yoga mat, with all the piercing mouse-dog ferocity he could muster.

"Chulo!" said Sarah. "Stop it!" She wagged her finger at him. "Sorry." She turned to me, rolling her eyes in the Chihuahua's direction, "So, how was it?"

All I wanted, after eleven unusually brutal hours in the taxi and a ninety-minute commute each way to the garage, were four Advil, a scalding shower, cucumbers on my eyes, a cup of hibiscus tea from Kalustyan's, and my lumpy twin bed. But Sarah was sweet, and genuinely curious, and I did my best to form words for her, and to ignore the bared teeth of Papichulo.

"Oh"—I rubbed my temples—"it was OK." I didn't have the energy to tell her how hellacious the shift had been: between my first fare beater—a man wearing too much blue eyeliner who claimed he only had fifteen dollars for the thirty-dollar fare when I dropped him off at a shabby, lemon-colored duplex in Kew Gardens—my first flat tire (and a forty-five-minute trip back to the garage in Queens to get it changed), and an NYPD officer who told me to "stop driving like an asshole!" as I was racing to Port Authority, trying to make it to the bathroom before I peed my pants, I had taken home a grand total of thirty-two dollars. A humiliating sum. After three months on the road I was still averaging just fifty or sixty dollars a shift, which was also pretty humiliating. But it was my own fault: it usually took me the first seven or eight hours of the shift to earn enough to cover the $130 lease fee for the cab (plus gas and credit card fees). In the three or four hours that remained before I had to turn in the taxi, when I was free to make money for myself, I hardly had the stamina to keep chasing after fares. By then, all I wanted was sustenance. To that end, maybe about a month after I'd started hacking, after picking up a woman coming from a blind date in Union Square who told me the best part of her rendezvous was truffled macaroni and cheese at Dogmatic (just three dollars a tin!), I began to scout out restaurants from the driver's seat, taking every opportunity to ask passengers where they liked to eat, going out of my way to follow up on their recommendations, and writing about them on my blog.

Sometimes people's tips were out of my price range, like duck with mirabelle plums at La Mirabelle, a traditional French restaurant on the Upper West Side, which my passenger, a violinist from Toulouse who was going to Lincoln Center, insisted was the only place in town where he could find decent duck. But more often than not I could afford to try things my passengers suggested, like the lamb burger with harissa and fresh mint and pickled onions at Vareli, a "Mediterranean bistro-ey place in Morningside Heights" that a kinky-haired woman who'd hailed me on West 96th Street, with a toddler, a folding stroller, a Bed, Bath & Beyond bag, and a boogie board in tow, had told me about. I hadn't taken it personally when she'd lost her temper after the credit card machine in the cab stopped working, and these days, every time I drove the taxi anywhere near Morningside Heights, I craved that lamb burger.

Papichulo was working himself into a real fit of canine hysteria now, snapping at my ankles between ever more menacing barks. I didn't know whether to laugh or to run. "Chulo, that's enough!" said

Sarah, taking him in her arms and caressing his trembling back. "It's Layne. She's your friend!"

I escaped to the bathroom. Somewhere in the middle of scrubbing off the filth from the cab, I noticed a new book sitting on the back of the toilet. (When he wasn't composing techno symphonies, or searching for a job that would allow him to continue composing techno symphonies, Sarah's husband, Romeo, a conventionally handsome Italo-Argentine with bleached blond hair and the beginnings of a belly, liked to read in the bathroom. He chose interesting stuff: art zines, a photographic history of graffiti on the New York subway, *Heartsnatcher* by Boris Vian, an unsung writer/poet/musician/inventor from France whom Romeo considered a genius.) Now David Byrne's *Bicycle Diaries* was on top of Romeo's pile of zines. I dried my hands and picked up the book. Below the title was a simple, almost forlorn silhouette of a tall, thin man riding a bike toward an invisible horizon. The table of contents was a list of cities.

Reading through that list—Berlin, Istanbul, Buenos Aires, Manila, Sydney, London, San Francisco, New York—I felt the same overwhelming, full-body thrill I felt the first time Mom and Dad took me to LAX to pick up Grandma (I was eight). We'd ended up in the international terminal by mistake, and I noticed the list of cities in block letters on the Departures board: Paris, Rome, Rio de Janeiro, Tokyo. "Mom!" I said, tugging on her hand to break her stride, pointing at a procession of leggy flight attendants carrying matching suitcases. "Mom! When are *we* gonna take the airplane?" "Not now!" she said, as a man announced breezily over a loudspeaker something like "Last call for Pan Am flight 835 to Shanghai."

I finished spackling my face with clay mask and took *Bicycle Diaries* to my room, running my finger over the list of cities, wanting to read about all of them at once. "By the late '80s," wrote David Byrne, in the introduction, "I'd discovered folding bikes, and as my work and curiosity took me to various parts of the world, I usually took one along." I flipped through the first section on American cities and started reading in earnest when I got to the chapter on Berlin: "There are little stoplights just for the bikers," he noted, full of wonder. "Even the turn signals! . . . How do they do it?" Most of his observations were dry, down-to-earth, peppered with jabs at the Bush administration and snippets from conversations with gallerists and fellow musicians. Reading him, I sensed that he, unlike many travel writers I'd come across, was driven neither by starry-eyed escapism nor by a desire (subconscious or not) to replicate the comforts of home in a different context, nor by an obligation to say nice things to please a local tourism board. Byrne was curious, honest, never too effusive: "Berlin is lovely in the summer and there's lots to see," he wrote. "The food is great—not as exclusively pork and potato oriented as it used to be."

I read the lines again: "Berlin is lovely in the summer . . ."

I switched off the reading lamp and closed my eyes, which burned from being open for too long. Byrne's photograph of a pristine bike path, paved with stone, lined with trees, tracing a languid curve into a Berlin park, floated into my mind. "Berlin is lovely in the summer . . ." I rolled onto my back and pressed my hands to my stomach, feeling the beginnings of a familiar pull.

21

I wasn't sure why the cop started flashing his lights at me when I turned left onto 72nd Street from Park Avenue, but I slowed down, and my pulse sped up, as I merged to the right with the squad car on my tail.

"We're getting pulled *over*?" said The Bride, who was sitting shotgun. She grabbed my arm with one of her tiny manicured hands.

"It's OK," I told her, though my heart was beating fast and my stomach was on edge after two coffees and chicken and rice with lots of harissa from the Famous Halal Guys cart on 53rd and Sixth. "It's OK."

"Shit!" she said, letting go of my arm. "Shit, shit, *shit*!" She started to chew on one of her long coral fingernails.

I put the taxi in Park and glanced in the rearview mirror at The Bride's entourage: a pair of sour-faced bridesmaids in teal-green satin, and a middle-aged man with an orchid pinned to the lapel of his dark suit who was holding an enormous robin's-egg-blue box in his lap containing what I guessed was The Dress. The three of them had been engrossed in their own conversation, perfectly content to let me deal with their girl on my own, until they spotted the cop. Now the man was clenching his jaw, and the bridesmaids were raising their painted eyebrows, looking at each other and mouthing the word *Shit!* as they watched the policeman saunter up to the driver's side window.

"Did you know one of your brake lights is out?" said the cop, crossing his arms. I stared at his biceps, bursting out of his short sleeves, not knowing what to say. I heard The Bride panting next to me. I had a glimmer of inspiration. I kept my mouth shut and turned to her. Hyperventilating though she was, she understood that this was her cue.

"I'm getting *MARRIED* today!" she wailed at the cop. "I was supposed to be there at eleven *THIRTY! PLEASE* don't do this now!"

No one in her entourage said a word—the three of them were leaning back, plastered against the back seat as if trying to get as far away from our conversation as possible. I gave the cop a pleading look.

He bent down to get a better look at The Bride, taking in the shellacked curls, the rhinestone tiara, the layers of impeccable makeup, and the mania in her wide green eyes. A smirk flickered over his face.

"OK," said the cop. "Go ahead. But you better get that light fixed."

I hit the accelerator before he could change his mind. *Unbelievable,* I thought, gazing gratefully at The Bride. She may have been the most frightening passenger I'd encountered in five months of taxi driving, but she'd just saved me from another ticket. There was no way that cop would have let me drive away with a busted brake light if she hadn't been in the passenger seat. (It seemed to me that the NYPD looked for any excuse to ticket yellow cabbies: I'd gotten two tickets so far, at $150 apiece, both when I was trying to use the bathroom at Grand Central Terminal, where NYPD squad cars had taken up most of the parking spots at the taxi stand on 41st and Lex.)

"Oh my God, oh my God, oh my God," said The Bride, fanning herself as we continued west on 72nd Street. "I don't feel well."

There were pearls of sweat on her forehead.

"I think I'm gonna faint."

Oh, no, you're not. I turned up the air conditioning to maximum. "Did you eat?" I asked her.

"Yes."

"Do you need a barf bag?" I started fumbling through my big red purse, which was resting, unzipped, on the front seat between me and her.

"No!"

I pulled my hand out of my purse and looked in the rearview mirror, trying to catch the eye of someone in her entourage, but the three of them were whispering among themselves, pretending not to be paying attention to us.

"OK, then," I said, "let's try again. Take a deep breath—"

"I *can't*!"

"Yes, you can."

We'd been going back and forth like this from the moment I'd picked up her and her entourage at the Waldorf Astoria—which, I thought now, was the moment I'd fallen down the rabbit hole.

"I can't *breathe*!" said The Bride.

"Yes, you can. Come on. Like this: in through your nose"— I inhaled through my nose, shrinking my nostrils—"and out through your mouth." I let out a long, loud sigh, letting the air catch in the back of my throat.

She closed her eyes. "Oh, my *God*." All she could manage was a short, raspy inhale.

"Good girl," I said. "Keep it up."

The closer we got to Fifth Avenue, where I was looking forward to dropping her off, the more difficult it became for The Bride to breathe. She continued to fan herself, fidgeting in her seat, tugging on the seat belt as though she were trying to free herself as we approached the green wall of Central Park. When I turned off the meter and hit the brakes, she started to hyperventilate again.

"Go in!" she said.

"What?"

"Go in!"

"I can't go in!" I pointed at the barricade, and the sign that said PARK DRIVE CLOSED: DO NOT ENTER! "See the signs?" I shook my head. "No cars."

"Hold on!" She rooted around in her handbag, pulling out a crumpled but official-looking piece of paper with a green seal and waving it in my face. "I have a permit!" She was shouting now. "Please, please, go in!" She pointed at a man on a racing bike who turned into the park and disappeared behind the trees: "Follow him! You won't get in trouble! I'm late. *Please!*"

I took my foot off the brake. I had less than five seconds to decide which would be worse: the wrath of The Bride or the wrath of the NYPD. The car behind me was honking.

"Please!" She grabbed my arm again. The veins on her neck swelled. I looked in the rearview mirror. There was no comment from the man or the bridesmaids. *Now what?* their eyes seemed to say.

The car behind me was still honking, longer and louder as the seconds passed. *Oh, hell,* I thought, swerving around the barricade, driving into Central Park, gripping the wheel with both hands as I rounded the bend in the pedestrian-only road, hoping her permit was for real.

"Do you know where the Boat House is?"

"Not exactly . . . ," I said.

"Just keep going!" she said, as we coasted toward a fork in the road. "Go! Go! Go! Run over whoever you have to! Just go! God, I'm so late. I'll tell you where to go!"

But "Oh, my God!" was all she could manage when we came to the fork in the road. There were no signs for the Boat House. No one in her entourage knew the way, either.

I veered right, though I wasn't sure why. The asphalt under the cab felt sickeningly smooth, absent the potholes I'd grown accustomed to on the streets of Manhattan, where I could almost feel the lumps in the bedrock below the surface. On the Park Drive, the taxi seemed to float, as if the tires could barely hold on to the road.

Please let this be the way, I thought, passing cyclists and rollerbladers and runners in shimmering spandex. All of them turned around when they heard the rumble of the Crown Vic's motor. A man on a unicycle gave me the finger. A couple in matching sun visors yelled something I couldn't hear through the closed windows. I didn't need to hear it. What the hell are *you* doing on *our* road? I drove as slowly as The Bride would let me.

This can't be right, I thought, trying to see around the bends up ahead, searching for a sign, or the Boat House itself, but all I could see were trees.

"She doesn't know where it is," I heard one of the bridesmaids whisper.

I kept one hand on the wheel and shoved the other into my purse, feeling around for my Manhattan pop-up map, when I spotted a wooden building with a copper roof under a ring of stooping trees.

"There it is!" said The Bride, reaching across my line of sight, wagging her finger at the windshield. "That's the Boat House!"

I smiled. "I see it," I said, trying to steer around a pack of runners.

"Run them over!"

"I'm not gonna run them over." I waited for the runners to jog past before I drove over a low curb and braked next to one of the stooping trees.

"Take me to the door!" she said, not noticing the artfully trimmed hedges that stood between us and the French doors at the entrance.

"This," I said, "is as far as I can take you."

"Fine!" She jumped out of the passenger seat and bumped her head on a tree branch. The shellacked curls didn't budge. "I'm OK," she said, smoothing her hair.

The man in her entourage reached through the partition and handed me the fare, without a word, plus a two-dollar tip. The Bride opened the back-seat door and snatched the blue box off his lap.

"Break a leg!" I called after her, as she raced toward the Boat House.

"Tiffany!" said the man. "Slow down!"

The bridesmaids got out, not closing the cab doors. I collapsed onto the steering wheel, burying my head in my arms.

A few seconds later, there was an unfriendly knock on my window. *Now what?* I raised my head, not wanting to open my eyes. It wasn't a cop, but a runner, in full-length Lycra. "You know," said the runner, a drop of sweat dangling from the tip of his nose, "you're not supposed to be in here."

"I know." I raised my palms in an "I'm innocent" gesture. "But she . . ." I pointed at the Boat House, but The Bride was long gone. "A bride made me drive her here! What was I supposed to do?"

"You better turn on your hazard lights and drive as slow as you can," said the runner, icily. "I don't know what the cops are going to do to you."

"But I have . . ." That's when I realized The Bride had made off with her permit. "I—oh, shit."

Time stretched to the slowness of a nightmare as I followed the twists and turns of that too-sleek road, sitting on the edge of the driver's seat, wishing I could explain myself to the exercising people in my path, who glared at me and the taxi as if they were ready to pounce. Around every curve were more angry exercisers—I was sure they would have hurled eggs at me if they could have—and I started to get the feeling I was driving in circles, as though I'd never find a way out of the forbidden green maze.

I don't know how long it was before I spotted a break in the trees. *OK!* I thought. *Almost there.* I sped up. *Please don't let there be any cops. Please.* I pressed harder on the accelerator, envisioning the taxi as an untraceable yellow streak as I raced out of the park. When I rounded the last bend before the exit, I slammed on the brakes. *No, no, no!* I blinked hard, hoping I was hallucinating. I opened my eyes. No, this was real.

I wasn't seeing one cop. I was looking at a throng of NYPD squad cars, plus a pack of police vans, plus about fifty uniformed officers guarding the entrance to the park.

I started to sweat all over. I tried to think fast. I considered a car chase. But this was no solution: I still felt uncomfortable driving over forty-five miles per hour in Manhattan.

I parked the taxi behind the line of squad cars. What could I do? What could I say? I got out of the cab and scanned the crowd of officers, zeroing in on the chubbiest one. Why? If I ran, I figured he couldn't catch me.

The chubby officer's cell phone rang, and he stepped away from his colleagues to answer it. *Breathe,* I thought, waiting for him to finish his conversation. *Will this never end?*

"Hello, Officer," I said, as he snapped his phone shut.

He ignored me, his eyes fixed on what I now realized was Fifth Avenue, his thumbs hitched in his gun belt.

"Officer?" I clasped my hands behind my back, following the cop's gaze to the city workers in orange vests who were setting up barricades on the sidewalk. "What's going on?"

"Israel Day!" he said, jerking his chin at a Star of David flag mounted on a street lamp. "The *parade?*"

"Oh!" I said. "Israel Day! Uh . . ." The cop was glowering at me like the Queen of Hearts at Alice. "Officer. I'm really sorry. I know I'm not supposed to be here, but"—I pointed at the taxi, parked at the end of the line of squad cars—"but this bride, she forced me to . . ."

He put his hands on his hips. "She *forced* you?"

"She needed to get to the Boat House." I could feel the other officers looking at us now. "She was late. For— For her wedding."

The cop shifted his weight from one hip to the other. There was nothing but annoyance on his fleshy face as he shook his head at me, then at the cab, then at me again. I held my breath.

"Awright," he said finally. "Get outta here."

"Really?" I gaped at him. "Are you sure?"

"What do you mean 'am I sure'?! What are you gonna do? Leave the cab there all day? Get outta here!"

That night, after my shift, on Skype with Mom and Dad, as I was telling them about the chubbiest cop—and sprinting back to the taxi and turning on the ignition and gunning all eight cylinders out of the park while the other cops on Israel Day patrol pointed at my cab, looking as incredulous as I felt as I flashed across Fifth Avenue— a speech balloon popped up on my monitor.

So you're driving a taxi?! It was Joaquín.

"Oh!" I said. My stomach bottomed out.

"What?" said Mom.

"Nothing." I left his message suspended on the screen. "What'd you say?"

"I *said*," said Mom, "I can't believe that bride only tipped you two dollars!"

"The girl was hysterical, Virginia," said Dad.

So to speak . . . , I typed.

I couldn't not respond to Joaquín's email. No, I'm not in Buenos Aires, I'd written, making myself wait a week before I answered him.

"Honestly, Leroy. She made her break the law!"

What about your writing? Joaquín typed.

It's a long story . . .

"What's that noise?" said Mom.

"Are you typing something?" said Dad.

"No." I hid my hands in my lap, even though they couldn't see me—Mom and Dad didn't have a web camera, and neither did I.

"Well, I just don't understand these brides nowadays. They think they can act like movie stars!" Mom sighed into the microphone, "Hey! What time is it? Eleven thirty? Oh, *barf*! Leroy. We gotta get going. You haven't even shaved yet! And I still have to make the lasagne—"

"Lasagne?" I said. "OK, OK, I have to go, too . . ." Mom and Dad and I took our time saying goodbye, the way we usually did.

Are you still there????? Joaquín wrote.

Yes . . .

I heard the front door open and the patter of Papichulo's claws on the hardwood floor in the hall.

¿Y vos? I started typing again, my hands shaking a little. ¿Qué tal? Are you in Buenos Aires?

Sí.

Papichulo was outside my door, growling.

I miss our talks, Joaquín wrote.

So do I, I typed, but I deleted it before I hit Enter.

I missed talking with Joaquín even more than I missed dancing with him. Could I tell him that? I wanted to tell him so many things: about New York, and the taxi, and the tango in the taxi, about the things I'd been reading, about Ginsberg and Kerouac, and how much they reminded me of him. While Kerouac had been chasing uninterrupted rapture ("Why should I compromise with anything else . . . ?"), Ginsberg was teaching himself to observe what he called the "dearness of the vanishing moment." Ginsberg had it right, I thought. And so did Joaquín, in his way—it was because of him, whether he knew it or not, that I was learning, little by little, to recognize the dearness of the vanishing moment, to appreciate the beauty of things in flux.

You're a great teacher, I wrote, trying not to be distracted by the sound of Papichulo's claws scraping against my door. Do you know that?

"Chulo!" said Sarah, from what sounded like the kitchen. "Stop that!" Papichulo started to whine.

A minute went by. Two minutes. "Chulo, baby, c'mere!" The Chihuahua grunted and scampered down the hall.

I got up and lay on my lumpy twin bed, pushing my palms against my belly. Talking to Mom and Dad, I'd been craving a snack. I heard the water-drop sound of a new chat message and lunged back to the computer.

Y vos sabes que te quiero. And you know that I love you.

What? I stared at the screen, at the flashing cursor. No, I didn't know. I had always believed, from beginning to end and afterward, that he meant more to me than I did to him.

Are you still there? he wrote.

I don't know.

Joaquín A. is typing . . . read the Skype prompt in the chat window. I waited, tugging on my lower lip, watching the ellipsis dissolve and reappear.

You're a wonderful person, he wrote.

And I'm sorry.

I stood up and stretched my arms to the ceiling. Why now? Did it matter? I let four minutes go by, maybe five, wishing there were room to pace. I went back to the computer. There was a yellow Away cloud next to Joaquín's name. *Just tell the truth.*

I sat on my folding chair, letting my fingers hover over the keyboard.

Te quiero también, I typed.

The Away cloud stayed there.

There was a light knock on my door. "Layne?" It was Sarah.

"Come in."

"Want some stir-fry?"

I looked at my laptop. The monitor was dimming, preparing to fade to black. Through my open door came waves of garlic and ginger-scented air.

"Sure." I stood up, pushing in my chair.

"Everything OK?" said Sarah, glancing at the computer.

"Everything's fine." I pressed on the corners of my eyes with my knuckles to stop the tears. Our *te quiero*s were platonic, I knew—even though we had sent them through cyberspace. I closed my laptop and followed Sarah into the kitchen.

22

The sun was going down in Spanish Harlem when Isabel and I reached the top of the subway stairs at 110th and Lex.

"Where is this place?" she said.

"This way," I said, steering her by the triceps.

"How do you know?"

"Taxi driving." Now that I knew which way the avenues ran, I could surface at almost any subway station in Manhattan and get my bearings in a few seconds. I didn't consider myself a good cab driver yet—after five months of hacking, I could still get turned around in Greenwich Village, or in downtown Brooklyn—but at least I was developing a sense of direction.

"Wow," said Isabel, who could not read maps, and would routinely leave her apartment in Astoria an hour before she was supposed to meet anyone anywhere in Manhattan, to give herself time to get lost.

We crossed Third Avenue. A yellow taxi pulled up to the red light and braked well behind the faded white lines of the crosswalk.

"He's empty," I said.

"Do you always check?"

"Yeah." Even when I wasn't driving, I would look to see if a cab had a passenger. It was a strange new reflex, one of several strange new reflexes, which also included chasing after jaywalkers, and flying into a rage whenever a double-parked vehicle was blocking my way—but these were disturbing impulses, disproportionate reactions, and I wasn't sure whether I should tell Isabel about them.

We continued east on 110th Street, past an empty school yard where the basketball hoops had no nets. The streetlights thinned out. We walked faster. When we turned right on Second Avenue, we saw it, next door to Devil's Ink Tattoo, a storefront giving off enough lime-green neon to illuminate the whole block: WALKERS-WOOD CARIBBEAN / AMERICAN RESTAURANT, the sign read. Alex and Jillian, the final passengers I'd picked up on my last shift, had told me this was their favorite Jamaican place in Spanish Harlem. "Don't go on Sunday," Jillian said, before I dropped them and their daughter Miriam off at the Central Park Zoo. "Edward's not there, and there's no rum cake."

It took a minute for our eyes to adjust to the neon and fluorescence inside Walkerswood, where the blaze of artificial light reminded me of walking through Times Square. There was a TV mounted on the wall, hospital-style, to the right of the entrance, tuned to *Jeopardy!* In the back was a counter encased in bulletproof glass. Saffron-colored pages from the menu ("Welcome to a Taste of the Caribbean") and a NO SMOKING sign were stuck to the glass with blackening pieces of Scotch tape.

"Edward isn't here," said the man behind the counter, a pudgy middle-aged man in a burgundy T-shirt with a birthmark on the side of his nose. He told us his name was Fred.

I looked at Isabel, disappointed. "Do you still have rum cake?" I asked him.

There were two pieces left. He wrapped them in wax paper for us while we studied the menu: jerk chicken, chicken curry, smothered steak, oxtails . . .

"Oxtails?" said Isabel.

Fred took an aluminum pie tin from a shelf under the counter and approached the steam table on the far wall of the kitchen, where all the food had a dull shade, as though it had been simmered past the point of fatigue. He scooped oxtails and rice and peas (red beans) and sweet plantains into the tin until it buckled.

"Here you are," he said, handing us the open pie tin, and two plastic forks, gesturing toward the scattering of empty Formica tables. "Sit anywhere you like." The "Final Jeopardy!" round was just starting.

Isabel and I beamed at each other as we took our first bites of oxtail. The meat melted off the bone, steeped in the flavor of its own juices in the simple brown sauce.

The rest of it was just as delicious as Alex and Jillian had promised: golden fried sweet plantains were still a little firm, not at all greasy, and our rice and peas had a richness I couldn't trace. I got up and knocked on the glass to get Fred's attention. He was riveted to the TV—so engrossed it took him a few seconds to notice me standing there. I turned around and looked at the contestants scribbling down their questions to the "Final Jeopardy!" answer. The category was nineteenth-century authors. The clue: "She wrote some lesser known novels under the pseudonym A. M. Barnard. Her most famous novel was loosely based on her childhood experiences."

"Who was Louisa May Alcott?" said Fred. The lilting ticktock of the think music had barely started.

"Sounds right to me." I waited for Alex Trebek to announce the commercial break, and then I asked Fred, "What do you put in your rice?"

He snickered, looking down at his feet.

"Come on. Tell me. You know I won't be able to make it like you."

Fred rubbed the back of his neck, looking up at the ceiling as though asking permission from someone on high. Then he whispered, like he was sharing something he wasn't sure he should be sharing, "Coconut milk."

"Coconut milk?"

"Mmmm hmmmm." He nodded, handing me two more plastic forks for rum cake, and pointed the remote control at the gap in the glass, turning up the volume on the TV. The commercial break was over. "Let's start in the middle," said Alex Trebek, "Andrew McCluskey, he had three thousand dollars and he wrote down . . . Who was Louisa May Alcott. He came up with the *correct* nineteenth-century author's name. Nice going . . ."

"Nice going," I said to Fred.

He grinned.

Isabel unwrapped the rum cake, dark as espresso, and so soaked with alcohol it practically dripped. It tasted like caramelized sugarcane.

"So, lady . . ." She brushed a crumb off her lip. She'd painted her nails with candy-apple polish that would look cheap on most women, but made her hands look ready for a royal ball. "Tell me. Is it getting any easier?"

"Is what getting easier?" I unfolded the wax paper around the second piece of rum cake and took a forkful.

"Driving the cab."

"Oh." I stopped chewing for a second. "Well . . ." To the casual observer, I was improving. I thought about the petite lady with the plum lipstick I'd picked up two shifts ago, at the bus stop outside St. Luke's Hospital, at ten minutes to seven in the morning. When she told me she was late for work, I gunned it through the beautifully timed green lights on Amsterdam Avenue, channeling the spirit of Mom, the family lead foot, who liked to set the cruise control on her minivan to eighty-five miles per hour. "You're a hell of a driver, *mamita,*" said the lady with the plum lipstick, when I dropped her off on 149th Street, at three minutes to seven. Maybe I was becoming a better cabby, but the city was starting to wear me down, and I was beginning to wonder if I was losing my humanity.

To escape, if I was anywhere near 42nd Street, I would stop at the Mid-Manhattan Public Library—the poor, drab cousin of the grand, marble-pillared main branch on the other side of Fifth Avenue—wandering around the stacks longer than I should have, wondering what was left of the New York of O. Henry and Joseph Mitchell and E. B. White—that is, the city I was searching for, full of eccentrics and underground saloons and new sounds and far-out art. I came to the conclusion that it wasn't possible for someone to understand New York, or appreciate its shadow side, without having driven here at least once. A person had to go behind the wheel to experience the full extent of its frenzy, to know the desperation of its strivers, who measured time in milliseconds and held yellow lights in contempt. Slow down? Not on your life. In the taxi, it felt like everyone on the island was clamoring for their lucky break. In the taxi, I could see the city's fangs, and, more and more, I was beginning to show mine.

There was half a piece of rum cake left. I put down my plastic fork and pushed it toward Isabel. "I'm getting better," I said, running my fingers over a jade streak in the marbled Formica, "but I'm also getting scary."

She slid the cake back in my direction. "What do you mean?"

"You really wanna know?"

She nodded.

"OK." I moved my chair closer to the table. "On Sunday, I wanted to go to the bathroom at the Wellington Hotel." I lowered my voice, even though Fred didn't seem to be paying attention to us, and probably couldn't hear me above *Wheel of Fortune*. "You know I like to stop there. The doormen are really nice, and they always let me use the bathroom. And sometimes, if I have time, I like to get a chocolate chip cookie from Petrossian. I told you about those cookies, right? With the pecans? Did you try them?"

"Not yet."

"OK. Never mind. I mean, not never mind, but we will. You have to try them. Oh, man . . ." I rubbed my stomach. "Anyway"—I waved my hand in front of my face—"on Sunday I stopped . . . No. I was *try*ing to stop, at the taxi stand at Fifty-sixth and Seventh, right in front of the Wellington. But I couldn't park. And you know why? Because there was an SUV there. Taking up the last spot, right under the sign that said NO PARKING ANYTIME: TAXI STAND."

"Uh-oh."

"Yeah. So I double-park and I go up to the SUV and knock on the window. It's this man holding a Yorkie in his lap. Doo dee dee, la dee da, totally in his own world. They both jumped a mile when I banged on the window. I didn't care. I started yelling at the guy. 'You can't park here!' " I shook my fist, the way I had then, so Isabel could get the full effect. " 'This is a *TAXI* stand!' The guy got this really terrified look on his face. Then he pushed the Yorkie off his lap and drove away as fast as he could. That's when I noticed he had Georgia plates. I probably scared him off New Yorkers forever."

Isabel crossed her arms over her stomach, laughing. "Oh, no!"

"Oh, yes," I said. "And last night! I was walking in Midtown, and I saw this lady cross the street against the light. Totally. Oblivious. She didn't even look to see if any cars were coming. And she was wearing all black!"

"OK . . ."

"So I chased after her, and I stopped her, and I told her she was endangering her life. 'No one can see you when you cross the street like that!' She looked at me like I'd lost it. And then she just kind of snorted and walked away."

Isabel was still giggling. But she covered her mouth when she saw I was serious.

"I'm telling you, it's true. People are so cavalier when they're walking around!" I had been, too, before I drove the taxi. I had to think of Orwell: "It is curious," he wrote, "how one does not notice things." Indeed: I had never noticed how dangerous it was, how much I was throwing off the city's rhythm, every time I crossed the street against the light—until I saw it from the driver's seat.

"Well," said Isabel, "yeah . . ." She was doing her best to sympathize, but her eyes were widening into a kind of mystified-petrified expression I was beginning to recognize from my time on the road. Now was not the moment to tell her about the trip downtown with the man in the midnight-blue suit.

I'd spotted him just as I was pulling away from the taxi stand on 20th Street: a tall, thin man with a weekend sailor's tan who was walking with willfully squared shoulders, turning toward the street now and then with a searching, almost vulnerable expression on his face. I pulled over to pick him up before he raised his hand.

"Liberty and Broadway," he said, as he lowered himself into the cab. Like many of the men I took to Wall Street, he carried nothing in his hands.

I put the cab in gear. He rested his elbow on the window frame and said nothing. At this point, I liked to think I could feel when a passenger wanted to talk, and when he preferred to ride in silence. Silence had become my default setting in the taxi, and by now I was starting to identify different kinds of quiet behind the partition: there was impatient silence (as in the lady in pink silk who huffed and puffed after I missed the first two signals on the way to her real estate showing), drunken silence (when I picked up a trio of college students in skinny jeans on Varick and Spring who fell asleep on the trip to Williamsburg), suspicious silence (when I mistakenly took a banker across the Brooklyn Bridge, en route to the Financial District), curious silence (with a group of Japanese boys who surreptitiously snapped pictures of me on the way to Macy's), and compassionate silence (as on the trip with a Ukrainian woman with a gold front tooth who didn't seem to mind when I got lost on the way to her mud treatment at the Oasis Health Center in Brighton Beach).

But melancholy silence, mixed with varying degrees of existential longing, might have been the most common form of quiet I perceived in my passengers, who, I assumed, had few opportunities to sit still in New York. This was the silence I sensed in the man in the midnight-blue suit—until we got stuck behind a FedEx truck blocking the eastbound traffic on 18th Street.

A minute went by, then two minutes. I looked in the rearview mirror: a line of cars was forming behind us. My passenger began to sigh, crossing and uncrossing his legs.

BEEEEEEEEEEEEEP! BEEEEEEEEEEEEEEEEEEEEEEP!

I looked in the rearview mirror again. The line of cars stretched all the way to Ninth Avenue. The sound of their horns was escalating from annoyed to furious. My passenger's sighs were getting louder, too. This, I decided, was the worst part of driving a cab in New York: how desperate people were to get where they were going, and how responsible I felt, even in congestion I could not control. As hard as I tried, I couldn't detach myself from the urgency behind the partition, and, in the case of the man in the midnight-blue suit, the message in his eyes was plain: *Fix this. It's your job.*

BEEEEEEEEEEEEEEEEEEEEEEEEEEEEEP! BEEEP! BEEEP! BEEEP! BEEEP!

Don't just sit there! I thought. *Do something!* I put the cab in Park, leaving the engine running, and raced over to the FedEx truck.

"HEY!" I shouted at the driver, a doughy man in a baseball cap hunched over a sheet of wax paper spread out on the steering wheel, eating a submarine sandwich. He looked up when he saw me waving my arms, swallowing hard, as though he hadn't quite finished chewing.

"I have a *CUSTOMER!*" I shouted at him, louder still, pointing at the cab. "You can't block the street like this! Can't you hear that?" I extended my hand toward the growing rank of honking cars, and then I made slicing motions with my arms in the direction of the curb, like a runway worker at the airport. *"MOVE IT!"*

The FedEx driver pointed at his sandwich. "When am I supposed to eat lunch?"

BEEEEEEEEEEEEEEEEEEEEEEEEEEEEEEEEEEEEEP! BEEEP! BEEEP! BEEEP! BEEEEP! BEEEEEEEEEEEEEEEEEEEEEEEEEP!

"Are you *KIDDING* me?!" I yelled, emboldened by the crescendo of horns behind me. The angry New Yorkers were on my side now.

"MOVE!" I roared at him, close to hysteria, if not hysterical. If I had learned anything from The Bride, it was that hysteria could take you far on the streets of New York. A mystified–petrified look flashed over the FedEx driver's face, and for a second I felt a pang of guilt: he looked genuinely frightened. But I had a passenger: What choice did I have?

BEEEEEEEEEEEEEEEEEEEEEEEEEEEEEEEEEEEEEEEEP! BEEEEEEEEEEEEEEEEEEEP! BEEEEEEEEEEEEEEEEEEEEEEP! BEEEP! BEEEEP! BEEEEEEEEEEEEEEEEEEEEEEEEEEEEEEEP!

The FedEx driver pulled the wax paper and the sandwich onto his lap, grabbed the gearshift, and angled his truck toward the curb, just far enough to let me, and the cars behind me, pass.

The honking procession turned against me in an instant. They didn't see, or didn't care about, my negotiations with the FedEx driver. Now I was the one blocking traffic. I raced back to the cab.

"Phew!" I said, settling back into the driver's seat, glancing in the rearview mirror as we coasted down West 18th Street. Had my passenger seen me, standing in the middle of the street, gesticulating on his behalf? I sat up tall, prepared to accept his gratitude, but he was staring at his cell phone. Was it a given that I would do battle for him like that? Was it understood that I would throw a tantrum, and interrupt the FedEx driver's lunch, for the sake of getting this man to Liberty and Broadway as quickly as possible? *Fix this. It's your job.* Yes, I supposed it was.

"I don't know," he said, looking up from his phone, a distracted smile on his thin lips, "how you can drive in New York."

"Neither do I," I said, as a man in a black tutu crossed against the light at Fifth Avenue. I slowed down to keep from hitting him. My passenger laughed. He was still chuckling when I turned right on Broadway, and when I finally stopped, at Liberty and Broadway, he tipped me a dollar and showed me his cell phone. There was a picture of me: a short, dark-haired thing in Capri pants, flailing my pale arms at the FedEx truck. Even in profile, you could see the murderous look on my face.

"Let's go," I said to Isabel, piling our plastic forks in the empty oxtail tin, rewrapping the remains of our rum cake in wax paper.

"We'll be back," Isabel told Fred.

"My customers always come back," he said.

We backtracked to the subway station, a little bit blind in the darkness after an hour or so in the neon and fluorescence of Walkerswood. I turned to Isabel, who was walking with her arms crossed tightly across her chest. Was she trying to protect herself from me, or the night?

"You know what?" I said, while we waited for the light to change on Third Avenue. "I wish everyone could drive a taxi, just for a day. I think the city would be a different place." But even then, I thought, as I watched another empty cab drive past, I wasn't sure I would feel like a citizen of New York.

23

I was driving west on East 45th Street, in the middle of a noontime traffic jam, when my bladder started to twinge. I turned up the radio so as to drown out the stirrings in my body: Celia Cruz was singing, and there was that infectious joy in her voice: *A-gar-ra-te fuer-TE . . . Y ya no te suel-TES . . .* (Hold on tight . . . and don't let go yet . . .). I hoisted myself up, trying to see around the U.S. Mail truck ahead of me. My bladder twinged again, more emphatically this time. *Never again,* I thought, *will I underestimate the power of an iced coffee at Café Grumpy.*

I'd driven straight to Café Grumpy after another run-in with a fare beater—a man in safari shorts and a Red Sox cap who let me take him all the way to La Guardia, where his credit card was declined. "Don't you have any cash?" I asked him. He shrugged, halfheartedly, and showed me his empty wallet. "How can you do this?" His answer was another unrepentant shrug, and that's when I realized he was high—and all I could do was fume as he dragged his suitcase out of the cab and disappeared behind the automatic doors in the Delta terminal. "Move on, honey bunch," I remembered Mary Jo telling me. "Chasing after those idiots is dangerous, and a waste of time."

But I was still furious by the time I got to Café Grumpy— a place I'd learned about from a law student who'd ridden in my cab a few shifts ago, where the coffee was as marvelous as the name— and ordered a large iced coffee to go, after which I had to visit Port Authority twice in thirty minutes to use the bathroom.

And now, at 45th and almost Park, my hands still tingling from the caffeine, I had to go to the bathroom once more. *Uh-uh,* I thought, *we're not doing this now.* My bladder twinged again, indifferent to my resolve. I surveyed the congestion: the U.S. Mail truck, which had been inching forward until that moment, stopped altogether and turned on its hazard lights. I tightened my grip on the steering wheel.

"Do not let anyone see you sweat," I remembered Mary Jo telling me. She had been reading my blog, where I'd been documenting my misadventures behind the wheel, trying to keep the stories light, and stay true to my theme, weaving in anecdotes about eating tips from passengers whenever I could. But Mary Jo could sense the tension, and the lack of pleasure, beneath my words. "Don't worry about your fantasies going to bits," she said. "Right now you're still getting acclimated to the job."

Right now, no matter how I positioned myself in the driver's seat, my bladder continued to twinge and throb. I looked around. What were my options? There was no way I could go around the U.S. Mail truck, even if I threw a Bridal Fit and forced him to pull over: East 45th Street was too narrow, and so were the sidewalks. I could turn on my hazard lights, leave the cab in the middle of the street, go look for a bathroom—but what if traffic started moving? I considered the empty iced coffee cup. *No way.* There had to be another solution.

I glanced up at the mail truck—it was going nowhere, its hazard lights still flashing. I turned off Celia Cruz and squeezed every muscle in my pelvis, but it was useless. My kidneys were aching, and I knew what this meant: If I didn't find a bathroom in the next sixty seconds, I was going to pee my pants.

I undid my seat belt. *Are we really doing this?* It was body over mind now. I put the taxi in Park. Slid the driver's seat back as far it would go. Picked up my *New York City 5-Borough Street Atlas,* which was the size of a sheet of elementary-school construction paper, and laid it across my lap. Then I pulled down my pants. *OK,* I thought, grabbing the empty iced coffee cup from the holder on the console, *here we go.*

I situated the cup underneath me and let go, gingerly at first, but then, when I saw I was on target, I held the cup steady and relaxed as I felt it fill up, the plastic hot under my fingers. Tears of humiliation and relief rolled down my cheeks when I finished. I felt a MacGyver sort of triumph as I fitted the lid back on the cup.

My pants were still down when a middle-aged lady with a pixie haircut knocked on my window: "Are you free?"

"No!" I said, clutching The Atlas to my hips. She glanced at my bare knees—could she see the pants around my ankles?—and raised her eyebrows. "Please," I said, taking one hand off The Atlas and waving her off with the other. She scurried away, rearranging her pashmina shawl and shaking her head as if she were trying to forget what she'd seen.

I pulled over as soon as I extricated myself from the traffic jam on 45th Street, dumping the contents of the iced coffee cup in the gutter, throwing the cup in the trash, rubbing hand sanitizer into my fingers and palms until my skin burned. I didn't care that I'd made only twenty-four dollars on this shift so far—I drove straight to the Mid-Manhattan Public Library, ignoring the raised hands of potential passengers along Fifth Avenue.

I've reached a new low, I thought, hanging my head as I walked up and down the fiction aisles, avoiding eye contact with every person in my path. *No one can call me a poser now,* I thought, staring at the New York literature shelf, not registering the titles.

I wandered into Travel, where I usually ended up. There was a stack of books on a metal reshelving cart, and I started to pick through it. Somewhere in the middle of the pile was a Lonely Planet guide to Berlin from 2006. I pulled it out, turning to the section on taxis:

It's no exaggeration to say that your average Berlin cabby can hold forth respectively on any subject from the best sausage in the city, through the meanderings of Nietzsche . . .

Sausage and Nietzsche? I thought. *You've got to be kidding me.* I flipped to the introduction:

Since reunification, Berlin has undergone a massive evolution . . . Gone is its self-perception as a beleaguered and schizoid city existing beneath the ominous presence of the Wall . . .

Maybe this was starry-eyed travel writing, but I didn't care: I wanted to believe it, as much as I wanted to believe David Byrne's dreamy descriptions of Berlin in his *Bicycle Diaries*. I checked out the Lonely Planet guide from the library and walked back to the taxi in a reverie.

A clean-shaven blond man in a navy-blue sport coat hailed me on 42nd Street a few minutes later.

"JFK," he said, swinging a laptop bag and a briefcase in after him.

It was 3:11 p.m. I could only imagine the state of the Long Island Expressway and the bumper-to-bumper on the Van Wyck. There was no way I could take him to the airport and get the cab back to the garage on time, but I really needed the cash.

I started the meter, and my passenger dialed his cell phone. ". . . Yeah, the merger's in place. But Steve couldn't believe it when I handed him my resignation. And you should've seen the look on Terry's face!" He untied his tie and yanked it off as we entered the Midtown Tunnel. "Wait a second, I'm losing you," he said as we drove further into the darkness. "Can you hear me? Aw, shit." He hung up.

"How are you?" he asked, when we emerged from the tunnel, the professional edge gone from his voice.

"Oh," I said. "I'm doing OK." I smiled at him in the rearview mirror, and he gave me a funny look. He was on his phone again.

". . . Yeah," he said. "I gave myself an hour and twenty minutes to get to the airport. Yeah . . ." He was wiggling out of his sport coat, one arm at a time. "Plenty of time."

I looked at the clock. It was 3:35 p.m. The traffic on the Long Island Expressway was moving at an average speed of ten miles an hour.

". . . Well, I *am* in a little bit of traffic," he said, glancing at the yellow cab next to us, which had a Guinness ad tent mounted on its roof. The slogan, written in smoky white letters on a black, beery background, said FORTUNE FAVORS THE BOLD.

You're about to be in a lot of traffic, I thought.

He leaned his head back, let out a tired but exultant sigh, and dialed another number as I forced the taxi onto the Van Wyck Expressway, where the congestion intensified and our pace was even slower. I couldn't drive more than five miles an hour. Every thirty seconds or so, we came to a complete stop. This was worse than I feared. I gritted my teeth.

By 4:00 p.m., my passenger had finished his phone calls. He leaned forward and stuck his head through the partition. "I'm starting to freak out a little bit," he said, eyeing the swarm of brake lights ahead of us. "Are we gonna get there by four thirty?"

"Yes," I told him, though I didn't believe it. We hadn't even cleared Jewel Avenue, the first exit off the Van Wyck, yet.

"Shit! I can't miss this fucking flight! This *sucks!*"

Why, oh, why, did I pick this guy up? In six months of cab driving, and seven trips to the airport (four to La Guardia, three to JFK), I'd gotten turned around from time to time, but I'd never made anyone miss a flight. No taxi driver had ever made me miss a flight either, though I'd come close in Buenos Aires, stuck in a jam on the only highway to Ezeiza. I'd started to freak out a little bit, too, then—but I'd known, somehow, the taxista would get me to the airport on time. *"No te preocupes, muñeca,"* he'd said. *"Ya llegamos."* Don't worry, doll. We're almost there. I didn't have that confidence now, moving between zero and five miles an hour on the Van Wyck, which looked like a parking lot stretching to infinity. I didn't see how we could make it to JFK by 4:30.

My passenger shoved his briefcase off the seat. "Can't you go another way?"

"At this time of day, the surface streets aren't gonna be any faster," I told him. The truth was, I didn't know how to get to the airport any other way. Would a GPS have helped? I didn't know. I didn't have one. Our taxi school instructors told us we'd never learn the city if we used a GPS, and besides that, it was supposedly illegal for yellow-cab drivers to use one. I opened The Atlas to look for an alternate route, but I almost rear-ended the cab in front of us, trying to read the map. *Stay here,* I thought. *Just stay here.* If I got off the Van Wyck, I was sure I'd get lost.

"Fuck!" said my passenger, when I hit the brakes again.

I rode the rear ends of the cars in front of us, nosing into the fastest-moving lanes, going after every inch of forward momentum I could find. *I am a rower on the River Styx—*

"Fuck!" said my passenger, glaring at me in the rearview mirror.

It was 4:14 p.m. We had two miles to go before Linden Boulevard, where the congestion, according to the electronic signs on the shoulder, was supposed to clear.

"Fuck!" he said again, when two big rigs merged onto the Van Wyck, squeezing traffic even tighter.

I stopped looking at him in the rearview mirror, focusing instead on the odometer as it struggled from one tenth of a mile to the next. I tried to visualize the airport, or, more specifically, depositing my (justifiably?) infuriated passenger at the airport, in time for his flight. *Please let us get there. Please.*

At 4:21 p.m., we made it to Linden Boulevard, where the congestion actually did begin to clear. We accelerated to twenty-five miles per hour. At 4:23 p.m., the road opened up for real, and I clung to the steering wheel with both hands, summoning all the power of the Crown Victoria's V8 engine, driving the cab as though it were sounding a siren, zigzagging around and past every car in our path, past the cargo area and the rental car parking lots, past the taxi driver holding lot.

"Which airline are you flying, sir?"

At 4:29 p.m., one minute before my passenger's deadline, I hit the brakes in front of American Airlines Departures, terminal 8. He threw a wad of cash through the partition, seized his laptop and briefcase, scrambled out of the cab, and slammed the door without waiting for his receipt. I counted the money: he'd paid the fare, plus two dollars. I dropped the crumpled bills on The Atlas and put my head down on the steering wheel. "Holy shit," I whispered, "I hate this job."

"Moving right along, young lady!" I looked up. A knock-kneed cop in a fluorescent vest was patrolling the passenger drop-off area, waving his walkie-talkie at me. "Mooooove it!"

"All right! All right," I said, pulling away from the curb, cutting off a Super 8 Shuttle bus, driving toward the exit signs. "I'm going!"

And as I followed the racetrack curves of the road from the airport to the expressway, I remembered that first taxi ride from JFK with the cabby from New Orleans, and how uneasy I'd felt then, in spite of how gracious he'd been. In some way, I was thinking now—no closer to feeling passion for New York than I was that day—it was as if the city had been telling me it was time to go from the moment I arrived.

PART III

Berlin

Unknown to many, the city of Berlin actually sits on top of a massive water table. The air in this metropolis is unusually clean and fresh for a large city. That is because the earth is constantly being saturated with water from underneath. The air is always being cleansed and purified. That is why there is the old song "Berliner Luft" ("Berlin Air").

Das ist die Berliner Luft Luft Luft,
so mit ihrem holden Duft Duft Duft,
wo nur selten was verpufft pufft pufft . . .

This is the Berlin air air air
With its sweet scent scent scent
Where things seldom fizzle chug chug . . .

Whenever I arrive back in Berlin and step out of the airport terminal, I take a deep breath. The air is so different and fresh. Die Berliner Luft.

—Alexander Frey, musician

24

"You're going to learn all that by the time we land, right?" said the man in the long felt coat standing in the aisle of the 737, a garment bag slung over his shoulder, grinning at my German phrase book. He was waiting for a woman in a red jumpsuit to resolve a struggle with her rolling suitcase, which was too big for the overhead compartment.

"Ha!" I said, scanning the "essential words" on the inside cover— *Entschuldigung, Ich verstehe nicht, bitte sehr.* I looked up at the man with what must have been a helpless expression on my face.

"You know what Mark Twain said," he began. "You can learn English in thirty hours, French in thirty days . . . and German in thirty years!" He winked at me and squeezed past the woman in red.

The pilot interrupted the easy-listening boarding music and, in a clipped but cheerful voice, asked ladies and gentlemen to please stow their items and take their seats so we could leave on time for *Bear-LEEN.*

"Bear-LEEN," I whispered, as the plane took off and circled over Jamaica Bay. I gazed out at the flat roofs of Queens, blanketed in haze, at the jagged outline of Manhattan, like a heartbeat vector on the horizon, and pulled my notebook out of the seat-back pocket, rereading a passage I'd copied from "My Lost City," F. Scott Fitzgerald's heartbroken goodbye letter to New York:

> Full of vaunting pride the New Yorker had climbed here and seen with dismay what he had never suspected, that the city was not the endless succession of canyons that he had supposed but that it had limits . . . I felt that, for the moment, the city and

I had little to offer each other ... frayed nerves were strewn
everywhere ... Thus I take leave of my lost city ...

So do I, I thought, when I read Fitzgerald's words the first time—in
that moment, they had released me from my own doubts about taking a leave from New York. But now I read them differently. Didn't
you have to possess a thing somehow, in order to lose it? I didn't
think of New York as "my" city. I didn't know if it would ever be
"my" city. Was I running off before I could find out? Had I been
expecting the impossible of this place from the beginning?

Was I doing the same thing now, expecting the impossible of Berlin? I thought about the fire I'd felt in the last few weeks, a rekindling
of appetite, so to speak, as I put together a Kickstarter campaign to
support a series of taxi adventures in Germany: How will the food
quests play out, I'd written in my proposal, in a city not exactly known
for its gastronomy?

I was stunned when people contributed more than what I'd
asked for: It's 12:54 a.m., I wrote to my backers the night my project
reached its funding goal. I have to get up in 96 minutes to go to the
garage and pick up my cab and start my shift. But I can't sleep. Because
I just discovered that you've all helped me make the Berlin adventures
happen ...

I rushed gratefully, feverishly, through the logistics of spending July
and August in Berlin, feeling the wind at my back as I shopped for a
cheap plane ticket, researched neighborhoods, and combed Couchsurfing listings for a place to stay, all the while finishing as much
work as I could for my virtual jobs before I left, figuring out what to
do with the things that wouldn't fit into my suitcase, and reading all
the Berlin literature I could find at the library. (Christopher Isher-
wood was especially interesting: "It is strange," he wrote, "how people
seem to belong to places—especially to places where they were not
born.") I was writing my blog with revived passion, too, composing a
list of fifteen of my favorite cabby-recommended dishes in New York
City that went viral and got picked up by *The Wall Street Journal.*

But I wondered now, on board Air Berlin Flight 6438, how much
of my fascination for Berlin was rooted in despair over my unhappy

relationship with New York. Dazzling, aloof, unrelenting New York. City of high-hanging fruit and new gray hairs.

"What are you looking for, kid?" said Dad, when I told him about Berlin.

"I'm not sure. But I think I need a break from hacking."

"So do I," said Mom.

She'd been reading the stories on my blog about my run-ins with the NYPD and the FedEx man, about the accident in the iced coffee cup and the trip to JFK with Mr. 4:29—though I'd written them as comedies, I'd lived them as tragedies, and Mom knew this, of course. She also knew that I'd abandoned all those romantic notions about driving the taxi, including the one about learning to hack as the equivalent of learning to lead in tango. Being in the driver's seat didn't mean knowing where I would end up: I couldn't choreograph what might happen in the taxi any more than Joaquín could map out his tangos at the *milonga*. Driving a cab, I told him, the last time we'd chatted on Skype, is just a new way of following. And leading, he wrote back, is an illusion *al final*.

I flipped through my phrase book as the plane settled into the great circle route over the Hudson Bay. Reality was this: I didn't speak a word of German, and according to Mark Twain, and the man in the long felt coat, I wouldn't be able to speak it any time soon. Before this trip, I'd spent a total of three unimpressive days in Germany (two in Frankfurt, where I sat through a brutally cold night at the train station on the way to Prague, and one in Munich, on a nine-hour layover where the only things I could afford to eat were soft pretzels).

And people were skeptical when I told them I was going to Berlin for the summer. "Why Berlin?" said the software engineer from Hoboken who'd started talking to me when we got caught in the middle of a traffic jam on 23rd Street, on my last shift. I told him the cab drivers in Berlin were supposed to know as much about Nietzsche as they did about sausage.

"Who cares about sausage?" he said. "Why don't you go to Rome? Or Paris?"

.   .   .

I stared out the window at the city's spiderweb grid as the plane descended into Tegel airport. *Bear-LEEN.* As intriguing as it sounded in the travelogues I had read, the image of the city I had formed in my mind was impressionistic at best: it was whatever the visual equivalent of "the cultural capital of Europe" or "the epicenter of cool" might be. I'd seen photos of the Brandenburg Gate (where people had danced on the Wall when it came down twenty years before) and the TV tower (a retro construction of a space-age future, marking Berlin's skyline the way the Empire State Building marked New York's) and David Byrne's bike paths, but I couldn't envision the city the way I had Buenos Aires and New York before I'd been there. The sounds of Berlin were easier to imagine: I pictured people moving to something like Kraftwerk *(Wir fahr'n fahr'n fahr'n auf der Auto-bahn / Wir fahr'n fahr'n fahr'n auf der Auto-bahn . . .)* the way I'd imagined people dancing tango on street corners in Buenos Aires.

Taking a taxi from Tegel felt novel and luxurious. The driver apologized for his English as we glided over the open road in his cream-colored Mercedes.

"Your English is better than my German," I told him. After the plane ride, almost nothing in the German phrase book lingered in my memory. At baggage claim, caught up in the relief of spotting my suitcase (it didn't matter how often I flew—I considered it a miracle every time my luggage arrived when I did), I'd bumped into a German man as I pulled it off the conveyor belt. By the time I could spit out an approximation of *Entschuldigung* (excuse me), he was marching out the exit doors in his socks and sandals.

I rolled down the window. I hadn't slept on the plane, and my eyes were red and swollen, and I was wishing I didn't have to pay a visit to a stranger named Steffen to pick up the keys to the apartment I was going to rent. But the sun was shining between fast-moving clouds, and coming from New York, where everything seemed so tightly penned in, the streets so choked in comparison, I couldn't help but smile, feeling as though I'd climbed from a dim basement to some luminous upper floor. I reached through the open window and felt the air—lush and warm on my skin—and as we drove along a canal fringed with healthy-looking weeds, there seemed to be so much space to breathe it. "Berlin is lovely in the summer . . ." I inhaled, reaching my hand farther out the window into the watery northern light. Oh, yes, it was.

"You are from California?" said the taxi driver, who looked about my age, though there were many gray flecks in his dark hair.

I nodded.

"My name is Taza," he said. "I am from Ankara." Taza typed Steffen's address into his GPS and drove south and east, into a neighborhood where every second storefront seemed to be a döner kebab stand. I stared at the slabs of meat, which looked like punching bags on spits. My mouth watered when I smelled fat melting into beef. Or was it lamb? I didn't care. I wanted some.

"Tell me," I said, looking at Taza in the rearview mirror. "Do you have a favorite restaurant, in Berlin?"

He thought about my question for a beat. "Mmmm"—he scratched his temple—"yes."

Woo hoo! I thought. *I just got here and I'm getting tips.* I dug through my purse and pulled out my notebook. "What is it called?"

"Uuaaaaaa . . ." He turned around. His eyes were puzzled. "Turkish shwestera?"

"Mmm hmmm." I flipped to a blank page in my notebook. "I like Turkish food, but it doesn't have to be Turkish food—"

"I am one shwestera," said Taza. "She is thirty years old."

Oh, no. What's a schwestera?

". . . Und I am brother . . . He is forty years old . . ."

"Oh . . ." I closed my notebook. The döner kebab stands were thinning out, replaced by Soviet-style apartment blocs standing tall at right angles. *So this is the East . . .* I'd always imagined Berlin in the geographical center of Germany, with the Wall marking the dividing line between East and West. Then I looked at a map: Berlin was only sixty miles from the Polish border. During the Cold War, the city was deep in East German territory, carved into four sectors, with the Russians in charge of the East. The English, the French, and the U.S. had divided up the administration of Berlin's western sectors, which became, in the words of the Australian author Anna Funder, "an odd island of democratic administration and market economy in a Communist landscape."

I kept quiet as we passed people on bicycles, who seemed to outnumber the cars on Karl-Marx-Allee. No one was wearing a helmet. I noticed a girl with a shaved head, coasting behind the others, and looked back at her as we drove by: there was a red light clipped to her messenger bag, to the wide strap she wore across her chest. When she rode through the shade, the light flashed on and off like a heart beating outside her body.

"I put the keys here," said Steffen, as he lifted the cigarette-burned cushions on a mustard-colored couch. "Somewhere . . . I think . . . here . . ."

I leaned my suitcase against the doorjamb while Steffen searched for the keys to the studio I was subletting not far away, in a neighborhood called Friedrichshain.

I looked for a place to sit. A plastic patio chair in the far corner, turned upside down, was the only chair in the room, and there was a wooden speaker propped between its legs. I sat-stood on my suitcase, punch-drunk and exhausted after flying over six time zones, as Steffen—a chubby-cheeked, curly-haired blond in glasses with rectangular frames who looked like he'd just graduated from college— tossed the couch cushions on the floor. He was in love with Berlin, he told me, as he ran his hand around the sofa frame, feeling for the keys, and had been from the day he moved here, from a village in Mecklenburg, in northeast Germany, five years ago. He didn't think he'd ever leave.

"And what will you do in Berlin?" he asked me. He gave up looking for the keys in the couch and moved to his desk, shuffling through papers, opening and closing drawers.

"Oh," I said, gazing at the window facing the street. The plastic shade was pulled down, but sunlight was sneaking around the sides, catching an empty beer bottle, coloring it amber. "I have this crazy project where I get in random taxis and ask the drivers to take me to their favorite places to eat . . ."

I turned when I heard Steffen's roommate walk in, switching his PlayStation controller to his left hand and holding out his right hand to shake mine. "I'm Ivo," he said, smiling—wait, were his teeth green? His light brown hair was tied in a low ponytail that extended in a long, thin line to the middle of his back. "What is it you are doing in taxicabs?"

Ivo's eyes shone when I told him about the taxi adventures, about Buenos Aires, and New York, and Nietzsche and sausage. I tried not to stare at his teeth.

"*You* drive a taxi?" said Steffen, who stopped tearing apart his desk to look me up and down.

"You write?" said Ivo. "Me, too!" He rested his PlayStation on his belly. "Science fiction. And I just finished a children's book."

"She doesn't care about your children's book," said Steffen, pushing Ivo out of the way as he moved to the closet. "We are in a punk band," he said. "I play drums. Ivo plays bass. We have one CD."

"Don't ask how we found money to make it," said Ivo.

"Online poker"—Steffen grinned, yanking open the closet door—"and medical trials."

"For real?" I laughed.

Ivo nodded. "Thank God we survived."

"Of course we survived," said Steffen. He pulled a backpack out of the closet. We heard something jingle. "Hey!" he said, unzipping the top pocket. "Here they are!" He fished out the keys, lobbing them toward the ceiling and snatching them out of the air like an outfielder before he handed them to me.

"Thank you, Steffen."

Ivo watched me stuff the keys into my jeans pocket. "What will you do," he said, stroking his goatee, which came to an elfin point below his chin, "if the cab driver can't speak English?"

"Hmmm . . ." I thought about the ride with Taza—he was friendly, but we'd barely been able to communicate. "I don't know."

"Here," said Ivo, "give me some paper." I pulled out my notebook. He turned to the first blank page, and I stood next to him as he wrote: *Bringen Sie mich bitte zu Ihrem lieblings Platz für gutes Essen.*

I studied the words. Ivo's handwriting, curly, baroque, slanting left, looked like it was from an earlier age. "What does it mean?"

"It means 'Please bring me to your favorite place for good food.'"
He grinned. "In German."

The words "DIE YUPPIE SCUM" were spray-painted in turquoise
on the wall of my new (temporary) apartment building on Dirschauer
Strasse, a few tram stops from Ivo and Steffen's place, in Friedrichshain, in what was once East Berlin. I pushed open the glass front
door, rolling my suitcase into a light-filled foyer with ceilings maybe
fifteen feet tall. The walls and the floor tiles gleamed, spotless and
white, leading to a spiral staircase with a blond wood railing. This
place was much more posh than I'd imagined.

All I knew about Friedrichshain, from a few days of research on
the internet, was this: Until the Wall came down, it was a working-
class district. After the Wall came down, it became one of the wild-
est neighborhoods in the city, where young people from all over
Germany and squatters from West Berlin built their paradise, making art and throwing parties in abandoned buildings. Everyone was
invited. Though the neighborhood was becoming more and more
mainstream, anarchists, according to an anonymous blogger who
called himself An Englishman in Berlin, were still holding out in
Friedrichshain, burning cars to protest gentrification and police raids
on their squats. (Someone had even started a website, the Englishman
noted, to track the number of luxury cars anarchists set on fire each
day. If the Google Map on brennende-autos.de was accurate, the
highest concentration of car burnings over the last three years was in
Friedrichshain.)

I parked my suitcase in the middle of the foyer and pulled a slip
of paper out of my back pocket: Karl Hoffman, Dirschauer Str. 8,
10245 Berlin-Friedrichshain. Karl Hoffman, a journalist who was
spending the summer in Weimar, a friend of Steffen and Ivo's I'd
found via Couchsurfing, was subletting his studio to me. Karl Hoffman, I realized now, had given me his address but no apartment
number.

I lugged my suitcase up the stairs. There were no names on the
doorbells. I tried the key in the doors on all four floors. A dog started

yelping behind one of them. The key Steffen had given me fit none of the locks. I dragged my suitcase back down to the foyer, sweaty and frustrated—the contentment that had come over me in the taxi with Taza, and at Ivo and Steffen's place, began to subside. Was I in the right building? I looked at the metal mailboxes mounted on the wall. A mail lady with sunburned cheeks entered the foyer just as I spotted Karl Hoffman's name on a box in the bottom row.

"*Sprechen Sie Englisch?*" I said.

"*Nein.*"

I rolled my suitcase out of her way, not knowing what to do as I watched her slide letters through the mail slots with brisk, indifferent hands. She finished and turned to leave.

"Wait," I said, catching up to her before she walked out the door. I showed her the slip of paper with Karl's name on it. "Do you know," I spoke slowly, "where this is?" She pointed out the back window of the foyer, to a building I hadn't noticed, on the other side of a court-yard crowded with bikes. "*Hinterhaus,*" she said. "*Da hinten.*"

"Ah!" I said. "*Danke shown.*" I rolled my suitcase out the back door. Drum and bass music bounced around the courtyard, almost overriding the screeches of an electric saw slicing through cement. The building next door was under construction.

I climbed the stairs of the back building, which had none of the yuppie-scum elegance of the front one: the yellow-brown carpet on the stairs was tattooed with old stains, and had the sweetish reek of stale beer. I tried my key in all the doors, until it finally turned, in an apartment on the third floor, across from a door with a blank dry-erase board like the one I'd bought for my college dorm room.

I opened the door and pulled my suitcase inside, stepping into a hallway carpeted in lurid, institutional blue. On the left side of the hallway was a bathroom nearly as big as my bedroom at Romeo and Sarah's. I had to stand on my tiptoes to see myself in the mirror above the sink.

The institutional blue carpet continued to the bedroom/kitchen/living room/office at the end of the hall. The only traces of Karl were on the bookshelves that ran along the back wall of the studio, where I found *Die Liebe in den Zeiten der Cholera;* a guide to recent architecture in Berlin, in English; a book of selected poems from Goethe, in German and English; a pile of maps from Croatia; and a red reading lamp. Next to the bookshelves was an unmade futon bed—Karl had left a note on a bundle of sheets: "We are CLEAN!!" I opened the door that led to the bamboo-lined balcony, which faced the courtyard between the front and back buildings. From here, the drum and bass music, which was coming from my upstairs neighbor's window, canceled out the sounds of the construction next door.

The balcony was just big enough for a plastic table and one plastic barrel chair. I brought them inside—this would be my desk setup—and put them by the wall opposite the bookshelves, near the kitchen area, which had a stainless-steel sink, a foot of stainless-steel countertop, a two-burner electric stove, and a mini-refrigerator that was empty except for a bottle of Beck's.

I opened the beer, sank into the plastic chair, and looked around the room, which was big enough for dancing a conservative tango. The mini-refrigerator shuddered and started to hum. A breeze wafted through the balcony doors, tousling the filmy curtains. *What are you looking for, kid?* I closed my eyes and sipped the beer, taking deep, greedy breaths after each swallow, far less tired than hungry.

25

I leaned against the mock brick wall next to the *Geldautomat* on the corner of Warschauer Strasse and Revaler Strasse, across from a supermarket called Kaiser's, a few blocks from my new sublet, flipping through my notebook, searching for the page where Ivo had written *Bringen Sie mich bitte zu Ihrem lieblings Platz für gutes Essen,* working up the nerve to hail a taxi as I tried to resist the smoky perfume of the döner kebab stand on the other side of the street.

I'd never attempted a taxi adventure in a place where I didn't speak the language. Until the ride from the airport with Taza, I hadn't wanted to think about how much of a handicap this could be. I put away my notebook and took out my German phrase book, turning to the page titled "Language Difficulties."

"Eek shprek-he kine doytsh, eek shprek-he kine doytsh," I muttered over and over, glancing at the diamond-shaped stones in the sidewalk as a group of boys in wrinkled T-shirts strolled by holding bottles of Berliner Pilsner by the neck, as if the beer were an accessory, or an appendage. *I don't speak German, I don't speak German . . .*

How many taxi adventures had I attempted now? A hundred? Two hundred? I'd lost count. Anyway, it didn't matter how many, nor that cabbies were now my colleagues—in a new city, even in this new city, where the balmy air went down like a tonic, it felt like the first time. A teenage girl cycled past, silk flowers woven through her spokes, some kind of terrier without a leash trotting alongside her. I looked both ways before I stepped through the bike lane, over the curb, onto Warschauer Strasse. *"Eek sprek-he kine . . ."* My stomach seized up the way it used to when I saw a ball rocketing in my direction on the soccer field. *"Eek sprek-he kine doytsh."* I squinted into the oncoming traffic and raised my hand.

The noontime glare on the windshield made it impossible to see who was driving the four-door Mercedes taxi that stopped for me. I opened the passenger-side door, letting my thumb slip out of the phrase book. The driver was a woman. She looked like she might be in her fifties, wearing royal-blue sunglasses and Gummi Bear earrings to match. There were circles of bubble-gum-colored blush on her cheeks.

"Guten Tag!" I said. *"Eek sprek-he kine . . . Uh . . ."*

The taxi driver smiled. She had short blond hair, mottled with gray, that flipped outward in haphazard waves. The sun caught one of her Gummi Bear earrings, turning it a transparent blue.

"Can I help you?" she said, as I looked through my phrase book, trying to find the page I'd lost.

"You speak English?"

"I do."

"Hallelujah." I opened the car door a little wider and pointed to the passenger seat. "Is it okay if I sit here?"

"Of course." She picked up her purse and set it on the floor in the back. "Where would you like to go?" Her accent was elegant: a little German, a little British.

"Uhmm . . ." I pictured the map of Berlin I'd been study-ing the night before, trying to remember landmarks that were far enough, but not too far away. "How about . . . Could you take me to Alexanderplatz?"

A warm gust of wind drifted into the cab through the open windows, ruffling her hair. "Where in Alexanderplatz?"

"I don't know. Anywhere around there would be fine. I'm look-ing for an adapter."

"An adapter?"

"A plug, you know the plugs here are different—"

"Oh!" she said. "You can find this at Saturn, I think."

"Saturn?"

"Yes." She turned on the meter. "There they have all the elec-tronic things."

We drove south on Warschauer Strasse. I studied the taxi license taped to the dashboard. Her name was Waltraut Quoidbach. It was typed in purple letters, next to a picture of her with fuller cheeks and reddish hair. Above the picture, in bold black handwritten letters, was the word "ZILLE."

"My real name is Waltraut," she said. "It's a very German name, a very *Wag*ner name, and I don't feel very like this. Everybody calls me Zille." She pointed at her license. "My uncle gave me this nickname. He was my godfather." She smiled. "He called me Zille because I look like the pictures of a painter called Zille. He painted poor people, people who were a little bit fat and always smiling, and they all made fun of each other all the time. And I was like this in my youth. A very funny child. Like he painted."

I followed her gaze westward as we crossed the bridge over the S-Bahn tracks. The TV tower glittered like a disco ball in the sun. I liked Zille. She reminded me of Nidia. Not physically—Zille was smaller, softer. But her openness seemed unconditional, uncensored, like Nidia's. I dug through my purse, looking for my hack license. I wanted her to know we were colleagues, or sisters, in a way.

"You drive a taxi?" Zille laughed, doubling over the steering wheel. "Ha! Oh! That would be fun! New York is . . . Oh, but it must be hard."

"Yeah." I nodded. "It's hard." But now I was four thousand miles away from the garage. "Is it hard here, too? How many lady cab drivers are there in Berlin?"

"Oh, not a lot. It's about ten percent of all of them."

"Ten percent?" This sounded like a lot to me. "In New York, it's only one percent!"

She pushed her sunglasses higher on the bridge of her nose. "Because it's a man job," she said. "It was always a man job. It always will be."

"Why?"

"Because mostly the men *think* they are the better drivers. Which is not true at all! We women, we don't have to show how *potent* we are all the time. And sometimes"—she cleared her throat—"it's really better to have a woman driver. For example, prostitutes. When they are going home, they don't want to have a male driver. So they call me."

"Well, that's understandable—"

"Isn't it?"

I looked at her license again. "How long have you been driving a taxi?"

"Twenty-*seven* years. And I am a naturopath also. For thirty years I do this work."

"Are you serious?"

She nodded. "Most of the days, I drive the taxi. And I see patients, in between."

"Do you have a specialty?"

"Oh, no . . . People come, I ask them what their chief problem is . . . You know . . . Many people come because they don't sleep, for example."

"Could I make an appointment with you?"

"Ha!" she smiled. "You can. Of course!"

She turned right, onto Mühlenstrasse, where I'd taken myself for a walk the night before, and we drove past the East Side Gallery, once part of the Berlin Wall, now a mile-long stretch of murals on the River Spree, and a monument to peace, where people liked to pose for pictures.

"You were driving the taxi before the Wall came down," I said. "Is that right?"

"*Ja.*" She nodded, glancing out the window at the murals, which morphed into a horizontal rainbow as we sped by. "In West Berlin. It was like driving in a small island." She took off her sunglasses, setting them on her lap. "And the other was always the enemy. The Russians. We were separated. But you know something? Even when we were an island, we had so much green and water we could live without feeling suffocated."

"Can I ask you—"

"Ask me."

"When the Wall came down . . . what was it like?"

"In the taxi?"

"In the taxi," I said, "and in general."

"Hmmph!" She put her sunglasses back on. "We had to know from one day to the next day one half of the city we never went to before. We made a *lot* of faults." She laughed, without smiling. "Oh, *ja!*"

"I can't imagine—"

"And it was also very difficult," she went on, "because a lot of names of streets change again after a year. You learn it and you know and you go there and it is not what it was."

I'd read about this phenomenon before I'd come to Berlin. After the Wall came down, Ho-Chi-Minh-Strasse reverted to its original name: Weissenseer Weg. Leninallee became Landsberger Allee. Wilhelm Pieck Strasse, named after the first president of East Germany, was now Torstrasse.

"And so it was a lot of movement. A lot of new things," said Zille, "but I'm very grateful because I am from all the inhabitants of Berlin somebody who's seen *every* part of the city, which is not normal."

In the beginning, she told me, many of her colleagues refused to drive to the East. The East was strange for her, too, at first. "But it's only in my head," she said. "I tell myself, 'They are family. They are Germans. They are Berliners, too.' But on the other side, I don't have to like every part of my family. And when I don't see them for forty years, how can I love them the next day?"

We came to the end of the East Side Gallery. I tugged on my seat belt to loosen it and turned around to take another look, noticing the narrow, rounded ledge at the top of the Wall. *How did people dance on that?* I wondered, remembering the images I'd seen on the news, of people jumping up and down on the Wall, the day it "fell" in 1989. I was fifteen. Growing up during the Cold War, having convinced myself that I was likely to die in a nuclear bomb blast, seeing it end this way, with dancing and fireworks and champagne, was unreal.

"Do you remember where the Wall used to be?"

"I remember every time I cross it," she said. "Now it's like a band of stones you can see when you look down at the street, like a line that goes through the city." She reached out the window, pointing down at the asphalt. "Every time I cross these stones, I'm happy. That I can cross it. Knowing that never again in your life someone can say 'You can't cross, you can't go over there, you can't stop there.'" She shook her head. "This is a sensation which only people who lived here can understand."

I didn't know where we were in relation to Alexanderplatz, but now I had to crane my neck to see the candy-striped needle at the top of the TV tower, and I guessed that meant we were close. I looked over at Zille. The sun caught one of her earrings again, casting a blue Gummi Bear shadow on her neck. I was finding it difficult not to be amazed—no, that wasn't right. I was finding it difficult to be amazed and to stay in reporting mode at the same time: *Are you getting this? And this? And* this?

But reporting mode didn't seem quite right, either. Beyond trying to figure out when to ask her where she liked to eat, I couldn't stop worrying about whether and how I was ever going to capture the extraordinariness of Zille—and the extraordinariness of encountering her now, on my first real attempt at a taxi adventure in Berlin—on paper, or on the screen, as it were. And as much as I didn't want to categorize the experience while being in the midst of the experience, I couldn't help but think that I had just hailed my fairy godmother.

"Did you ever want to leave Berlin?" I asked her.

"I studied in Paris," she said. "But I came back. I prefer Berlin to Paris."

"Why?" We stopped at a red light. A man in a muscle shirt was towing a sofa on the back of his bike through the intersection.

"Paris is beautiful," she said, "but the people are not."

"How do you mean?"

"They talk only about trees, or eating. It was boring!" The light turned green. The man with the sofa had made it to the other side of the intersection and was waving at a group of tourists, who were taking pictures of him with their cell phones. "Berlin is Prussian, you see. We say, 'When you leave me alone, I leave you alone.' The French call it *laissez faire, laissez aller,* and you see it in every part of Berlin. For example, in the opera. You have a lady with evening dress and all the jewelry, and then just beside her is a punk with holes in the trousers and maybe a yellow haircut"—she ran a hand through her hair, fluffing out the sides—"and they look at each other and they smile and they enjoy the music. And nobody looks at them. Well, maybe a little bit. But it's nothing! In Munich or Düsseldorf and some areas, maybe also in Frankfurt, you cannot see this. They will throw the punk out, or don't let him in. This is what I like here."

"I like that, too."

She made another right turn, pointing through the windshield at a brick palazzo with a square, medieval-looking tower at one end. "This is our City Hall," she said. "Now we are in Alexanderplatz."

"We are?" I grabbed my notebook. "But I wanted to ask you also—"

"*Ja?*"

"A bit of a random question," I said, turning pages in a hurry, searching for a blank one. "Where is your favorite—what is your favorite thing to eat in Berlin?"

"My favorite thing to eat in Berlin?" Zille turned her head this way and that as if trying to jog her brain.

"Yes."

"Oh . . . uh . . . hmm . . . Well . . ."

"Yes?"

"You know typical Berlin food is not good."

"Oh?"

"For example, no one eats *Eisbein* in Berlin. Well, not me, anyway."

"*Eisbein?*"

"This is like . . . How can I explain? It's like a big piece of pig knuckle."

"Oh."

"*Ja.*"

"And when you want something good?"

"Well . . ." She laughed, peeking over her shoulder, pulling up to the curb, next to a massive concrete plaza surrounded by (what I guessed were) department stores built during the socialist era. "I like Italian food!"

"Ah-ha!" I smiled. "And do you have a favorite place?"

"Ummm, *ja.*" She stopped the meter. "This is a family business, you know. And mother is cooking—"

"Oh!"

"And also because my sister is living in Italy and I'm over there a lot, so I like the food."

"Is it far away?"

"No, it's not far away."

"Could you take me there?"

"Now?" She laughed. "What about Saturn?"

"Maybe later I can go to Saturn."

26

The M10 tram stopped at Eberswalder Strasse before I had a chance to ask the woman standing next to me if I could take a picture of the flames tattooed to her calves. I thought about riding to the next stop, but there wasn't time—I was already running behind, and I had no idea how long it would take to walk from Eberswalder Strasse to the beer garden, where I was meeting Julia, a woman in Berlin who had sent me an email out of the blue, not long before I'd left New York. I saw your picture in *The Wall Street Journal,* she wrote. You were sitting on top of a taxi with some baklava. Are you really coming to Berlin? Let's have a beer when you're here.

Yes! I thought, stepping off the tram, crossing the street under the U-Bahn tracks, glancing at the people lining up for ice-cream cones as I hurried down Kastanienallee. *Let's have a beer . . .*

"Julia?" I said to the woman with platinum-blond hair and china-doll skin who was waiting at the entrance to the beer garden. She was holding a cell phone and looking around with a small, expectant smile.

"Layne?" she said, her smile widening when she recognized me. "I'm so glad to meet you!" She shook my hand in both of hers.

"I'm sorry I'm late—"

"Don't be silly," she said, dropping her cell phone into a zebra-print shoulder bag. "Come this way." I followed her into the beer garden, past a sign that said PRATER in silver-spangled letters. The bike racks were filled to capacity, as were the rows and rows of taxicab-yellow picnic tables, where there must have been two hundred people basking in the afternoon heat, swigging half liters of beer. "This is the oldest beer garden in Berlin," said Julia. When we got to the counter, she switched from her lilting, British-inflected English to German and ordered us two pilsners. "Here you go," she said, handing me a heavy mug with foam cascading down the sides. "Let's find a seat."

"Ist hier noch frei?" Is this spot free? she asked two men bowing over plates of white sausage and yellow-brown mustard. They nodded. *"Weisswurst,"* she said, glancing at their plates as we sat down. "From Bavaria. You eat it with sweet mustard. It's de*lic*ious. Even when it's this hot outside." The German guys smiled at her—Julia was stunning, but in an unselfconscious way, one of those people who have such an abundance of beauty they seem happy to spread it around. She raised her glass to mine. "Cheers! And welcome!"

"Cheers!" I lifted my mug with both hands and drank. The beer tasted clean, slightly bitter, not quite cold. I made a mental note about the *Weisswurst*.

"How are you liking Berlin so far?"

"It's a dream," I said. I never imagined, reading her email a few weeks ago from my cramped room at Sarah and Romeo's, that I would be sitting here with her, at this sun-dappled table, under these old chestnut trees, among all these people who looked so happy and at ease. "But I've only been here a week." I was trying to be cautious. But the more I came to know Berlin, the more I liked it, and it wasn't as if the city were engaging in any kind of heavy seduction. Seduction didn't seem to be in its nature—it struck me, over and over, that the city was simply being itself. There was the Antiquariat on Niederbarnimstrasse, just a few blocks from the studio I was subletting, where they sold used books by weight, for 2.50 euros a kilo, and the people drinking beer on the S-Bahn, as if every day were Mardi Gras. And I loved the miniature sculptures of "cork men" in yoga poses atop the street signs, and the fact that you could buy a bike inner tube from a vending machine on the sidewalk, or a bratwurst from the "Grillwalkers" who circled Alexanderplatz with barbecues strapped to their bellies. And of course there was the taxi ride to Saturn with Zille: "The Italian place she likes isn't open at lunch," I told Julia, "so she couldn't take me there in the end. But I have the address. I still have to go—"

"I'll go," she said.

"You will?"

"Of course." She smiled. "I like Italian food." She slipped on a pair of Jackie O. sunglasses. "Come on," she said. "I want to show you something."

We finished our pilsners and walked back to Kastanienallee, where I noticed, now that I wasn't in a rush to get to the beer garden, a disproportionate number of tall, slender, gorgeous people, promenading at a hangover pace, smoking, not wearing bras, showing off their tattoos (though not one could surpass the artistry of the flaming calves on the tram), possibly making their way to one of the cafés that served brunch until six p.m. I tried not to stare at a man in a Speedo, a beach towel draped around his neck, coppery shoulders glistening in the sunshine. The nearest beach, if you didn't count the beach bars on the River Spree, was over two hundred kilometers away. "Was this what you wanted to show me?"

Julia giggled. "People like to call this street 'casting alley,'" she said, "because of all the good-looking people walking around."

A few steps later, we heard what sounded like a waterfall, and a lot of drunken shouting.

"What's that?"

"I don't know. Come on."

I followed her to a street called Oderberger Strasse. "Holy guacamole!" I said when we turned the corner.

Someone had opened the hydrant in front of the firehouse, and water was shooting into the air with the force of a geyser, glinting in the sun, flooding the cobblestoned street. Bare-chested boys were bounding through the spray, guzzling beer, and pulling girls in sundresses into the water with them. Toddlers jumped into puddles, squealing with delight as they kicked water at their parents. A shoeless woman with blond-gray dreadlocks stood in the middle of the street, hands on her hips, head tilted back, mouth open wide, to catch what drops she could. A handful of firefighters was surveying the scene from the steps of the firehouse, smiling as if to say, "Frolic all you want."

"Are all German firefighters this much fun?" I asked Julia.

"We had a really long winter," she said, beaming behind her sunglasses.

"I've lived in Berlin eight years," Julia told me, a few days later, at Muntagnola, the Italian restaurant Zille had suggested I try. "And I still love it."

She plucked a piece of bread from the basket and drizzled some olive oil over the top, and as we sat across from each other at a sidewalk table under the red-and-white-striped awning on a tree-lined street in Schöneberg, in what was once West Berlin, Julia said she never imagined she could stay anywhere for eight years: She was born in Hamburg, but grew up in the Philippines, and in Africa, and she'd lived in London, where she had taught herself computer programming, and in Ireland, and Frankfurt. Her passion was movies, especially Woody Allen movies, and movies from France. By day, she worked as a software quality assurance manager. At night, she was studying to be a movie subtitle translator. "When I came to Berlin," she said, "I didn't want to leave."

"Why?" I took a bite of bread—soft and dense, with a chewy crust that had the slightly charred residue of a brick oven. Muntagnola was more upscale than most of the cabby-recommended restaurants I'd ever been to—pastas cost around thirteen euros, and the wine list could tempt a person into extravagance—but if the bread was a sign of things to come, I didn't mind. "What made you stay?" I asked Julia, closing my menu.

"The feeling," she said, glowing a little, like someone talking about a new love. "I mean, Berlin's not beautiful. It's not like Paris—there's no fantastic architecture. It's not big and fast, like New York. It's not sophisticated like London. But here, I feel free."

"So do I," I said, and Julia smiled, though it probably sounded premature, and presumptuous of me to say, and though I wasn't sure myself, after ten days in Berlin, how much of my affection for the city stemmed from the exuberance of escaping New York. Still, it was as if every day corroborated the feeling that it had been right to come here: everything in my immediate sphere, minus the reports for the Argentine satellite company, was moving in a steady upward curve.

I thought about the email I'd gotten the day before, from a reporter named Heike at RTL, a prime-time German news show: My colleagues and I love the idea of your taxi adventures. Would it be possible to do a short interview with you? I didn't know how Heike had found me, and I had no idea that her message was a sign of things to come.

I ordered for both of us: two kinds of handmade pasta, and two glasses of Sicilian white wine, which, according to our waiter, had been made from grapes grown on land confiscated from a Mafia boss after his arrest.

"You speak Italian?" said Julia, after the waiter left.

"A little."

"I only know one phrase in Italian—"

"What's that?"

"Roma non fu fatta in un giorno," she said, with a French accent.

I laughed. "Rome wasn't built in a day?"

"You wouldn't believe how useful it is."

The waiter brought the wine. We toasted to Berlin.

"You know what I just read?" I said, and it occurred to me, while we drank, that though we barely knew each other, Julia and I were simply picking up where we'd left off. "Before World War I, Berlin was known as 'Elektropolis.'"

"Elektropolis?"

"Back then it had to do with industrialization more than anything else," I said. We took another sip of wine—which smelled like apricots, and was nice and dry. "But when I read it, I thought, now Berlin's a different kind of Elektropolis. Don't you think?"

"Hmmm . . ." She thought about it for a moment. "I've never heard that before," she said, smiling into her glass, "but I like it."

Our pasta came: tagliatelle with zucchini flowers for me and *strangolapreti* (priest stranglers) for her, which looked like round, green jewels in sage butter, made with spinach and ricotta and sprinkled with pecorino cheese—they were similar to gnocchi, but stuffed with raisins and pine nuts and, Julia and I agreed, beyond even the deliciousness of gnocchi.

. . .

That night, I lay awake on the futon, replaying the meal in my mind, wiggling my feet to the rhythm of my upstairs neighbor's drum and bass. It was impossible to sleep in Elektropolis—and it wasn't just the music (which wasn't my music, but somehow made me feel hip by association, as if I were an extra in a movie with an ultramodern soundtrack).

Around two a.m., the door to the front building slammed. Someone was parking a bike in the courtyard. I turned on the red reading lamp and pulled out my notebook. I was beginning to feel as if the cosmos were atoning for the ass-kicking in New York and had decided I was to lead a charmed, if temporary, life in Berlin. *Change your latitude, change your karma?* I tapped my pencil on my lip. No, something else was at work here. I knew by now, if I knew anything by now, that relocation, on its own, was just a cosmetic fix—

"Ooh, ooh, oooooh, OOOOOOOOOOH . . ." A woman moaned into the night from somewhere in the front building. A man's ecstatic "Aaaah, aaaah, aaaaaah, AAAAAAAAAAAAAAAH!" followed, seconds later, drowning out the drum and bass.

27

The taxi driver smiled when I poked my head through the passenger-side window. He had the face of a wizard in a Gothic fairy tale: thick eyebrows flaring upward like flames, a pointy nose sloping downward, with a cleft at the tip, and a black beard, going gray, that grew well below his chin. He was wearing a bowler hat, and a string of prayer beads around his neck.

"Guten Tag!" he said. *"Wo möchten Sie hin?"* Where would you like to go?

He nodded when I asked him if he spoke English.

"My favorite place to eat? Hmmmm." He squinted, running his finger over the cross-hatched lines under his eyes. "I have to think . . ."

I climbed into the front seat. After the ride with Zille I always got in the front seat of the taxi. I felt like I was being too forward when I rode shotgun in Buenos Aires, and in New York, too, as if I were opening the refrigerator in a stranger's house and helping myself to a snack. But in Berlin it felt like the natural thing to do.

I noticed the picture the taxi driver had taped to the meter, a still shot of a scene from *City of God:* the two lead characters, a fledgling photographer from the slums and his bronze dream girl, were sitting close on a beach in Rio de Janeiro, liking each other too much to kiss.

"I got back from Brazil two weeks ago," said the taxi driver. "I go in winter, to a little town on the coast, about two hundred and fifty kilometers north of Rio."

He shifted out of Park, and I let myself relax into the front seat, remembering the feeling I had the first time I landed in Rio, on one of my border-hopping trips to renew my Argentine tourist visa. As soon as the plane touched the tarmac, I applauded, along with the

Brazilian woman sitting next to me, who smiled into the sunlight streaming through our window and said, "Everyone should come to Brazil one time before they die."

We coasted downhill on Warschauer Strasse, over the Oberbaum Brücke, across the River Spree. YOU ARE NOW ENTERING THE TOURISM SECTOR read the graffiti on the U-Bahn tracks, above what had once been the path of the Berlin Wall, between Friedrichshain, in the East, and Kreuzberg, in the West.

"I was born in Turkey," said the taxi driver, as we followed the course of the elevated U-Bahn tracks that ran down the middle of the street like a zipper. "I came to Berlin in 1980. To Kreuzberg." He was eighteen, he told me, and it was a crazy time. "In the eighties, Kreuzberg was a place where anyone could go." He twisted his prayer beads between his finger and his thumb. "And I am a painter, so—"

"What do you like to paint?"

"I paint mostly with acrylic, but I also take photos and make sketches in the taxi." He stopped at a red light on Kottbusser Tor. Ladies in headscarves were sorting through tomatoes at the produce stand across from the U-Bahn station.

"Is driving a cab a good job for an artist?"

"No." The light turned green. He merged into the traffic circle, yielding to the cyclists. "Although sometimes you get interesting passengers and good dialogue. But other times"—he said, straightening his arms against the steering wheel—"people forget to be human."

"That's true." I nodded, thinking of the man who'd hailed me on Eighth Avenue on his way to work at the Ritz-Carlton. "Come on!" he said, smacking the partition when I hit the brakes after spotting a cop. "Let's go! Look at all those green lights!" And I would never forget the woman with no eyebrows who got into the cab near Union Square, en route to a hair appointment: "I took a cab instead of a train," she bellowed into her cell phone after I missed a light on Park Avenue. "Unfortunately, I don't have the right cab driver."

"I think an artist should love people," said the taxi driver. We were still riding alongside the U-Bahn tracks, and the architecture was shifting from warm to cold, Jugendstil giving way to concrete blocks from the 1970s.

"And what about a taxi driver?"

He laughed, dropping his head back, holding on to his hat. "I have driven a taxi for twenty-five years," he said. "Without compassion, this job is impossible."

He took me to Sen Viet, his favorite Vietnamese place in Kreuzberg.

"During the war, a lot of people came to Berlin from Vietnam," he said. "That's why you see so many Vietnamese places in Berlin." (And the Vietnamese diaspora in Berlin, I learned later, cut along a Cold War pattern: while East Germany invited guest workers from North Vietnam starting in the 1950s, West Germany welcomed thousands of asylum seekers from South Vietnam after the fall of Saigon. Years after the Wall came down, the divisions between the North and South Vietnamese communities in Berlin were still perceptible.)

The taxi driver double-parked and walked me into the restaurant, which surprised me a little, though he acted as if it were a given. The manager greeted him like a number one cousin, thumping him on the back as he shook his hand. The small, crowded black-and-white dining room smelled like garlic and mint.

"You should try red curry with chicken and peanuts," said the taxi driver, pointing at the specials menu chalked on the wall. "I would like to eat, too, but . . ." He nodded at the cab, whose hazard lights were flashing. "I hope you like the curry." He waved goodbye to the manager, handed me his card, tipped his hat, and walked out.

I did like the curry. It wasn't quite spicy enough, but cilantro and lemongrass were all over the place, and there were more than enough sweet, sour, and salty layers of flavor to make up for any missing chili peppers.

When I got back to the apartment a few hours later, I looked at the pictures on the taxi driver's website. I liked his paintings, too. Light seemed to shine through the bodies and the faces, as though he'd painted them on glass.

"The message of my pictures is very simple, but heart-driven," he wrote, in the "Philosophy" section of his site. "Less technical sterility, less computer people, more humanity and tenderness."

I clicked on a photo of one of his paintings, called *Kuss 1* (*Kiss 1*), a picture of a man and a woman embracing in the middle of a dissolving skyline. "You will see soft forms and warm colors," he wrote of the painting. "Blue stands for hope. Recurring red and pink tones, the colors of love and danger."

I lay awake that night, like I did most nights here, listening to the rat-a-tat-tat of the neighbor's drum and bass and the echoes of techno and ska from the clubs on Revaler Strasse as I surfed the internet and went through Karl's books about Berlin: "I . . . wish to extend a thank you to that unknown East German borderguard in his observation tower," wrote Duane Phillips, in a guide to recent architecture, "who, at midnight, was tapping his machine gun to the sound of David Bowie, during a transvestite circus performance at Tempodrom in Potsdamer Platz in 1980. At that surreal moment, I fell in love with Berlin . . ."

My insomnia—I told Zille, when I'd gone to her for some naturopathic help—had everything to do with the excitement of being in Elektropolis, I was sure, and with the chain reaction in the German media after my interview with Heike at RTL: every few days now, I was getting emails from journalists wanting to talk to me about *Taxi Gourmet*. I celebrated every one of these messages, interpreting them as yet another sign that I was where I was supposed to be, though after weeks of sleeping so little—I wasn't always remembering to take the tranquilizing herbs Zille had given me—I was operating in a stupor when it came to the jobs that paid the bills, and it was becoming more and more difficult to stay focused on them. The next morning I almost hung up on the Argentine satellite company's chronically unhappy customer in South Africa, who called me three times in two hours to complain about an outage apparently caused by sunspots.

I made a third cup of coffee, trying to concentrate on a Customer Care report: "All systems are running smoothly except the link in Gabon, which continues to be unstable," I wrote. "Customer requests global operations center personnel to closely monitor link to determine reasons for volatility." The coffee made my fingertips tremble as I proofread the report. My hands were still tingling when I walked out the door to meet Julia.

I didn't understand why she was insisting I come to Prenzlauer Berg to watch karaoke—"Everyone who comes to Berlin should see it at least once," she said—but I liked spending time with Julia, and I was glad when I spotted her, sitting high up in the hillside amphitheater known as the Bearpit, in Mauerpark. I wove through the crowd and squeezed into the seat she was saving for me, looking around, trying to imagine this place as it once was, as part of the Wall and its "death strip," where East German border guards would shoot people trying to escape to the West, but I couldn't.

After the Wall came down, Julia explained, Berliners reclaimed this border for themselves. It was as if a military base had been transformed into the Haight-Ashbury of the 1960s: Now Mauerpark was a place for picnics and jam sessions and May Day riots. Every Sunday, there was a flea market—and a locally famous karaoke show hosted by Joe, a bike messenger from Ireland. I gazed at the people gathering to watch the show—hipsters and street artists and skinny-legged musicians carrying instruments on their backs, jugglers and basketball players and women in bikini tops—and I wondered what other city could have staged a metamorphosis like this.

"How are your taxi adventures going?" said Julia, as a man in gold leggings scooted past us, falafel in hand, making his way to one of the last free spaces in our row.

I smiled as I described for her the cab driver with the face of a wizard who wintered in Brazil, and his paintings, and the red curry at Sen Viet—and the ride with Ivo and Steffen, who had joined me for an adventure on one of their non-rehearsal days. We'd ended up at Hasir, on Adalbertstrasse in Kreuzberg, the restaurant where döner kebab was invented, or so our waiter claimed. Sure enough, later on, I found an article in the *Daily Telegraph* that corroborated the waiter's story: On March 2, 1971, Mahmut Aygun—who came to Berlin from

Turkey at age sixteen, as a guest worker—observed all the drunk people stumbling past his kebab stand in the middle of the night and had a moment of inspiration. What if they could take their meat with them? The future, he decided, lay in stuffing kebab in flatbread. Forty years later, his sandwich had allegedly surpassed sausage as the most popular fast food in Germany.

"It takes so little effort to be happy here," I said to Julia, as a man in a black fedora parked a pushcart with a rainbow umbrella across from the amphitheater and began mixing drinks ("Mojito / Caipirihna / Sex on the Park, 3 Euro"). Granted, I hadn't been in Berlin two months, and the only discouraging incidents so far, if you could call them discouraging, had to do with language: getting turned away by a string of cab drivers at Alexanderplatz who claimed they didn't speak English, and not being able to go as deep as I would have liked in the conversations with some of the cabbies. I'd even had one ride in which hand gestures and face contortions were the only way the driver and I could communicate, and ended up back at Gel Gör, a twenty-four-hour *köfte* (sausage) parlor where they butchered their own veal. I didn't have the heart, or the German, to tell the cabby that one of his colleagues had already brought me there. Still, I had never had more fun writing about my taxi adventures. And when I was out and about, and people approached me on the street and asked for directions—did I look like I knew where I was going?— I would shake my head and say, "I'm sorry, I'm not from here." And I *was* sorry—not only because I couldn't help them, but even more so because this wasn't my city. "But maybe it's because I don't live here."

"Maybe," said Julia, slipping on her Jackie O. sunglasses. "Maybe not."

The Stray Cat Strut started to play, and Joe, the MC from Ireland, picked up the microphone and stepped into the center of the stone circle that was now to be the karaoke stage. "Heeeey! Is that too loud at the front? It's okay? What? What do we call this? The what pit? The BEAR-pit!" There were no more seats in the amphitheater. People were starting to gather on the grass behind the stage. "Oh!" said Joe, looking a little dumbfounded, as though he couldn't quite believe we'd all shown up. "It's so lovely to see everybody this afternoon!"

There was only euphoria in the Bearpit for those brave enough to sing. An hour later, Julia and I were losing our voices, hollering as loud as we could, along with the rest of the crowd, for every person who took the stage (but especially for two guys from England who peppered their version of "Blue Suede Shoes" with leprechaun leaps, and a girl in a ruffled skirt who did full split jumps to Kate Bush while staying in key). I couldn't remember the last time I'd been part of an audience like this. There wasn't a drop of irony in people's enthusiasm.

"Only in Berlin," said Julia, between acts.

"Maybe I should stay longer."

"I think you should."

A man with a TV camera was panning the audience, zooming in on a girl in a grass skirt who was hula-hooping in the front row.

"Look!" said Julia, tugging on my sleeve, pointing past the hula hooper: the crowd was parting, clearing a path for an old man with a frizzy gray beard who wore the expression of a downtrodden prophet and moved toward the stage as if he didn't have the strength to bear the weight of his clothes.

"It's him!" she said, clasping her hands.

"It's who?"

Joe the MC took the plastic KaDeWe bag the old man was carrying and handed him the microphone, which he cradled close to his chest.

"Who is it?" I asked again, as the first notes of "My Way" sounded through the speakers.

"Listen," said Julia.

"Zum schluuuuss . . . ," the old man sang, and we watched him transform with each note from someone dejected into someone in full flower, unfurling his spine, puffing out his chest, raising his eyes to the audience, bursting into a radiant, toothy smile, as though he were taken aback by the beauty of his own baritone. The crowd, including Julia and me, roared.

". . . Da stehen wiiiiir—"

The old man sang as though there had never been a Sinatra, as though this were *his* anthem, and this was his one and only chance to lend it his voice. As the song went on, he held on longer and longer to the notes, lifting his arm to the sky.

"Ich habe geliiiiiebt . . . gelacht . . . geweint . . ."

Julia and I stood with the rest of the audience as he finished the last verse—if we were excited before, we were in a frenzy now. When he lowered the microphone, the ovation echoed beyond the Bearpit. From our perch in the amphitheater, we could see heads turning across Mauerpark, toward the source of the clamor. The old man bowed to every corner of the crowd, eyes closed, luxuriating in the applause as if it were a warm bath.

"Isn't he fantastic?" said Julia.

"Who *is* he?"

"He comes here every week," she said. "He either sings 'My Way' or something by Céline Dion. I think he might be homeless. He always wears that same suit, no matter how hot it is, and he always carries that plastic bag from KaDeWe." KaDeWe was Berlin's poshest department store—Zille told me that after the Wall came down, it was the first place many East Berliners wanted to go in her taxi.

The old man picked up his KaDeWe bag and walked off the stage, pressing through the crowd, smiling and nodding as though in a daze as people patted him on the back. "I want to thank him," I said.

He was halfway across Mauerpark by the time Julia and I caught up with him. I tapped his tweed shoulder. He turned around, stiffly, as if his body were frozen, as if a spell had been broken.

"I just—I want to tell you," I said, pressing my palms to my chest, "you were wonderful."

He smiled faintly, his eyes cloudy with incomprehension. Julia translated. *"Danke,"* he said, dropping his gaze.

I dug through my purse, looking for a blank piece of paper. I pulled out my German phrase book instead, opening it to the title page.

"Would you sign this for me?" I said. I handed him a blue Bic. The only other person I'd ever asked for an autograph was David Boreanaz, when he was playing Angel on *Buffy the Vampire Slayer*—and that was in the mail. That was lust. This was something else—much more than an old man singing "My Way." Here was someone who'd gone beyond technique, beyond virtuosity, someone who was singing what he had lived—not what he hoped people might like to hear.

"Autogramm?" said the old man, mystified lines creasing his weather-beaten forehead.

Julia nodded.

I handed him the phrase book, still open to the title page. He wrote his first name—and only his first name—in loopy, deliberate, elementary-school cursive.

"Detlef," I said, reading the name at the bottom of the page. *"Danke."*

He beamed and passed me the Bic.

I emailed Karl after I got back to his apartment, asking if I could sublet his place for another month. I guess you like it then ☺, he wrote back, within minutes. It's actually open till October. How's your gourmet-tripping going so far? Twenty minutes later, I finished negotiating with Air Berlin: seventy euros bought me one more month in Elektropolis. I turned on Celia Cruz and danced around the room. *One more month in Bear-LEEN!* I spun and spun until I couldn't keep up with Celia, plopping down at my desk, opening the phrase book to the title page as I caught my breath. *One more month,* I thought, studying his signature, *where Detlef lives.*

28

You stayed in Berlin because of an old man singing karaoke?
I could imagine someone asking me, in the taxi, at some hypotheti-
cal point on the road. Out of context, it did sound strange. I stared
out the window of the M13, looking but not seeing as the tram
stopped and went from Friedrichshain to Weissensee, thinking of
ways I might explain my decision to a future passenger in New York:
Detlef personifies something about Berlin . . . Too abstract? *Detlef is the
city incarnate . . .* Too general? *Detlef sings to the art-for-art's-sake side
of the city . . .* Too purple? Of course, I would add, Detlef wasn't the
only reason I wanted to stay longer. *But he's the most unusual pearl on
the string,* I thought, as the tram veered north, retracing the route I
had traveled with Verena, the pretty, green-eyed reporter from the
Tagesspiegel, in a taxi a day ago.

It was drizzling when I got off the tram at Antonplatz, and I
peered inside the cabs lining up at the taxi stand, but I didn't recognize any of the drivers. I walked on, turning onto Langhanstrasse
as the lights began to come on in the windows of the apartment
buildings, lending a little warmth to the stark façades. I was looking
forward to meeting Verena once more, for the second part of our
taxi adventure, at a restaurant called La Bandida, at "Crazy Hour."
(ALLE LONGDRINKS & COCKTAILS 3,90€! read the lettering between
the neon Pepsi signs in the windows, VON 18:00–???!)

I counted six other customers besides Verena in the dining room,
which looked like a Quentin Tarantino rendering of a Mexican
saloon: sombreros with silver sequins hung above the bar, and someone had painted fake pinkish bricks on the walls, along with a mural
of a Jose Cuervo label held up by a three-pronged cactus. We chose
a table near the entrance, under an ad for Desperado beer.

A waiter in a ruffled shirt handed us menus embossed with a gold outline of a long-haired woman in a Mexican costume doing a flamenco stomp. Verena watched me run my finger up and down the laminated menu pages. "Fajitas, nachos, spaghetti . . . Oh, my."

"Would we be here if the taxi driver hadn't shown us this place?"

"Well . . ." I thought about Thomas, the cabby who'd driven us here yesterday, at lunchtime, when La Bandida was closed. At first he claimed he never ate out, but after a little coaxing in German from Verena, he closed his book—a Ken Follett novel with an exploding submarine on the cover—and said, "Well, there is an Argentine steak house I like . . ." He'd started driving a taxi in 1987. He was born in Berlin, in Friedrichshain, in what was then East Berlin, and, yes, he had been driving when the Wall came down. In a single day, he said, he'd had to learn the other half, the western half, of the city.

"Sprechen Sie Spanisch?" I asked the waiter in the ruffled shirt when he came to take our order.

"Nein." He laughed. *"Deutsch, oder Türkisch!"*

I watched the bartender deliver a pair of rainbow-striped cocktails to a middle-aged couple with matching mullets who were sitting in the corner, holding hands across their table.

Verena ordered what Thomas told us he liked to order at La Bandida: 180 grams of entrecôte, a baked potato, and a side of kidney beans with speck.

"This," said Thomas, pointing at the Crazy Hour sign when he'd brought us here the day before, "is our restaurant." He parked the cab, undid his seat belt, lit a cigarette. "My wife is a cook by profession," he said, leading us to the entrance. "She spends all day in front of the stove, so I am the one who cooks at home. On weekends, I like the barbecue. And when I don't want to cook, we come here." He tried the door. *"O, nein!"* It was locked. "I am so sorry!" he said. He threw his cigarette on the sidewalk. Verena and I told him not to worry. We'd come back at Crazy Hour.

"Is it like what you remember from Argentina?" said Verena, as I took a bite of entrecôte.

"Not exactly." The steak was good—marinated in a peppery vinegar sauce, tender and fatty in a grain-fed sort of way—but nothing like the *bifes* I remembered from Buenos Aires, which tasted like grass

and earth. "Putting sauce on a steak in Argentina is pretty much sac-
rilege," I said. "They only use salt. And I don't think"—I circled my
fork over the mound of kidney beans and speck with caramelized
onions and jalapeño—"I don't think I ever saw a bean on the menu
at a steak house in Argentina. But these . . ." I waited for Verena to
take a bite. "They're fantastic, aren't they?"

"Mmmm!" She nodded, glancing at her watch. It was eight o'clock.
The bartender turned off Buena Vista Social Club and started play-
ing Whitney Houston. This did remind me of Buenos Aires, where
I'd probably eaten the greatest *bifes* of my life while listening to Rod
Stewart and Britney Spears. There, the only *parrillas* that played tango
music seemed to be the ones catering to tourists.

"From 2003 to 2004," I remembered Thomas telling us, a few
blocks before he dropped us off at La Bandida, "I drove a cab for people in Parliament. This was not a job for me," he said. "I had a boss,
and he was very strict. And the passengers were complicated. They
would always talk about how wonderful things were in Germany."
He squeezed the bridge of his nose under his glasses. "And I was
struggling, barely making a living. Driving the taxi wasn't enough,
you know? I used to repair televisions, but after the Wall came down,
this kind of business was kaput. So I had to find another job."

"What did you do?" I asked him.

"I started to drive trucks. I drove to Italy, Portugal, Spain. I still
drove the taxi. But after some time I got my own car, my own taxi.
Now," he said, blue eyes bright against his sunburned face, "I am my
own chief."

"Our cab driver," said Verena, "Thomas." She put down her fork.
"There is a word in German that describes a person like him."

"What is it?" I said, arranging a last bite of steak and beans and
speck on my fork.

"I don't think this word exists in English."

The waiter in the ruffled shirt came over to clear our plates.

"The word," said Verena, watching the waiter retreat behind the
bar, "is *Lebenskünstler.*"

"What does it mean?"

"If you translate it, it means 'life artist.' But it's more than that.

It's like . . ." She looked up at the ceiling, stroking the tassels of her pink scarf. "It's a word for people who make an art of living by being resourceful, finding different ways to get by."

"*Lebenskunstler,*" I repeated, as Whitney Houston ripped through the chorus of "I'm Every Woman" and the waiter brought us the bill. I pulled out my notebook and wrote down the word. "Is that right?" I showed Verena. She smiled, took my pen, and added an umlaut over the *u*.

I hurried from La Bandida back to the apartment, dropping my purse on the futon, kicking off my sandals, opening my laptop and willing it to wake up quickly so I could start researching the word. Verena was right: There was no equivalent for *Lebenskünstler* in English.

The clubs on Revaler Strasse were warming up for the night as I sat at my computer, oblivious to the hour, sifting through every *Lebenskünstler* definition I could find, as if searching for the solution to a riddle I hadn't realized I'd been grappling with, until now.

Most of the explanations didn't seem to do justice to the word as Verena had described it. A *Lebenskünstler,* read one German-to-English glossary translation, is a "chilled-out dude." A British literature and culture scholar named Kelly Sear Smith included the word on a list of "Compounds and Curiosities" in German. A "Lebenskünstler," she noted, was a "life artist who manages to get his living in an eccentric way . . . think of Kramer on *Seinfeld.*"

After midnight—I glanced at the clock when I heard deep house music coming from somewhere downstairs—as the walls of the apartment began to reverberate, I finally found a *Lebenskünstler* definition that seemed to fit Thomas: "Oscar Wilde once purportedly said, 'I put my talent into my work, but my genius into my life,'" wrote Andrew Hammel, on his *German Word of the Week* site. "A suitable introduction to this week's entry. *Lebenskünstler.* Literally translated it means 'life artist.' He is a *Lebenskünstler.* Someone who pieces together his living from various activities that, collectively, bring in just enough money to live. No office, no suit, no boss, no rules . . ."

Yes. I read it again: *No office, no suit, no boss, no rules.* Here was a single German word that summed up Thomas's freedom-driven approach to life. Here was a word, I thought, as I copied the definition into my notebook, that implied that there was nothing wrong with trading security for freedom, with opting out of the nine-to-five, with driving the cab and working for the crazy Argentine satellite company and keeping up the taxi adventures, even if it meant eating a lot of garbanzo beans. I felt as if I'd been walking around for the past five years with an undiagnosed malady, and now someone was telling me, "No, in fact, you're not ill at all. Here in Berlin we have a word for your condition—which, by the way, is perfectly normal. The word is *Lebenskünstler.*"

29

One day, then two, then three went by after the ride with Thomas. It was September, and my departure date loomed, a darkening cloud on a not-too-distant horizon, and I still hadn't found a way to start the story about him. *The word is* Lebenskünstler, I thought, but it didn't feel right to force the idea into a paragraph in a six-hundred-word blog post. I went back to my notes, remembering snippets of our conversation. How did you know where to go? I'd asked him, when he told Verena and me about driving to West Berlin for the first time. Wasn't West Berlin a blank spot on the maps in East Germany? After he learned the way to KaDeWe, he said, it wasn't so bad. I thought about Zille. I imagined her and Thomas, traveling in opposite directions in the days after the Wall opened up—she from West to East, he from East to West—into the halves of their city that were totally foreign to them. Every time I tried to describe their crossings-over, the story would go flat.

I took a walk around the block, notebook in my pocket, hoping an opening line would come to me. DON'T FORGET TO GO HOME! read the headline on one of the posters outside the clubs on Revaler Strasse. *But I* am *home,* I thought—and what an unfamiliar thought this was. Two months here weren't enough. Neither were three.

Every city had its failings. I wanted to know: What was Berlin's flaw? What about the idea that it was "a city condemned forever to becoming and never to being"? Maybe Karl Schleffer was right: In the last hundred years, Berlin had gone from decadent metropolis to Third Reich headquarters to the city of the Wall—and was now the reunited capital where anything seemed possible. Forever becoming, without a doubt. But in my eyes, this was no flaw—how else could the city brave its history? I stepped around the remains of a TV some-

one had dropped from a high window. For me, Berlin's magnificence
lay in its restlessness.

"So you're big in Berlin, eh?" said Dad, on our Sunday call, when I
told him and Mom about the taxi ride with Verena, and the email I'd
gotten from a journalist named David at *Spiegel*.

"How did they find you?"

"I don't know." But I assumed it was how the other reporters
had found out about my project via that first TV spot with Heike
on RTL.

"All this press stuff is like having another job!" said Mom.

"Don't worry! They'll get tired of the story sooner or later. And
anyway"—I swallowed a sigh—"I'm leaving soon."

David translated for me, a few days later, when we climbed into a cab
at the taxi stand across from Brandenburger Tor, with a shy but kind
driver named Eren, who had been fasting for Ramadan but was happy
to show us a Turkish restaurant near Kottbusser Tor called Konyali,
where they baked *konya etli ekmek* (flatbread with beef, sumac, and
flat-leaf parsley) to order in a brick oven. David was compassionate,
and perceptive, and a vegetarian—he ordered the cheese version of
Konyali's flatbread. He was also genuinely interested when I told him
about Thomas and Zille and the other cabbies I was meeting in Berlin, and wanted to understand the spirit behind my project. "We're
so focused on where we're coming from and where we're going," I
told him, "on getting from A to B. Most of the time we're not paying
any attention to what happens between A and B. On a taxi adventure,
you *have* to pay attention. It's all about the in-between."

Something detonated when David's story went live: I had more
visitors to my blog in six hours than I'd had in six months. But the
hullabaloo was as brief as it was terrific—two days later, my web
statistics went back to normal, and everything was as it was before,
which was more of a letdown than I wanted to admit. But I also got
an odd email:

Hi Layne!

My name is Rumen Vassillevski. It's a Bulgarian name because my father is Bulgarian.

I read about Your blog in SPIEGEL and find it really interesting.

I'm a Berlin cab driver since fifteen years and I'm also a little gourmet.

Maybe I can help You with some informations for Your blog.

By the way I have a Berlin Taxi blog: autofiktion.com.

Right now I'm still in Bulgaria in my holiday.

But I will go back to Berlin just today.

Tomorrow I'm already "On The Road"!

Best Regards,

Rumen Vassillevski

"A little gourmet?" Julia laughed, closing her laptop. "Are you going to answer him?" We were at her flat on the northern edge of Mitte, sitting on her puffy white sofa, finishing bowls of fettuccini primavera with cream and fresh dill.

"I already did," I said. "He sounds like a weirdo." I rested the tines of my fork on my lip. "But in a good way."

"I agree," said Julia. She set her empty bowl on the glass coffee table and unwrapped the dark chocolate bar I'd brought, breaking it into pieces before she passed it to me. Her pale blue eyes, usually expansive and clear, were pensive. "How much time do you have left?"

"Three weeks," I said, taking a bite of chocolate, its flavor not registering. The closer I came to my departure date, the more I struggled with the idea of leaving Berlin, though I had no choice: my tourist visa was expiring, I'd already changed my plane ticket once, and if I didn't want to forget what little New York geography I knew, it was time for me to get back into the driver's seat. The truth? I hated the idea of going back to hacking. I had been thrilled, every day I'd been in Berlin, not to be driving the taxi in New York. As determined as I was to love the job, and New York City, I didn't feel devoted to either one.

"I know you'll come back," said Julia.

I wanted to believe her.

When I called Rumen the next day to work out the details of the food tour in his taxi, I thought he sounded mean on the phone. I wasn't sure if it was his voice—like James Earl Jones with a German accent—or his way of negotiating.

"Everyone expect something for free," he said. "I am a licensed city guide: when I make a tour it is normal if it should cost forty euro per hour."

Was this the same Rumen who'd written those funny emails (I'm really surpriced to hear from you!, he'd written in response to my response. My favorite is Asian kittchen. Especialy Thai and Vietnam. But as a half German of course I know some German places. Whatever I will think about it!)? The same Rumen who had had the idea for the food tour in the first place? It sounded like he was changing the terms.

"I don't expect anything for free," I said. "I mean, I drive a taxi, too. But if it's forty euros, I can't afford more than an hour—"

"One hour?"

Now I was annoyed. "Maybe it's not worth it for you. We don't have to—"

"OK!" he said. "We will meet us. One hour is OK."

"OK. And if it's OK with you, I'd like to invite some friends of mine—"

"Friends?"

"They're travel bloggers. And I told them about you, and they're very curious."

"Fine," he said, hanging up before I had a chance to say goodbye.

Three days later, I was walking to Jessnerstrasse to meet Rumen, hoping he wouldn't show up for our tour. I buttoned up my jacket and crossed my arms, ducking under the drizzle. Summer was over. The trees were letting go of their leaves, and the city was getting cooler, darker, folding into itself in mid-September. I loved it still: That morning, at the used-book store on Niederbarnimstrasse, the lady who was weighing my paperbacks at the cash register peered out the window at the cloudy sky and said, "You don't come to Berlin for the weather. You come for the people."

I noticed only one taxi parked on Jessnerstrasse. A tall man in a navy-blue rain jacket was wiping it down, his back to me. I tugged on my sleeves, pulling them down over my hands.

The man turned when he heard my footsteps. *Oh, no,* I thought when I saw him.

"Hello!" His voice was even deeper in person than on the phone—it had a Beethoven symphony sort of weight to it. "You are Layne?" he said, looking me up and down and extending one of his giant hands in my direction. He had beautiful eyes, deep-set, blue-gray. His sandy blond hair was cut in a buzz, and he wore an aviator watch. I guessed he was in his mid-forties.

All I could do was nod as I shook his hand, which was warm and coarse. *Oh, no,* I thought again, feeling myself falling into the monosyllabic idiocy that overtakes me when I find someone really attractive. "Rumen Vassillevski?"

"It is nice to meet you."

"You, too." My face was on fire.

I looked up the street and spotted a man and a woman in nylon windbreakers walking in our direction. It was Dan and Audrey, thank goodness. They were a couple from the U.S. who'd quit their jobs in Prague, sold their stuff, started traveling around the world in 2006, and were still on the road four years later, documenting their adventures on a site called *Uncornered Market*. We'd found each other on the food and travel circuit on the internet and arranged to meet in person when we discovered we'd be in Berlin at the same time. They said yes right away when I'd invited them to come along on the food tour with Rumen.

The four of us shook hands, graciously, awkwardly.

"Should we go?" I said, a little too brightly.

"German food is today's highlight for you," said Rumen, steering the taxi through the traffic on Frankfurter Allee as though slaloming around the cones in a sports car commercial.

"Oh, really? I thought Asian was your favorite—"

"We are in Germany and so you have to know the German food. It's a *must!*" He moved his whole body when he spoke, as if the seat weren't big enough to contain him.

"Well, OK." I laughed, pushing a strand of hair out of my eye, regretting that I hadn't put more effort into fixing my hair that morning. "This is cool, because I've been on a lot of—well, not a lot, but some taxi adventures in Berlin, and none of the cabbies have really shown me any German food yet . . ." My face was still warm. Dan and Audrey were chuckling in the back seat.

"I will show you something *unique* in German food." Rumen grinned. "You never would find, you never will find, and maybe this, especially this restaurant, will not exist for a long time."

"It's new?"

"No, it's luck. Because it's, um, it still exists from the socialist time. This restaurant. And it's for poor people. But the food, or the meals, are okay. And it's at a very central place, close to the Alexanderplatz. And I don't know how they can exist by these prices and by these clients."

"Is the food good?" I said.

"Of course." He nodded "It's one hundred percent German!" He giggled—an impish, high-pitched giggle that seemed totally out of sync with the heft of his body and voice. *"And . . ."* He paused. "You have to try the *Dead Grandma.*"

"What is Dead Grandma?"

Dan and Audrey started laughing for real.

"You will see!" said Rumen. "Usually"—he parallel-parked the taxi on Karl-Liebknecht-Strasse with three turns of the wheel— "I eat German food only at my mother." He turned off the ignition. "She is born in Berlin, in Neukölln. Later we moved in a village in East Germany."

"And your father is Bulgarian?"

"Yes." He undid his seat belt. "Every year I make my holidays in Bulgaria. I go always in the mountains. I don't like the coast."

"Why?" said Audrey.

Rumen smiled. "In Bulgaria we say the Mafia isn't part of the government, the government is part of the Mafia—"

"Wow." Dan laughed.

"And this is the reason the prices on the Black Sea coast are so high."

We climbed out of the cab, gazing up at the TV tower as we followed Rumen to the restaurant. There was a brown and yellow sign in old German script over the entrance. Käse König, it was called. "Cheese King?" I said, looking up at the sign. "Or the King's Cheese?"

"I am not sure," he said. "Anyway, it's not so important."

We went inside, inhaling the scent of caraway seeds, eyeing the steam-table buffet behind the counter, which contained an assortment of unidentifiable purees in hotel pans, in overcooked shades of green and brown. Rumen rubbed his hands together and greeted the woman at the cash register, who smiled at him like a willing accomplice as he ordered one plate of *Tote Oma* (Dead Grandma) for us to share.

"This is very interesting!" he said, handing me a Corningware plate with boiled potatoes, sauerkraut with caraway, and the pièce de résistance: a puddle of lumpy, brown-pink mush surrounded by a ring of red-orange oil. "I just learn that Dead Grandma has another name, too." He pointed at the mush. "You can also call it *Katastrophe!*" He put his hands on his hips, leaned his head back, and let loose a thunderous guffaw. There were a few elderly customers in the cafeteria, and they looked up from their lunches, surprised by the volume of his laugh.

"Catastrophe?" I was laughing, too. Dan and Audrey were studying the Corningware plate, smiling politely.

"What's in it?" I said. "Wait." I waved my hands. "Never mind. I don't want to know."

"It's *Blutwurst*," said Rumen, "and *Leberwurst*. A mix!"

"Blood sausage and liverwurst?" said Audrey.

"Genau." He nodded, passing us forks and stepping away from the table.

"Hey," I said, "where are you going?"

"I have to go check the taxi," he said. "Maybe I could get a parking ticket! Don't worry! I will wait for you outside. *Guten Appetit!*"

He slipped out the door. We each took a bite.

Dead Grandma, or *Katastrophe,* wasn't as repulsive as it looked.

"I think I can taste paprika," I said. "And nutmeg."

"It reminds me of the filling in a banh mi," said Dan.

"I think it's better with sauerkraut," said Audrey. "There's kind of a neutralizing effect."

"Well?" said Rumen, when the three of us got back in the taxi.

"It wasn't bad," I said.

"I don't know if we'd eat it again," said Dan, "but it was better than we thought."

"Really?" said Rumen.

"I've definitely had worse," I told him, which was true. Dead Grandma could not compare to the *chinchulines* (chitlins) that tasted like rancid vegetable shortening at the *parrilla* across from the casino in Buenos Aires.

"The problem with the German kitchen," said Rumen, looking over his shoulder as he pulled onto Karl-Liebknecht-Strasse, "is that they don't use herbs. And they use sugar in everything! That's why if I'm in Berlin, because my mother is not in Berlin, I prefer Thai and Wietnamese food. And now"—he raised his hand toward the sunroof—"I will show you maybe one of the best Wietnamese in town."

I looked at the clock on the dashboard. We'd been on tour for almost an hour already. "How did you start liking Thai and Vietnamese food?" I asked him.

"Now it's fifteen or twenty years ago," he said. "I lived in Frankfurt-am-Main, and there I discovered Indian food. Because at this time it was 'new' "—he made air quotes, keeping his hands on the wheel—"and then later I came to Berlin and in Berlin it was difficult to find Indian food because they didn't know at this time this cuisine. And from Indian food I came to Thai food! I like very much the coconut milk, the red curry with the chicken." He swallowed as if his mouth were watering. "And then from Thai I came to Wietnam, two years ago or three years ago, because at this time Wietnamese food started to become popular in Berlin especially."

"Just two years ago?"

"In my opinion. But I'm not a one hundred percent specialist," he said, changing lanes on Karl-Marx-Allee. "Please fasten seat belt because it's a little bit crazy . . ."

"Oh, yes, sorry." I didn't know how he could keep up the conversation and deal with the traffic at the same time. When I got involved in talking with my passengers, I either got lost or made careless mistakes, like smashing into side mirrors, or braking too hard.

We crossed the River Spree and drove into Kreuzberg, formerly part of West Berlin, where his favorite Vietnamese place was. "Before the Wall came down," he said, "the most important thing for me was to go one day to West Berlin. This is what I dreamed about. To live in Berlin was not so important. My dream was to go on the other side of the Wall."

"Where were you when the Wall came down?"

"I was there," he said. "Dancing on the Wall, at the Brandenburger Gate. By the way, this was the only place on the Wall where people could dance. The other parts of the Wall were too small. But at Brandenburger Gate they built the Wall very wide, very thick, so it could stop a tank."

"You were there?" I said. *How did it feel,* I wanted to ask him, *to dance on the Wall?* But it seemed like a silly network-newsish question.

"Of course!" he said. "All night, all day, was a party. The people in the West gave us bananas and champagne. And also every East German got some welcome money. You know what I bought with this money?"

"What?"

"A Tracy Chapman LP. And some West sausages. Because this was difficult to find in East Germany. There was a special *Imbiss* on the Ku'damm. There the *Wiener Würstchen* had a special taste."

"How did you find it?"

"I saw it," he said, smiling, "and I smelled it."

"Aha." I sat up straighter, positioning my legs so that my thighs didn't spread over the seat.

"Anyway, after the Wall came down, there was some kind of anarchy, especially in East Berlin, because there were not so many policemen on the streets."

"Is that why you came to Berlin?"

"I came to Berlin because anything was possible." He paused, looking at me, then at Dan and Audrey, as if to make sure we were paying close attention. "This is the main reason. But also because I could have two loud parties per year and the neighbors won't call the police—"

I laughed.

"And in Berlin I could ride my bike on the sidewalk and walk in the street with my beer!"

"But that's still true, isn't it?" I said. "I still have this feeling, like anything is possible—"

"No." He shook his head. "The best days in Berlin are over."

I stared at him. "What do you mean?"

"I mean in the beginning it was everything is possible—"

"Yeah?"

"But then it became boring. More and more normal people came to Berlin that weren't here in the nineties, and they have no idea what I'm talking about," he said, the buoyancy fading from his voice. "They can't imagine this freedom we had."

I looked out the window. We passed a man on a bike with a bongo drum belted to his back. *Over?* I thought. *No, no, no . . .*

"Well, how was it different?" asked Dan.

"Every living room was a pub," said Rumen. "There were parties where the professor was sitting next to the house cleaner and this was completely normal. This changed a lot. In the nineties when I started driving the taxi there were much more Berlin clients. Now most clients, they moved to Berlin for business, or for their partner. Or they are tourists. They come because Berlin is cheap. And what is cheap is not respected."

"What is cheap is not respected . . ."

"Exactly! They don't respect Berlin, or how it was. How can I make you understand?" He glanced over at me again. "In the last time," he continued, some of the fervor returning to his voice, "I understand more and more about my reason to come to Berlin. I always said I came to Berlin because of the city Berlin, and not because of a partner or a job! But now I know that Berlin was and is a real person for me—"

"For me, too." Despite its age—773 years old, and counting—I'd started to think of Berlin as an adolescent burning to be an adult, and New York as a man in midlife crisis.

"About New York, I'm not sure." Rumen laughed. "For me, Berlin is mostly my mother, but it can be my father too—*ach*!" He pointed out the window, at a sandwich board on the sidewalk advertising soy lattes. *"Sojamilk!"* He grimaced like he was sucking on a lemon. "Milk is from a cow! Not from *Soja*!"

I bit my lip. I liked soy milk, but I wasn't going to tell him that.

He parked the taxi next to the bike lane on Hasenheide, outside a Vietnamese restaurant called Hamy. To the right of the entrance was an open kitchen where two elderly Asian women in hairnets were stir-frying with furious concentration, flames licking the sides of their woks. After our Dead Grandma appetizer, none of us knew what to expect here, but I was still hungry, and I couldn't help feeling hopeful when I thought I caught a whiff of kaffir lime. We ordered pho and red curries and ginger tea and sat at the last empty picnic table outside.

"Have you seen my blog?" said Rumen.

His blog—*Autofiktion: Untrue Stories from the Real Life of a Berlin Taxi Driver*—was in German, of course. When I copied the posts into Google Translate, they read like gibberish. "I wish I could understand it," I said, "but I can't."

"Maybe it is better you don't understand."

"Why?" I laughed.

"What I write is a little bit crass, maybe a little bit provocative. Mostly about Berlin, how Berlin changes."

"I'll look at it again," I said. "Your photos are great, by the way." His pictures—of graffiti, road signs, found objects, construction sites—were scenes from the street so absurd many of them looked surreal.

"You like the photos?" His eyes lit up. I blushed again.

Our curry arrived, under a veil of shredded cabbage and fennel.

"This I like very much about the Wietnamese kitchen," said Rumen, waving his fork over the curry. "The contrast. They make always a little salad. In the Thai kitchen they only give you the hot curry."

"You really are a little gourmet," I said. I took a bite and started to cough as soon as I swallowed—behind purple basil and kaffir lime were red hot chili peppers. "It's delicious," I said, hitting my chest, taking a forkful of rice to tame the heat.

"Too spicy?" He looked worried.

"No." I cleared my throat. "Just spicier than I expected."

We ate, and I floated in and out of the conversation as Rumen talked books with Dan and Audrey. Had we read Michel Houellebecq? No? Iliya Troyanov? How about *Zorba the Greek*? No? But this was a must! "I read this book for maybe the tenth time this summer," he said. "Zorba is a hero for me. When everything falls apart, he dances."

I tried to take small, elegant bites, unsettled—least of all by the bizarre transition from Dead Grandma to red curry. *Was it true? Were the best years in Berlin really over?* I hoped no one at the table could see how intrigued I was by Rumen, who had loved this city far longer than I had, and seemed to love it still, even as he felt it slipping away from him.

30

"I never thought he'd be beautiful," I said to Julia as we waited in line at Schlemmerbuffet, a döner kebab stand on Rosenthaler Platz, the day after the Dead Grandma tour with Rumen. I gazed at the hunk of meat spinning lazily in the window and glanced over at Julia as we stepped closer to the counter. She had the look of a little girl with a pocketful of candy.

"What are you smiling about?"

"Oh . . ." She feigned an innocent look at the ceiling. "Nothing."

"Nothing?"

"Bitteschön!" said the man at the cash register. Can I help you?

She ordered—döner kebab with *scharfer Soße*—for both of us, and a man with a giant serrated knife started trimming thin slices off the spinning hunk of meat, letting the shavings pile up in the drippings before stuffing them into pieces of triangular flatbread.

"Julia," I said, as we settled into one of the Formica booths along the wall, "do you know something I don't know?"

Something glimmered behind the habitual tranquility in her eyes as she handed me my sandwich, sheathed in a piece of triangular tissue paper. "You know I told Dilek about your taxi project."

"Yeah . . . ?" Julia had introduced me to Dilek, one of her first friends in Berlin, weeks earlier. Besides her column in the *Berliner Zeitung,* she had written four books, and a play called *Turkish for Lovers.* Dilek, Julia explained, was friends with David at *Spiegel.* "Aha!" I wagged my finger at her in mock indignation. "So you told Dilek, and Dilek told David . . ."

"And Ru—What's his name?"

"Rumen Vassillevski."

"And Rumen Vassillevski found you in *Spiegel!*" Julia plucked a piece of meat out of her sandwich. "So he's cute, eh?"

"Yes," I said, glancing at my döner—meat, tomatoes, and onions spilling out of the flatbread like fruit in a cornucopia—trying to figure out how to eat it without getting it all over my face. "But I don't want to meet any beautiful men right now!" I had less than two weeks left in Berlin. Anything that made the city more endearing at this point only added to my despair about leaving it.

"But you know what?" I said, as we took our first bites—the meat was heavily, aggressively seasoned, almost too salty but not quite, the *scharfer Soße* vaguely spicy, a little bit sweet. "It's not just that he's good-looking. He's really—" I picked up a fallen slice of onion. "He knows so much about Berlin. And he *loves* Berlin. I kind of feel like he slapped me awake."

Julia resituated a tomato. "What do you mean?"

"I've been romanticizing like crazy since I got here. I had no idea how much the city changed since the nineties." *How oblivious I've been,* I thought, after the conversation with Rumen. Oblivious to what had come before, to how the city was transforming now. Why hadn't I noticed all those cranes jutting out of the skyline? Or the shabby-chic boutiques, and the single-origin coffee shops and the condo construction sites that had popped up—and the Jugendstil apartment buildings that had been torn down—just in the months since I'd been in Friedrichshain?

"The city couldn't stay like the nineties forever," said Julia. "Cities change! Berlin especially. Maybe your taxi driver"—she tucked a stray shred of lettuce back into her sandwich—"is a little unrealistic?"

"Maybe . . ."

"Do you think you'll see him again?"

"I don't know." At the end of our food tour, we'd shaken hands, and he'd only let me pay him for one hour, though the trip had lasted more than three. "There is no lead," I'd written on my blog that night, "no quote, no way to dive into describing today's taxi adventure in a way that would do justice to the man who led it . . ."

·   ·   ·

"Welcome to Alcatraz!" said Rumen, smiling a little sheepishly as he led me through one solid wood door, tall enough and wide enough for a carriage to pass through, then through another solid wood door just like it, into a cobblestoned courtyard, flush with weeds, to the back house of his apartment building, where he unlocked a steel door with a head-high window that resembled a dirty piece of graph paper. It did look like a jailhouse door, actually. I followed him up a dusty, raw pine staircase, hands in my pockets, my face hot. I want to invite you to have a MILCHKAFFEE, he'd written, exactly forty-eight hours after the end of our food tour. I make the best MILCHKAFFEE south of Frankfurter Allee . . . No, I didn't want to meet any beautiful men just now, but I'd still been hoping he would write. He wanted to show me some books and more of his photos, too, he said. Yet I wasn't entirely sure why he'd invited me to his place: Was he interested in me? Or interested in having me write more about him? Unlike the day I met him, he was clean-shaven, wearing black jeans and a matching jacket. I had to force myself to look him in the eye.

"Please," he said, "come in." He opened a door that led to a kitchen where the walls were papered orange, the air smelled like fried eggs, and blue-gray paint was peeling off the wide wooden floorboards. Above the kitchen table, across from the door, was a drawing of a man in sky-blue shorts holding a naked woman by the shins, as if she were a wheelbarrow.

"Come," he said, noticing me staring at the drawing. I followed him from the kitchen to the living room, my face still warm.

"Wow," I said, leaning against the door frame as my eyes adjusted to the orange-pink light filtering through the striped curtains. It looked like books were breeding in this room: standing two and three layers deep on lacquered shelves that spanned an entire wall, piled on the rolltop desk between the two south-facing windows, heaped on the canvas chair next to the desk, stacked on the wooden shelf under the glass-topped coffee table, along with back issues of *Der Spiegel*.

Poster-sized photos of a metal ashtray hung on the walls—"This ashtray I took from a train station in Bulgaria," he said—next to a map of Europe after the Cold War and pictures of Bob Dylan at various stages of his career. Two sofas and a futon, blanketed in cowhide and sheepskin, were arranged in a U shape. The low ceiling was plastered with crimson crepe paper.

"It's difficult to find places like this in Berlin anymore," he said, looking around the room as if he wondered how much longer it would be his.

"I believe you." It was the sort of room you would find at the end of a secret passageway.

"Please . . ." He extended his hand toward the sheepskin-covered futon closest to the coffee table, where two dainty squares of cream-colored cake sat, perfectly centered, on two square white plates. "Be comfortable."

I moved to the sofa and sat on the edge, eyeing the cake. *Be comfortable, he says.* I pulled the sides of my jacket together and folded my hands in my lap.

Rumen walked into the kitchen. "Now I make the coffee!" He returned to the living room holding an antique wooden coffee grinder. "Twenty euros," he said, smiling as he sat in his desk chair, sandwiching the grinder between his knees, "on eBay!"

I laughed. "Do you use it all the time?"

"Of course! I told you I make the best *Milchkaffee* south of Frankfurter Allee!" He cranked the handle of the coffee grinder until it didn't resist anymore, then went back into the kitchen.

I turned around and knelt on the sofa, examining the books on his shelves. There was his beloved Michel Houellebecq, plus Bertolt Brecht and Alexander Solzhenitsyn. Hermann Hesse had his own shelf. Nietzsche and Schopenhauer shared one. There were American authors, too: Jack London, Jack Kerouac, Charles Bukowski, Henry Miller, Mark Twain. An autobiography of Miles Davis. Eleven volumes of Freud. German-Bulgarian dictionaries next to titles in Cyrillic. A book of illustrations by Heinrich Zille—

"Zille!" I said, pulling the book off the shelf. "You like him, too?" After that first taxi adventure with Zille, I'd found a compilation of her namesake's paintings at the Antiquariat on Niederbarnimstrasse. Zille's uncle was right, I thought, as I studied the pictures: The resemblance was obvious. Zille had the same apple cheeks and upturned nose as the people in the paintings. I could imagine her stepping into any of those scenes, laughing, dancing, shouting across the courtyard of an overcrowded *Hinterhaus.*

"What is it?" said Rumen. I took the Zille book into the kitchen. He was standing at the stove, brewing the coffee in a Moka pot and warming milk in a metal pitcher. I showed him the cover: Zille's characters were holding hands, swaying in a circle on the dust jacket.

"Zille is a real Berliner who painted real Berliners," he said, as he turned off the flame under the milk and beat it for a few seconds with a whisk. "That is what makes him special."

I opened the book and flipped through the pages, but I couldn't concentrate on the pictures. The coffee started to bubble. Rumen let it percolate, waiting for the sound to fade before he turned off the burner and set the Moka pot on the edge of the stainless-steel sink.

"You know what?" I said, closing the book. "I've been thinking about what you said before, how in Berlin anything was possible—"

"*Ja . . .*" He took two glasses out of the cupboard, grabbed a hot pad, and pulled the milk off the stove, filling the glasses two-thirds of the way.

"I know I wasn't here in the nineties, but I still feel that way—"

He shook his head. "For me, this golden time is over," he said, pouring the coffee, which swirled through the hot milk and settled, like a diffuse nebula, at the bottom of the glasses. "You know what happened after the Wall came down? Many people who lived in East Berlin left East Berlin. Almost everything was empty in the East. And young crazy people like me came, and some crazy people from West Berlin came over, too. We wanted to make new things, not only parties! And money was not important—"

I nodded, holding the Zille book next to my chest.

"But then in the late nineties, more and more normal people moved to Berlin." He sighed, stirring the coffee into the milk with a long-handled spoon. "Because it was the capital and because it was cheap. Now the empty spaces, mostly they are gone." He took what looked like an electric toothbrush and started frothing milk with it.

"But—"

"There is no 'but.'" Rumen picked up the glasses of *Milchkaffee,* carrying them near their rims as he brought them into the living room and set them on the coffee table. I followed him, returning to my place on the edge of the sheepskin-covered futon.

"Do you like Mercedes Sosa?" he said.

I loved Mercedes Sosa.

"I saw her sing one time." He pulled a record from the stack on the floor. "I will never forget." He opened the dustcover on the record player and lowered the album onto the platter.

I closed my eyes and tried to listen. I didn't want to believe that Berlin's golden days were over. Or, more precisely, that I'd gotten here too late. Rumen sat next to me on the futon. Though his knee was at a respectable distance from mine, not even the sound of Mercedes Sosa's voice—smooth and unshakable, as if drawing force from deep in the earth—could put me at ease.

"So"—he raised his glass of *Milchkaffee*—"*Prost.*"

"*Prost!*" I said, clinking my glass with his with a little too much enthusiasm. I took a sip, quickly wiping away my milk mustache. "Oh!" I said. "You weren't kidding."

"What means?"

"This is really good!" The milk softened the punch of the coffee but didn't disguise its strength.

"*Danke schön.*" Rumen grinned and gestured toward the cake. Instead of frosting, the top had a layer of round, sugary crumbs. "*Streuselkuchen,*" he said. "It's my favorite. Try!"

I took a bite. It was very dry and very sweet.

"Maybe it's not the best *Streuselkuchen*—"

"I don't know." I took another bite of cake, unable to make it past the sweetness. "I have nothing to compare it to," I said. Emboldened already by the caffeine, I turned around, facing the bookshelves, and pointed to the titles in Cyrillic. "This is Bulgarian, right? Do you speak Bulgarian?"

He took a long swallow of *Milchkaffee*. "My Bulgarian is very poor," he said. "But you know what? If Nietzsche wrote in Bulgarian, I would learn Bulgarian!"

I laughed. *What better reason to learn a language?* I thought.

"Bulgarian isn't funny!"

I pressed my lips together, trying to stop giggling.

"Well, sometimes it is funny," he said. "*Egal,* Nietzsche! Let us go back to Nietzsche!" He ran his hand over the books on his Nietzsche-Schopenhauer shelf, pulled out a copy of *Also sprach Zarathustra,* and opened it to a page marked with green satin string. "How can I explain you? Nietzsche . . . He tries always to tell the truth. Look here." He handed the book to me, pointing at a sentence underlined in pencil.

"I can't read German," I said, handing the book back to him.

"*Ach!* Then you must learn German!"

"I will."

"You will?"

"Yes." Now I was determined to learn the language. "You know what I like about German?" I said. "There are whole ideas, whole ways of thinking about things, condensed into single words!" I swept my hands over the coffee table, almost knocking over my *Milchkaffee*—it was a sure sign that I was excited, when I started to knock things over. Rumen grabbed the glass before it toppled onto the table. "Ooops!" I said, my face getting hot again. "Sorry." I sat on my hands. "What I'm trying to say is there are words that take paragraphs to translate into English that have just one word in German."

"Like what?" He smiled.

"Like *Lebenkunstler.*"

"What?"

"*Lebenskuuunstler,*" I said, trying to pronounce the "u" with the umlaut. "Like you."

Rumen stopped smiling. "I am not a *Lebenskünstler,*" he said. "*Dafür kommt die Kunst noch zu kurz.*"

"I don't understand."

"I don't have so much art in my life."

"How can you say that? What about your blog? Your photos? Your books? The taxi?"

He shrugged. "That's not art."

"Yes, it is!" My voice was rising. "You don't have an office, or a boss. And you make your own rules. Isn't that what a *Lebenskünstler* is?"

He tapped his fingertip on the open book. "Let us go back to Nietzsche."

"But—"

He started to read aloud: *"Von allem Geschriebenen liebe ich nur das, was einer mit seinem Blut schreibt. Schreibe mit Blut und du wirst erfahren, dass Blut Geist ist."* He looked up at me. *"Das ist genial!"* He was beaming. *"Oder?"*

"But what does it mean?"

"If you write, you should write with blood," he said. "Nietzsche has only respect for a person who write with blood. This I try to do. But I must keep trying. It's not so easy."

"No, it's not." I sat back on the futon and looked up at the ceiling. Had I ever really written with blood? Had he?

"Did you study philosophy?"

"No," he said. "I was not allowed to study—"

"You weren't allowed?"

"You know I am from East Germany. Not everybody there could study what they want. My teachers, and the people at the university, they said I was too *individualistisch*." He resituated the satin string and shut the book. "I did not fit in the system."

I set my glass on the coffee table. To empathize was impossible, and I didn't get the sense that he was looking for sympathy, or indignation on his behalf.

"Anyway," he said, returning *Zarathustra* to its place on the Nietzsche-Schopenhauer shelf. "Now I want to show you something completely different." He reached for a folded-up map as thick as a book, with a red, yellow, and blue cover.

"Do you know this plan?" He sat down next to me again, handing me the map. I'd drunk the *Milchkaffee* too quickly. My heart was beating so fast and so loudly that I wondered if he could hear it.

"No," I said, opening it carefully. It was a Falkplan map of Berlin, which folded out in sections, one neighborhood at a time.

"This is not a normal map," he said. "My uncle, he was from the West, he was a fan of maps like me. When he visited us he would bring this map, and we would sit for many hours with him and study it. We had no maps of West Berlin. On our maps it was white. So both things were interesting for me: to look at the map and to see West Berlin on the map." He picked up his glass of *Milchkaffee*, tilting his head back to catch the last of the foam. "My uncle showed me on this map where my grandmother lived in West Berlin. And when the Wall came down some years later I could find her house."

"You never went to your grandma's before the Wall came down?"

"How could I go? It was not allowed."

"Wait." I shook my head. "You found her house because you remembered where it was on your uncle's map?"

"That's right."

I tried to imagine finding my way to an address on Staten Island, where I'd never been, from a memory of a map I'd studied last year. "That's crazy!"

"Not crazy," he said. "Maps are my religion."

I smiled. "I believe in maps, too." I handed back the Falkplan, watching him refold it with a reverent expression on his face. *Eight days left,* I thought.

"What time is it?" I stood up and peeked in the kitchen, glancing at the clock on the orange wall. It was almost five in the afternoon. I'd been at Rumen's place for three hours. "Oh!" I said, "I have to go."

"Go?" he frowned. "Where you must go?"

"I have to make a phone call." I leaned against the doorjamb, hands behind my back. "To the States." This was a lie. I needed to leave. Call it an unfurling, call it falling, call it infatuation or attraction or desire—whatever it was, it was too much just now.

"But you didn't see the photos!"

"I know. I'm sorry. Maybe we can look at them another time."

"Schade," he said. Too bad. He stood up, running his hands over the outsides of his pockets. I picked up my purse and the empty cake plates.

"No." He took the plates from me and set them back on the coffee table. "I will do it."

He walked me down the stairs, unlocked the steel door, followed me through the weedy courtyard, held open the solid wood doors that led to the street.

"Thank you for the *Milchkaffee,*" I said. "It was delicious."

"You are welcome." He stuffed his keys in his pocket, resting his hand on my shoulder. I could feel the warmth of his palm through my jacket.

31

The sun hid behind cotton-ball clouds as I walked south on Jessnerstrasse, back to the apartment, my heart thundering in my chest as though I'd made it out of a burning building just before its collapse. Or was I the burning building? I turned right on Weserstrasse, moving urgently toward nothing urgent—least of all my fictitious phone call to the States.

When I got to Wismarplatz, I stopped to admire a man with a two-toned Mohawk and a woman in leopard-print shorts playing Ping-Pong at one of the public tables on the sidewalk. *Du bist so wunderbar, Berlin . . .* I walked on, pausing again when I got to Boxhagener Platz, where the sun was making a late-afternoon appearance, and the people lounging on the patchy grass were stripping down, angling their bodies westward, soaking up whatever warmth they could from the weak autumn rays, listening to reggae from a boom box someone had strapped to a hijacked shopping cart. A man in an Adidas T-shirt was practicing handstands, baring his toned ivory stomach every time he went upside down. I recalled the warmth of Rumen's hand on my shoulder, which tingled at the memory from five minutes ago.

I noticed an empty L-shaped bench in the corner of the *Platz* near a clump of yellowing poplar trees, whose leaves were rustling as if negotiating with the wind, and I sat down. What an ungraceful exit I'd made! But I had to get out of there. *Schade,* he'd said, too bad. I thought about the forlorn look in his eyes and squeezed mine shut. So I'd found him in the end: the taxi driver who knew as much about Nietzsche as he did about sausage. He wasn't a Lonely Planet invention. *If Nietzsche wrote in Bulgarian, I would learn Bulgarian!* I believed him.

I felt the seat move, and I opened my eyes. A pretty redhead had plunked an overstuffed backpack on the other end of the L-shaped bench and was trying to keep it (the backpack) from tipping over.

"Hey, Miranda!" said a dark-haired boy who was carrying a guitar case, smiling at the redhead as he approached the bench. He kissed her on the cheek, righting the backpack as he sat down next to her. They looked like they were in their early twenties.

"I'm taking off in three hours," said the redhead, gazing down at the ground as the boy situated the guitar case between his legs. "I don't want to leave!" she moaned. "The year I lived here was the best year of my life, you know?"

"Better than Buenos Aires?" said the boy, resting a tanned arm on the back of the bench.

I stared at them, not quite believing what I was hearing. I couldn't tell where they were from. They both spoke English with slightly different Spanish accents. I started fumbling through my purse, trying to act as if I weren't listening, resisting an overwhelming urge to chime in.

"Better?" said the redhead. "I like the culture and the people of Buenos Aires. But I don't think the city is beautiful."

"And Berlin is?"

"Well," she said, "I think with more sunshine and some better architecture Berlin would be the best."

It already is, I wanted to tell her. It had taken me a while, but I was finally realizing that affinity with a city was not about aesthetics (or pace, or cosmopolitanism, or lack thereof). It was about the way a place made you feel, or, more precisely, what it elicited from you. *Just like a person,* I thought. *Every person brings out something different in us.* But how often did a person, or a place, encourage you—better yet, implore you—to come as you were?

The boy put his arm around the redhead. She sighed, leaning her head on his shoulder. "Hey," she said, "do you know if there's an internet café close by? I have to print my plane ticket."

I watched him help her on with her backpack. In eight days, I would be sitting where she'd been sitting. I hung my head, too blue to appreciate the synchronicity of the scene. Would the little red-haired girl come back to Berlin? Would I?

.   .   .

There was an email from Air Berlin when I got back to the apartment. Subject line: 01OCT TXL JFK. I stood up and started pacing the institutional blue carpet. *Maps are my religion . . . I did not fit the system . . . Do you like Mercedes Sosa . . . ? Enough!* I had to think about New York now. New York was where I drove the taxi. New York was where I lived. But where *was* I going to live? The ninety-minute commute from Romeo and Sarah's to the taxi garage was too long—I was looking for a new place. I'd finally posted an ad on Craigslist ("Food Writer Seeking Shelter in Queens") and heard from some scammers ("Due to my transfer from my working place and now situated in Nigeria, and presently my house is available for rent for $900 per Month"), but there were two options that sounded promising: one in Astoria, with a massage therapist from Puerto Rico who led a singing prayer circle in Bushwick once a week. The other—"$672 Rent-Stabilized near Subway, Midtown (Queens Plaza)"—was in Long Island City, with a writer who described herself as messy. She had a cat and, if the Google map was correct, lived five minutes (on foot!) from Team taxi garage.

I answered the writer with the cat, closed my laptop, and opened a book. What was Rumen doing? I replayed the afternoon in my mind, remembering how he'd set the table with shiny silverware and *Streuselkuchen,* how his eyes practically ignited when he read from *Also sprach Zarathustra.* Why had he invited me over? I still didn't know. What did it matter? I was leaving this place. *Let it go,* I thought. But I couldn't.

I wrote him the next morning. Subject line: **A crazy idea.** What would you think if I rode along during one of your night shifts?!

I like crazy ideas! he wrote back, a few hours later. It could be mine!

He picked me up two days later, around nine p.m., already a few hours into his shift. The night was cool, and so misty the asphalt on Dirschauer Strasse was gleaming. He was wearing a Pink Floyd T-shirt. Bob Dylan was playing at low volume. The dispatch radio, which he'd switched off during our food tour, was turned on. The female voice calling out cross streets in German sounded as if it were underwater.

He lifted a can of Red Bull out of the pocket in the driver's side door and took a gulp as I got settled in the passenger seat.

"So I told some people I was going to be driving with you . . ."

"Really?" He glanced at my face, then at my shoulders.

"Yeah." I'd put on a sleeveless white top with a cowl neck. Fifteen minutes ago, it had seemed like the only piece of clothing I owned that might impress him without seeming like I was trying to impress him. Now I felt both naked and overdressed. "Actually," I said, digging around in my purse, searching for a pen, "I'm doing research." I told him I'd issued an open call on my blog for "questions for a night driver."

"What kind of questions?" He drove west on Revaler Strasse, past the clubs in the old railroad yard—Cassiopeia, RAW Tempel, Suicide Circus—that wouldn't open in earnest for another three hours.

"About taxi driving," I said, pulling out my notebook, stowing my purse at my feet. He stopped at the corner of Warschauer Strasse. There was a long line at the döner kebab stand. "Mmmm." I closed my eyes, inhaling the smell of fat dripping down the meat on the spit. "For me, this is the perfume of Berlin."

"No," he said, "the perfume of Berlin is in the U-Bahn."

"The U-Bahn?"

He turned right on Warschauer Strasse. "You have to go underground and then you will know this . . . What is it? Smell? It's from the brake pads of the U-Bahn. Every town has different brake pads. And that's why the smell of Berlin is different from the smell of Frankfurt. Because of the U-Bahn."

He was smiling, his laugh lines showing up as shadows in his whiskers. I turned away, gazing out the window at the verdigris domes—we were at Frankfurter Tor now—continuing to regret that my shoulders were bare. I pinned them to the seat back.

"What about the questions?" said Rumen, accelerating past the M10 tram as soon as the light turned green.

"Oh!" I said. "Right." I reached for my purse again and ran my hand though the pockets until I found the index cards where I'd written out the questions from readers. There were more than I expected. "Some of these are even from taxi drivers."

"Good!" he said, scanning the empty sidewalks on both sides of Petersburger Strasse. "Right now there aren't so many passengers. Ask me something."

"OK." I relaxed a little, glad to retreat into questions that weren't mine. "The first one is from Florian, from Munich. Are you ready?" He nodded, taking another sip of Red Bull. "Florian asks, 'Is there a law in Germany that dictates all taxis be painted the atrocious beige-cream color?' "

Rumen didn't hesitate: "We have laws for everything in Germany," he said. "After the war the color of taxis was black. They look like cars for someone who died. The Berlin government changed it, in the sixties or the seventies, I think, to beige. The official name is R–A–L one zero one five. All taxis must use this—excuse me . . ." He reached into the glove compartment and turned up the dispatch radio. "One second . . ." He squinted as he listened to the lady announcing an address on the staticky speaker. "No," he said, "this is a client from an *Eckkneipe*." An *Eckkneipe*, I had learned from Julia, was a corner bar. "Not for us."

"Why not?"

"You must be very careful when you pick up a client from an *Eckkneipe*," he said, slowing down as we turned onto Torstrasse. "Most of the time, one or two persons have to bring the client to the taxi. In this case it is better to call an ambulance than a taxi. Because if the client is in the taxi, his problem becomes your problem. Problems. Whatever!"

I laughed.

He finished the last of the Red Bull and stowed the empty can in the pocket in the driver's side door.

I looked out the window. Two middle-aged couples in track suits were trying to flag us down. "Hey!" I said. "You've got—"

He was already pulling over. He'd spotted them before I had. *Oh, no,* I thought. *Four people.* I had to get out of the cab. That was the deal we'd negotiated before the night shift: if four people needed a ride, I would have to surrender the front seat, since there weren't enough seat belts to go around.

"I hope you will not get lost when you leave the taxi," said Rumen.

I undid my seat belt. "I'm a taxi driver, and I have a map. I won't get lost."

He reached out his hand. "Wait."

"Why?"

"First let me talk with them." The passenger-side window slid down.

"Hallo, guten Abend!" said Rumen, leaning over me and smiling at the couples on the sidewalk.

"Kit Kat Club," said the shorter of the two men. "If you please." He had a fake-sounding British accent and what looked like a fake mustache.

"I can take three of you," said Rumen, switching to English, "But not four." He pointed at me. "This is a colleague from New York. She is studying Berlin taxi drivers. She rides with me this night."

I tried to keep from smiling.

"Puhhaps," said the man, looking past me, "you might let the four of us ride with you in the back seat, then?"

Rumen shood his head. "Three can come only," he said. "You must have seat belts. I could lose my license—"

"Wait," I said. "I'll get out."

"No," said Rumen.

"Alrighty, then . . ." The man sighed, on the verge of rolling his eyes.

"Alrighty, then!" said Rumen, merging back into traffic.

"I made you miss that fare," I said, watching the passenger-side window slide closed. "That's not okay."

"That wasn't our passenger." He turned up the dispatch radio. "Let's go find our passenger."

It was a slow night for taxi driving. The only fare we found over the next hour and a half was a group of girls in platform heels and commando boots who smelled like hard liquor and jasmine flowers and stuffed themselves into the back of the cab before Rumen had a chance to say anything about seat belts. They told us they were from France, and they wanted to go to Berghain.

"It's too early for Berghain," said Rumen, switching to English again, putting the cab in Park. It was a little after eleven p.m.

"Then where should we go?" said the smallest one, pursing her glossy lips. Her skin was almost the same shade as her white-blond hair, which she wore in a pixie cut. She was sitting in the middle, on the tallest one's lap.

"I can take you to the new Tresor," he said. "After midnight, you can go to Berghain. In the moment there's nothing happening there."

"We don't care," said the girl with the white-blond hair. "Take us anyway."

Though it was just a fifteen-minute walk from my sublet on Dirschauer Strasse, and though Ivo and Steffen had told me it was "the greatest techno club in the world," I had never been to Berghain. I wasn't sure if Ivo and Steffen had either, but they knew all about the door policy: "When they look at your face, two things can happen. They will wave you inside *or* they will tell you to go away and never come back." I preferred not to know whether I would pass inspection.

"You know I could lose my license," said Rumen, grinning at the girls in the rearview mirror, "if I take all four of you right now."

"We are not going far!" said the tallest girl, who had enormous, kohl-lined eyes.

"And we will be very good!" said the brunette sitting behind me, whose breath was ripe with vodka.

"And tip you very good!" said the one with the white-blond hair.

The fourth girl, who had cupid-bow lips and a Brigitte Bardot gap between her front teeth, smiled and said nothing.

"Should I get out?" I said.

"No," said Rumen. "It's not so far away."

He turned off Bob Dylan and turned on the radio, pressing the Seek button until he found a techno station.

"*C'est formidable!*" said the French girls, bouncing in their seats. "Turn it up, please!"

"Girls . . . ," said Rumen, close to laughter, "you promise to be very good!"

"We *are* very good!"

It was 11:20 when we got to Berghain, which looked like an industrial temple from the Stalin era. The lights were off, inside and out, and no one was waiting in line behind the construction-site fencing.

"Is it open?" said the girl with the white-blond hair.

"I told you," said Rumen. "After midnight."

"I don't care!"

"Me, too!"

"We go!"

The girl with the cupid-bow mouth sighed and paid, and the four of them climbed out of the taxi. We watched them hurry down the dirt path behind the construction fencing, where I guessed they would wait as long as they had to for the club to open.

"Is it true?" I said. "Is it the best club in the world?"

"I don't know," said Rumen. "I never went. For me techno isn't music. But it's the only music the Germans invented in modern times, after the Prussian marches." He thumbed through the accordion folds of his big black wallet. "After the marches, the techno makes sense. It's the next step. But it's not for a human being." He snapped his wallet closed.

"How much did they tip you?"

"Thirty cents."

"Are you serious?"

"Ever since I drive the taxi," he said, "there is hardly anything I cannot believe." He shut off the techno.

I tried to relax into my role as co-pilot after we dropped off the French girls, but it was futile. As the night progressed, and I stopped paying attention to the names of the streets we were driving, I was sure Rumen could sense how on edge I was: more than once, when I looked over at him, he was smiling in the way he had at Käse König, half knowingly, half wickedly, as if he were relishing the awkwardness behind my questions. He also seemed to enjoy the curiosity of the few passengers we did pick up: a group of Irish tourists on their way to Mariannenplatz for fried chicken; a Turkish woman who wanted a *Kurzstrecke* (short ride) to the *Baumarkt* (home improvement store) next to Hasenheide Park, even though it was closed; a couple from Bavaria who'd just been to a supper club in Neukölln, who'd wondered aloud what I was doing in Rumen's passenger seat—and laughed a long time when we told them about Dead Grandma.

"You see?" he said, after we dropped off the Bavarian couple at a villa in Zehlendorf. "Sometimes a *Kurzstrecke* leads me to someone who wants to go a long way."

"Or someone you wouldn't meet otherwise." I was trying to see in the windows of the mansions behind the gates. "That's something I have to keep learning over and over," I said. "The way to the goal isn't always direct."

"It's the true." He loosened the shoulder strap on his seat belt. "I don't like this insecurity. But insecurity is the price of freedom."

And freedom, I thought, as he sped over the slick cobblestones, was both the means and the end, the one thing all cabbies held dear, the thing we were all seeking. But every cabby knew this freedom was relative. That we were free was only partly true. The truth—which was understood, and better left unspoken—was that we were more free than most.

At half past midnight, after more than an hour of circling the city with no passengers, Rumen drove back to Friedrichshain and parked at the taxi stand on Weserstrasse, outside the Baritone Bar. "Hunting doesn't work this night," he said. "Now we wait." We were the fourth taxi in line.

"OK." I sat back, rolling my shoulders in circles. He switched off the ignition and the dispatch radio. The silence in the cab felt dense and intimate. "How about a question from Claudia in New York City? Are you ready?"

He moved the driver's seat a little farther from the steering wheel and stretched out his legs. "Ready."

"What was your longest-ever ride with a passenger?"

"Six years ago." He smiled, closing his eyes as if to draw closer to the memory. "It was a two-hundred-seventy-kilometer trip to Hamburg. The clients had to catch a plane with an African airline. After I dropped them off, I made a sightseeing tour and went on a boat. For me it was a perfect day."

Someone got into the taxi first in line. Rumen turned on the ignition and pulled forward.

"Do you have more questions?" he said, putting the taxi in Park.

"Well . . ." I looked out the window. The Baritone Bar's picnic tables were empty. The temperature had dropped, and it was too cold, even for Germans, to sit outside. "There is one more question," I said. "From Franco, in Los Angeles." It wasn't exactly a personal question, but I'd been saving it for last. "You don't have to answer it if you don't want to."

"I don't?"

"That's right."

"OK . . ."

"Are you ready?"

"First tell me the question."

I read from the index card, though I'd memorized the question: "What's the most memorable thing a passenger ever did and/or told you?"

"Hmmmm . . ." He grinned, folding his hands behind his head. "That's one hundred percent secret," he said, "and one hundred percent passion."

"Oh . . ." My face went warm, and I was grateful for the dark. I folded the index card in half, fixing my gaze on a potted plant on the Baritone Bar's windowsill. "No problem. You don't have to say—"

The taxi queue was moving.

"She was looking for something special, like me," said Rumen, turning on the ignition again, pulling forward once more. "And she was nice-looking and not drunk. Well, only a little bit."

I laughed.

"She sat in the back of the taxi and she asked me to look at her. 'You are nice,' she said. 'What are you doing after? Can we have a drink somewhere?' We went to a bar and she told me about her. She studied architecture. She was very intelligent, and beautiful. Then I asked her if I could take her home." He paused, trailing his fingertip over his lower lip. "She lived not really far away but not too close, especially for a woman in heels."

"What was her name?"

"She wouldn't tell me her name! Then later she said it was Tamara. But in the morning I saw inside her shoe. You know what was the name in her shoe?"

"What?"

"Tamara!" He put his hand to his forehead. "Can you imagine this?"

"No." I laughed. "And yes."

I told him about the Englishman who'd asked me to breakfast on my first shift.

"Why didn't you eat breakfast with him?"

"I don't know. It was my first shift! What would you have done?" He grinned.

"You would've gone to breakfast."

"You must always eat breakfast."

I could have gotten out of the cab then, and found my way back to the apartment—we weren't so far away—and let Rumen continue with his shift. *Go while you're laughing!* I thought. He had answered all my questions. My journalistic duty was done. But it was as if my body were soldered to the passenger seat. I couldn't bring myself to leave.

"And now"—he fished a CD holder out of the pocket in the driver's side door—"for something completely different. Are you ready?" I nodded. He fed a disc into the player, raising the volume to maximum, pressing pause. "Dylan's 1997 album *Time Out of Mind* I can hear ten times in one night," he said. "If I write a book I really think about to start it with Dylan's words from the first song."

He pressed Play, and we listened to Dylan sing, in a pained, raspy voice, about deserted streets and weeping clouds and a woman he couldn't get out of his head, as dusky keyboards echoed in the background. The hair on my arms stood up. I looked out at the golden mist filtering through the air below the streetlights, the shadows of the linden trees on the street, the potted plant and the empty tables outside the Baritone Bar, the dreadlocked couple who whizzed by on bikes with skinny tires. All of it seemed part of the song somehow. Even as I was living it, I knew it was a perfect moment.

A middle-aged woman with spiky blond hair banged on my window. I flinched.

"Sind Sie frei oder was?" she said. Are you free or what? Confusion, then disapproval flashed across her face as she caught sight of the two of us reclining side by side in the cab, listening to "Love Sick," our hands near the gearshift, almost touching. She marched off before we could answer her.

Rumen sat up, glancing in the rearview mirror as the woman climbed into the taxi behind us. "Would you like to have a beer?"

I blinked hard, as if I'd been pushed out of a dark movie theater into daylight. "What about your shift?"

Bob Dylan was picking up the tempo. Rumen lowered the volume a little. "Now it's *tote Hose*. Let's have a beer!"

"Tote Hose?"

"Dead pants."

"Dead pants?" I laughed. "I have to remember that—"

"What about the beer?"

I pretended to be thinking it over. "OK," I said finally, "let's have a beer."

He pulled away from the taxi stand. Two blocks later, a group of thin men dressed in black waved at our cab like desperate hitchhikers on a desert road. *Oh, no,* I thought, as Rumen hit the brakes. There were four of them.

"Can you take us to Neukölln?" said the most underfed-looking one of the four, gesturing toward a pile of amps and speakers and guitar cases. "We're late for a gig." He was wearing a red bow tie, as were the rest of his bandmates.

Rumen and I looked at each other.

"You've got to take this fare," I said.

"I know." He looked down at the gearshift.

I got out of the taxi. The other musicians did a double-take when they saw me, their faces turning apologetic, as if they knew they were interrupting something. "Is it OK," the band leader asked, "if you take us?"

"Yes." I smiled at him. "It's OK."

Rumen opened the trunk, and he and the musicians started load-ing the equipment. I followed them around to the back of the cab. Rumen wiped his hands on his jeans. "We will see us later," he said, squeezing my hand.

"Yes," I said, "we will." I felt him and the musicians watching me as I walked away, stepping deliberately over the damp asphalt in what I hoped was the general direction of the apartment on Dirschauer Strasse. *I'm a taxi driver, and I have a map. I won't get lost.*

32

I spent the night after the shift with Rumen in a restless stupor, shuddering every time I remembered the feeling in the cab as we listened to Dylan, trying to write up a cool, neutral, professional version of the interview for my blog—he made me promise not to include the story about Tamara and her shoes—and wondering what might have happened if the musicians hadn't hailed us.

I have another question for you, I wrote him the next morning. It was a question from Rodrigo, my most loyal reader in Buenos Aires, whom I'd never met in person, who'd sent his query during the night, when Rumen and I were on the road: Did you see the movie *Night on Earth* by Jim Jarmusch, or *Taxi Driver* by Martin Scorsese? Rodrigo wanted to know. Do you feel related to any of the characters?

I will think about it, Rumen wrote back a few hours later. Maybe I can answer You when we see us again. Will we?!

We met on his day off, which was my last day in Berlin. Rumen wanted to give me a final tour of the city in his taxi. When he picked me up, the sky was leaden, and it started to rain as we drove west.

"I told you, in the late nineties, how more and more people came to Berlin," he said. "But did you know, in the last years, many people came to Berlin because of Knut?" He pointed at the Chinese pagodas at the entrance to the Berlin Zoo.

"Who is Knut?" I looked out the window, which was speckled with raindrops, at the pagodas, and at the statues of the two kneeling elephants guarding the entrance to the zoo. No one was lining up to buy tickets. Who wanted to go to the zoo in the rain?

"You haven't heard about Knut?" He steered around a double-decker tour bus. A spiral-bound Berlin street atlas slid across the dashboard. He reached over and pushed it back into the corner next to the driver's side door. "Knut is one ice bear born in the Berlin Zoo," he said. "As a baby ice bear his mother didn't want him. So one trainer had to care only about Knut, like a mother. He fed him with the bottle. He played Elvis on the guitar, to make Knut sleep. This man was like a hero in Berlin."

"How neat—"

"But when Knut was two or three years old, the man died. Maybe he was forty-five."

"What happened to Knut?"

"Now he has another trainer, I think."

"Oh." I sighed.

"What's wrong?"

"I'm sad."

"About Knut?"

"Yes." All the playful tension I'd felt in Rumen's taxi on the night shift had subsided. I pressed my hands to my belly as we drove by the zoo, then past Bahnhof Zoo, pushing against the pit in my stomach, wishing I could stop thinking about Air Berlin Flight 6441, departing Tegel at 10:25 the next morning. I hadn't even started to pack. *I'm coming back,* I kept telling myself. *I'm coming back!* In that moment—as the the wind severed the leaves from trees and cast them in puddles on the Ku'damm—it felt like a promise with no legs, grounded in nothing but the serendipities of a summer that was over.

Rumen pulled a lime-green CD out of the case in his lap and slipped it into the player. "And now . . ." The sounds of drums, Indian strings, and an ecstatic man singing into an echoing microphone took over the taxi as we drove west on Kantstrasse.

"Bhangra?" I laughed.

"You know bhangra?" he said.

"*You* know bhangra?"

"How do you know bhangra?"

"I went to an Indian wedding. All the old ladies were doing it." I bent my elbows and twisted my wrists, trying to mimic the moves of the grandmothers who'd outlasted almost everyone on the dance floor at my friend Sangeetha's wedding reception. The percussion sped up. I danced faster in my seat, as if to forget about my flight.

"You are crazy!" Rumen grinned, rolling down the windows, turning up the volume. The bass made the seats in the cab throb as we cruised down Kantstrasse. The people on the sidewalk stared as we drove by.

"So are you!" I hollered over the music.

"Richtig!"

He took me to all of his favorite places in what was once West Berlin: Zweitausendeins, his favorite bookstore on Kantstrasse, where I found a book about German bread and he bought a Muddy Waters CD for five euros; Rossia, a twenty-four-hour snack bar cum grocery store on Stuttgarter Platz, where he liked to eat stuffed cabbage rolls and buy mineral water from Georgia. On Kaiser-Friedrich-Strasse, we paid our respects at the memorial plaque to Herta Heuwer, the alleged inventor of currywurst, Berlin's equivalent of the New York hot dog: fried pork sausage sliced and sauced with ketchup and curry spices that British soldiers had originally brought with them to post-war Berlin. "Some people say they made currywurst first in Hamburg," said Rumen, "but this is nonsense!"

I clasped my hands over the hollow in my stomach again.

"Are you hungry?" he said.

The snack bar on the Ku'damm where he'd bought his first West Berlin *Wienerwürstchen,* the day after the Wall came down, no longer existed, so we went to Good Friends, a Chinese restaurant on Kantstrasse, for lunch. "This is where I bring many diplomats from China in my taxi," he said. We sat across from each other in straight-backed chairs and shared a plate of chicken livers in black bean sauce.

"If you want"—he ran the tines of his fork around the plate, drawing curlicues in the bean sauce—"I can take you to the airport."

"OK." I nodded, trying to read the expression in his eyes. Today they were more gray than blue.

I also said OK when he asked me, after lunch, if I wanted to have a beer at his flat. We rode east in the rain, listening to his new Muddy

Waters CD, saying little as we drove through the tunnels on the Autobahn.

"Where are we?" I said, when we merged back onto the surface streets.

"Neukölln," he said, maneuvering through the traffic outside the Estrel Hotel.

"And now?" I said, a few minutes later, glancing out the window at an olive-green love seat someone had left on the sidewalk.

"Treptow."

We crossed the River Spree and drove into Friedrichshain. We were getting closer to his flat. I started to fidget in the passenger seat, not knowing where to put my arms, or how to arrange my legs.

"Do you still get lost?" I asked him, as we passed the water tower next to the Ostkreuz S-Bahn station, whose purple-black shingles reminded me of a turret on a haunted house.

"What do you mean lost? In the taxi?"

I nodded.

"Of course! It's normal to be lost."

"Really?" We were on Jessnerstrasse—his *Strasse*—now.

"There is no cab driver who knows everything," he said, shifting into reverse. "Anyway, it's not the goal to know everything." He backed the taxi into a parking space across from his building. "The goal is to *find* everything, with the help of the map."

I held on to my purse and Rumen kept his jacket on when we got to his flat. We could hardly look at each other, standing in his kitchen, as he opened two beers—*thwack! thwack!*—and handed one to me.

I tried to read the black-and-gold label on the squat amber bottle. "From Bavaria?"

"In the last time it became more and more popular in Berlin to drink beer from Bavaria," he said. "You know the water in Bavaria, it's very, very good. So the beers are not so bitter like the beer from the north of Germany. Anyway!" He raised his bottle. *"Prost!"*

"Prost!" I said. We toasted, and I sipped. The beer was malty, and

bittersweet, with just a little bit of hops. He took a long swig. "Do you like the beer?"

"It's delicious," I said, turning the bottle around and studying the label some more.

"In the moment this is my favorite beer."

We drank: he in his jacket, me with my purse, searching for something to say. "Hey!" I said, setting the bottle down on the kitchen table a little harder than I'd meant to. "What about Rodrigo's question?"

He knitted his eyebrows.

"Have you seen *Taxi Driver* and *Night on Earth*—"

"Yes! I remember. Yes, of course, I have seen—"

"OK, I thought so. But that's not the question. The question iiiis . . ." I was already feeling the beer. "Do you identify with any of the characters—"

"Yes!" he said. "I was thinking about! I would like to be a mix from Robert De Niro, Roberto Benigni, and Armin Mueller-Stahl."

"OK." I laughed. "Explain."

"From Benigni, he's really funny and crazy and I like that he catch or tries to catch the opportunity to tell the pope his life, his problems. This is great, you know?" He took another swig of beer. "Robert De Niro is also crazy and a little bit too crazy, I think. But what I understand, what I like, he is angry man and the city and all its crazy people made him angry. This I understand totally. But he started to be wrong when he cared too much about Jodie Foster. This is a big mistake. Never care about junkies and prostitutes. It's too dangerous, and too—you can't win, I think. And then of course when he bought all these weapons—this is too much."

"Way too much."

"Armin I like of course because he's German from East Germany, and I like he put his own story in this movie. And I like then he came as a immigrant to New York and he had to learn the language. Armin Mueller-Stahl, he doesn't take his passenger too personally. This is the difference between Robert De Niro and Armin, maybe."

"Brilliant."

"Do you have more questions?"

"That was the last one."

"Good!" he said. "Come! Now starts your Berlin education."

We took our beers to the living room. "Please"—he gestured toward the sheepskin-covered futon—"take your seat." He pulled a red shoebox from the bottom of his bookshelf, sat down beside me, and flipped through the photos inside as if they were a card catalog. "This you have to see," he said, handing me a picture of a man in a marbled bodysuit, dancing alone on the Wall in front of the Brandenburg Gate.

"When did you take this?" I leaned in closer to look at the picture. Our heads almost touched.

"About two weeks after the Wall came down," he said, appearing not to notice my nearness, or being unfazed by it, as he rifled through the red shoebox. "Look here." He passed me photos faster than I could look at them. "These I took later. In ninety-two, ninety-three maybe."

I studied the pictures—of empty watchtowers, of a street vendor selling pieces of the Wall from a velvet-lined suitcase, of a squat called Villa Felix, in a Jugendstil apartment building that looked as though it had barely survived World War II—and I started to understand what it was he'd lost, after the golden nineties. The Berlin I'd met in 2010 was tame, grown-up, almost staid in comparison.

"Whoa!" I said. "What's this?" I showed him a picture of three tanks, painted in acid-trip colors, stacked like a Stonehenge replica near the Reichstag.

"This is an open-air exhibition from some artists in England."

"I can't believe that's the Reichstag!" The imperial building was missing its dome, surrounded by mounds of dirt and a wasteland of weeds.

"The Wall was next to the Reichstag. So this was former no-man's-land, or dead zone. It was only empty space." He guzzled the last of his beer. "Imagine a place like maybe two or three football places. One time I made camping there."

"In front of the Reichstag?" I let my head rest on the back of the futon. I wanted to take off my shoes.

He nodded. "At this time it was a quiet place. Nobody was there.

Like in the woods, or the park." He set his empty beer bottle on the coffee table.

"And now?" I left my shoes on, took a sip of beer instead. "I mean, when you look at these pictures—"

"Now?" He stood up and walked into the kitchen. I heard glass bottles jangle when he opened the refrigerator. "Now—" *Thwack! Thwack!* He popped the tops off two more beers, returning to the living room with a bottle in each hand. "Now, it's boring." He handed me one of the beers, clinking his bottle against mine before he drank. "And now some people come in my taxi and say, 'Oh, Berlin became so nice, so beautiful, so clean, blah blah blah.' They have no idea. Bloody tourists."

"I'm a bloody tourist."

"Yes." He looked at me, his irises a thin gray-blue rim around his pupils. "But you are interested in Berlin."

I lowered my eyes. Yes, I was interested. And now, seeing the city in a younger, wilder, more carefree incarnation—glimpsing parts of it that had vanished—was making me nostalgic for a past that wasn't mine.

"Maybe you think I am crazy," he said.

"No—"

"Maybe you think I am stupid to think so much about before." He gathered up the pictures and put them back in the red shoebox. "But you know what?" He fitted the lid on the box. "I miss my Berlin."

I miss it, too, I thought. *And I wasn't even there.*

For the next several hours, Rumen continued my Berlin education via YouTube, starting with footage of the East Germans pouring through the border checkpoint at Bornholmer Strasse the night the Wall came down: "This was the first point where the Wall opened," he said. "After the people heard this announcement from the East German government that they were free to travel, they went crazy, and they started to come to the crossing points. The guards became totally confused, and they just let the people go across. Can you imagine this?"

"Let's watch it again," I said.

We found footage of JFK's *"Ich bin ein Berliner"* speech. "Is he really saying he's a donut?" I asked. "I read somewhere he should have said *'Ich bin Berliner'* and not *'Ich bin ein Berliner.'*" Rumen held his beer bottle aloft. "JFK is not a donut! A donut is a donut! In Berlin it's called *Pfannkuchen*. And *not* Berliner! Only outside of Berlin they call a *Pfannkuchen* a *Berliner.*"

I wanted to bend and stretch the minutes as we sat side by side at his desk, angling closer and closer to his laptop, drinking beer after Bavarian beer. Whenever I felt him looking at me, I changed the cross of my legs, wishing, as I often did, that they were longer.

He showed me videos of every one of his favorite Berlin hymns: *"Berlin ist ja so groß," "Das ist Berlin," "Ich stehe auf Berlin," "Berlin, Du bist so wunderbar," "Berliner Frühling,"* "Born to Die in Berlin." Each song, and each beer, pushed me a little closer to delirium, until finally, around midnight, the dull empty ache in my stomach—which had persisted, in spite of all the chicken livers I'd eaten—gave way to dizziness. I was turning some precarious corner, caught somewhere between joy and despair: I'd finally found the thread in the labyrinth. And now I was about to drop it and walk away.

Who stood up first and started to dance? I wasn't sure. Rumen moved like a blissed-out clown with no inhibitions and no rhythm, raising his arms in victory for no apparent reason. I faked some salsa steps, flung my hair in front of my face, and watched him as I shimmied around the living room. I loved seeing him dance.

"This song is *'Schwarz zu Blau'*!" He turned up the volume and the speakers crackled. "From Peter Fox. He's a real Berlin boy! You have to know him!"

"OK!" I was drunk. Peter Fox was from Berlin. Whatever he was doing—hip-hop? reggae? dancehall?—sounded great to me.

"Hoooooooooooooo!" said Rumen, pointing at my feet. "You are a crazy dancer."

"So are you!"

We danced and danced, circling the living room, circling each other, sweating, smiling, still not touching. I collapsed onto the sheepskin-covered futon after we'd danced to all the songs on Peter Fox's first album.

"What time is it?" I said, slipping off my shoes.

"I don't know." He flopped down next to me, rested his head against mine. His skin felt hot. We sat like this for a few seconds, catching our breath, staring at the low crimson ceiling. He reached over, tried to untangle my hair. "Wait," I said, tucking some strands behind my ear. His lips were salty when he kissed me.

We were lying on our backs, holding hands under a thin wool blanket on the flattened-out futon, when he started to snore. I closed my eyes and listened to the sparrows, and the distant murmur of the S-Bahn—the last train of the night, probably—and the wind stirring the trees outside as if coaxing the leaves into quiet applause. I tried not to think about what time it was. The words from Liliana's favorite tango drifted into my head: *Que me quiten lo bailado.* Rough translation: No one can take away what I've danced.

It was still dark when I woke up, languid and disoriented, what felt like hours later, my hand still in his. He wasn't snoring anymore. The hair on his arms was tickling me. I let go of his hand. He took my hand back, pulling it toward his chest. I was falling asleep again when I heard the quarter-note wail of a German ambulance—or was it a police siren? I couldn't tell which direction the sound was coming from, but it wasn't far away. I remembered he was taking me to the airport. *What time is it?* I shut my eyes. I didn't want to imagine saying goodbye to him.

"I'm coming back to Berlin," I said.

The wail of the siren petered out. He didn't answer.

"Are you sleeping?"

"No." He loosened his grip on my hand.

I opened my eyes. Light was starting to sneak around the sides of the curtains.

He rolled over and sat on the edge of the futon, his back to me, and reached for his T-shirt, a rainbow tie-dye with "NEW YORK" written across the front in cracked, puffy white letters. It was a terrible T-shirt.

"I'm coming back to Berlin," I said again.

He nodded, his back still turned.

"Don't you believe me?"

"What?"

"I'm coming back." I sat up and grabbed a throw pillow, hugging it to my chest.

"I believe you."

"OK," I said. "Good."

He sighed, propping his elbows on his thighs.

"What's wrong?"

"I think—"

"What?"

"I think you are looking to me as a fixed point in Berlin."

"Huh?" I narrowed my eyes at his back.

"A fixed point. You are looking for a fixed point."

"What are you talking about? I never asked you to be a fixed point!"

"You didn't, but—"

"But what?" Something was pushing against the hollow in my stomach.

"I don't think you are being honest."

"With whom?" I flung the pillow on the floor. "I decided to come back to Berlin way before I met you!"

He sighed again, staring at the ground.

"It's the truth!"

The muscles in his jaw tightened as though he were clenching his teeth.

"Rumen?"

He wasn't saying anything.

"Fine," I said. "Believe what you want."

I scrambled off the futon and searched for my clothes, hands trembling as I zipped my jeans and picked up my purse, lifting the leather strap over my head. The more frantically I moved, the more immobile he became. I stood in front of him, wanting him to look at me, waiting for him to say something, blinking away tears. He reached under the coffee table and pulled out a package wrapped in a plastic grocery bag.

"Here." He held out the bag.

"What is it?"

"I made this for you." He was looking past me, at something on the wall.

"Keep it," I said.

The wounded look on his face was the last thing I saw before I walked out, not slamming the door.

PART IV

New York City

It returneth only, it cometh home to me at last—
mine own Self, and such of it as hath long been abroad,
and scattered among things and accidents.

—Friedrich Nietzsche, *Thus Spoke Zarathustra*

33

It was 7:30 in the morning when I got back to the apartment on Dirschauer Strasse. My plane was leaving in three hours. I raced around in the gray light—yanking my clothes off their hangers, tearing the sheets off the futon, stuffing all Karl's books back on the shelves. I had an hour to pack, to restore the place to its original, if scruffy, condition, to get myself ready to fly. I was too late for the S-Bahn. If I wanted to make it to the airport on time, I had to take a cab.

I swallowed past the lump in my throat and went online to get the phone number of a Berlin taxi service. To call a taxi: what a sorry scenario. *He was supposed to take me to the airport.* How I'd been dreading our goodbye at Tegel. But a sad goodbye would have been so much better than this one: every time I thought about the wounded look on Rumen's face, when I'd refused his gift, I felt a stab in my gut.

Oh! I thought, half an hour later, when I saw the taxi pull up—it was a Mercedes B-class, just like Rumen's. *Is it you?*

My stomach sank when the driver got out. He resembled Rumen only in his height: he was a stocky man in wire-rimmed glasses with waist-length, straw-colored hair. "You need help?" he said, pointing at my swollen suitcase. He loaded it into the trunk before I could answer him.

"To Tegel, yes?"

Composed was what I tried to be as he drove to Warschauer Strasse and turned left at Frankfurter Tor, onto Karl-Marx-Allee. I looked out the window at the workers' palace apartment blocks rising up on either side of the boulevard, remembering the ride down this street with Rumen: *"You have to try the Dead Grandma . . ."*

"Is it your first time in Berlin?" said the taxi driver.

I nodded, biting my lip.

He cracked his window, and the breeze tousled his hair, blowing long strands behind the lenses of his glasses. I slipped a hand in my purse, felt around for my cell phone, pulled it out—no new messages. I sighed. Hadn't I set myself up for this? What if I'd said no to that beer, and asked Rumen to take me back to Dirschauer Strasse after the chicken livers at Good Friends? Why hadn't I played it cool? Oh, who was I kidding? I was incapable of playing it cool.

The sun shone through a mass of billowy clouds, scattering shadows on the beige-peach tiles of the apartment blocks. How many times had I passed by these buildings that summer, mesmerized by their proportions, not knowing what to make of their Moscow wedding-cake grandeur? Passing by them now, the message was clear: I was a speck of dust, about to be wiped from this landscape onto another.

"Where do you fly today?" said the taxi driver. "New York? I have been in New York four years ago! *You* drive a taxi?" He let out a low-pitched whistle. "What it is like?"

"Well . . ." We were at Alexanderplatz now, which was empty except for a group of backpackers who were setting up a campsite near one of the entrances to the U-Bahn. "It's kind of like a video game."

He laughed so hard he started to cough.

"Will you come back to Berlin?" he asked a few minutes later.

"Yes," I said, sounding sure, though I wasn't. What about Rumen? And what about Elektropolis? Was it just a figment of my longing, in the end?

"You know," said the taxi driver, "Berlin, it changed a lot. I mean, it changes a lot." He pointed through the windshield, at an apartment building shrouded in scaffolding. "I think maybe the city has ten years left. And then it will be one big *gentrifizierte* SoHo."

I didn't sleep at all on the flight from Tegel to JFK. Every time I closed my eyes, the last moments in Rumen's living room would play

out all over again, and I would dissect them with masochistic preci-
sion. *A fixed point. You are looking for a fixed point* . . . I clenched my
fists under the tray table. *No!* I wanted to tell him. *You're wrong!* Then
I would rewind a little further, remembering how unsure he'd been
at first, when he kissed me, how he'd stroked my forehead, how warm
his fingers were, the way the skin in the center of his chest smelled,
like juniper, and honey . . . No. Like juniper and burning sugar.

Somewhere over Greenland, I started writing in my notebook
by the light of the map on the monitor on the seat back, as the girl
sitting next to me slept, arms crossed over her NYU sweatshirt. Was
I going in circles? Had I just repeated the same mistake with a different man in a different city? Was it possible that the streets had conditioned Rumen to live in brief—if passionate—intervals, the way
the *milonga* had conditioned Joaquín? Had I learned nothing about
the fleeting nature of things from all the taxi rides? Was I no farther
along than I was three years ago (three years ago!), when I started this
crazy experiment?

A flight attendant tapped me on the shoulder, smiling professionally under her Air Berlin sailor hat. "Chicken, or pasta?"

Here we go again, I thought, holding on to both armrests as the plane
descended into JFK. The Puerto Rican massage therapist with the
two-bedroom in Astoria had decided to go back to Puerto Rico,
and so Rebekka, the messy writer with the cat who lived around the
corner from the taxi garage, was going to be my new roommate—
for a six-month probationary period, without a contract, which we'd
agreed on when we'd talked over Skype.

Rebekka seemed nice enough: she was a freelance writer, like me,
originally from California, like me. When she wasn't doing journalism, she was working on a historical feminist sci-fi novel. *And she's
five minutes from Team,* I kept reminding myself as the plane taxied to
the gate, but in that moment none of these details were reassuring.
What was I doing back in this brown, unmerciful city?

. . . .

Rebekka smiled politely—a shyer version of her Skype self—when she opened the door to the apartment in Long Island City. She was about my age, tall and willowy, with short, dark hair curled under in a neat bob, and large hazel eyes that turned down a little at the corners. She slouched, her shoulders rounded in laptop posture, as she led me inside.

I forced myself to smile back at my new roommate, though I was a wreck after the sleepless flight, and the place smelled like cat pee and fish gone bad. I rolled my suitcase over the uneven hardwood floor, taking shallow breaths as I followed her down the hall.

"Here's a storage room," said Rebekka, shoving open the first door on the right, pushing a piece of a bed frame out of the way. There was a litter box on the windowsill, propped against the bars: "I try to keep the door open, in case she wants to go in here."

She showed me the rest of the place: in the kitchen, a pair of tabby cat oven mitts hung from magnets on the hood over the stove, and lumps of cat food were hardening in the metal dish next to the refrigerator. Litter box number two lived under the sink in the bathroom. Litter box number three was in the living room, across from a leather sofa whose armrests had been clawed to the stuffing, "She has some digestive problems," said Rebekka, "so I try to make it easy for her." I nodded, holding my breath.

The cat didn't have a name. She crept out from behind the sofa, tail aloft, dull, dark gray fur sticking out, on defense, when Rebekka opened the door to my room. "Hey, sweet girl!" Rebekka's voice rose several octaves, and she made smooching sounds as she smiled at the cat. "Heeere, kitty, kitty . . ." The cat circled the room with the caution of a huntress, ignoring Rebekka, glowering at me. *Oh, dear.*

My long, narrow room was a little smaller than the main room in the apartment in Berlin—palatial by New York proportions. There was a yellowing twin mattress in one corner and a card table in the other, in front of a curtainless, east-facing window. I left my suitcase by the door and walked up to the window: it had a view of Dena's coffee shop on 29th Street, and the traffic at the foot of the Queensboro Bridge, and the subway tracks as they curved into Queensboro Plaza. Even with the window closed, the noise—one part screeching

N and 7 trains, one part indignant honking, one part jackhammer and electric saw at the construction site in Queensboro Plaza—was tremendous, four thousand miles and a world away from the easy breathing of the S-Bahn, the bikes rattling over cobblestones, and my upstairs neighbor's drum and bass in Berlin. *Five minutes from the garage.* The cat rubbed against my suitcase, arching her back, tail still aloft.

I smiled at Rebekka. *Six months,* I thought. *I can live anywhere for six months.* I wanted to freeze all my senses.

That night I dreamed about driving the taxi. My passenger was a faceless man in a Panama hat who kept giving me a new destination every time we reached the last one.

The next morning, I woke up with the sun, which was streaming through the curtainless window facing 29th Street. I pulled out my earplugs—the construction hadn't started yet, but the honking had. I went to the window and looked outside. Yellow taxis were lining up at the entrance to the Queensboro Bridge, edging forward as they waited for the signal to change. When the light turned green, they charged ahead like thoroughbreds out of the gate. I watched them jostle for the lead as they raced onto the bridge, heading west, into Manhattan. *I have to get out there.*

But not today. I opened my laptop and checked my email. There were nine messages from the Argentine satellite company. One from Mom and Dad. One from Isabel. And one from Rumen.

My knees gave way when I saw his name. "What?" I'd been hoping, for the better part of the trip over six time zones, that he would write. After the way we'd left things, I couldn't believe he had.

I winced at the screech of the subway as it rounded the curve into Queensboro Plaza. I had always wondered who lived in the apartments whose windows you could see into from the subway.

I unplugged my laptop, pulling it off the card table and setting it in a sunny spot on the floorboards as I knelt to read his message:

Hi Layne!

I hope You had a good flight.

I have to apologies for what I said.

I thought a lot about this since You left.

But You know I'm from East-Germany, and here we are *sehr* direct!

Sorry—I'm joking but I'm very serouis in the same moment.

Anyway, it was a pleasure for me to tell You all the things about Berlin.

I realized that You are really interested in this city.

So I hope You will come back and we will see us again.

Greetings from Berlin/Friedrichshain!

Good Luck in your taxi! Good luck in NYC!

Rum

All is in limbo, I thought, leaning closer to the screen as I reread what he'd written. *But all is not lost.*

34

It took few days to work up the courage to take a test walk from the apartment on 29th Street to the taxi garage. I stood outside the chain-link fence, watching the day drivers straggle in after they finished their shifts, trying to take pleasure in my new, brief commute to Team.

"Ho-ZAAAAAY!" the dispatcher bellowed into the loudspeaker. His voice didn't sound familiar. "A-BOOOOO!"

Dit you have already your first shift? Rumen asked me. We were writing each other every day now, as friends, as colleagues, after we'd both apologized for the way we'd said goodbye in Berlin. Not yet, I answered him. Every time I pulled out my *New York City 5-Borough Street Atlas*—quizzing myself on Central Park transverses and alternate routes to JFK and La Guardia at rush hour—I felt like I'd forgotten what little geography I knew.

"HOW-ard!" The dispatcher's shouts ricocheted like thunderclaps through the parking lot. "A-ZEEEEEEZ!" My stomach seized up on the drivers' behalf.

I threaded my fingers through the holes in the fence, gazing up and down the rows of taxicabs in the Team parking lot. They looked like yellow boats docked in a dirty marina. I thought about the sailboat I'd seen at Pablo Neruda's house at Isla Negra, on the central coast of Chile, on one of my border hops to renew my Argentine tourist visa. Between Neruda's house, which he'd built in the shape of a ship—with portholes for windows—and the cottage where he wrote his poems, was a one-person sailboat perched on a pile of rocks, positioned at a tilt, as if it had just been hit with a mighty gust of wind. "Neruda liked to get in this boat," I overheard a young teacher telling her students, "and imagine he was a brave captain. But he was terrified of the ocean. For all he wrote about the sea, he wouldn't even put a toe in the water!"

My hands were sweating onto the steering wheel when I pulled out of the Team parking lot the next morning. *It's not the goal to know everything,* I remembered Rumen telling me, as I turned onto Northern Boulevard, watching out for new potholes. *The goal is to find everything, with the help of the map.* Maybe so. Nevertheless, I let myself fall behind the other cabs as I crossed the Queensboro Bridge, fighting an urge to drive straight back to the garage, even as I listened to the theme from *Superman.*

My first passenger was a priest who hailed me on 34th Street. He chuckled when he heard the *Superman* song. "Know how to get to Williamsburg?" he said. He was heavy-set, with a faint Brooklyn accent and a fading bow-and-arrow tattoo under his collar.

"Sort of." I turned down the music.

I got us to the Williamsburg Bridge, and the priest, who told me his name was Father Ron, took it from there.

"Taxi driving," he said, as he directed me through the Hasidic quarter, where men in fur hats and long coats walked with their hands folded and their heads high, "is an act of faith on both sides."

"True." I smiled.

"How long you been driving?"

"Not long." The question made me think of the *milonga,* where men liked to ask, after a song or two, how long I'd been dancing tango. "I was in Berlin this summer," I said, "so I've forgotten some stuff."

"Berlin, Germany? I've never been to Berlin." He scratched one of his salt-and-pepper sideburns. "But I have to tell you, I'm an old guy, and I don't have such a nice picture of it."

"You're not the first person who's told me that—"

"You're gonna make a right on Union," he said.

I nodded at him in the rearview mirror. "Even my parents felt that way. They automatically thought of the Wall."

"And Hitler," he said.

"And Hitler."

"But it must be more than that."

"Oh," I said, slowing down to make the turn, "it is."

I drove back to Manhattan after I dropped off Father Ron, thinking about divine intervention, and the impossibility of stopping for dim sum at Ping's. Within half an hour, I was stuck behind a garbage truck on West 88th Street, trying not to look in the rearview mirror at my passenger in the back seat, a freckled man in a spandex bodysuit I'd picked up two blocks ago, who was squirming and groaning, rather theatrically, I thought, as we waited for the trashmen to finish hurling bags into the business end of their truck.

"Can't you go around them?" said the man in spandex, sticking his head through the partition.

I'd been wondering the same thing. But there was barely six feet between the garbage truck and the cars parked to our right— I needed at least eight feet if I didn't want to smash the cab's side mirrors. Driving on the sidewalk wouldn't work either—every ten yards or so, there were trees in wrought-iron planters blocking the way. And it was too late for reverse: cars were lining up behind us, although no one was honking yet.

"I can't."

"Well, shit!"

Not everyone loves their cab driver, I thought, as the man in spandex brought a fist down on the back seat. The scene was familiar, all too familiar, but my reaction was not: I did not feel responsible for our predicament. What could we do but surrender to the garbage guys in wraparound sunglasses as they continued to pitch bags of trash at a pace that suggested they were pulling from an endless pile of refuse? I thought I caught them grinning at me, and at the growing queue of cars waiting for them to finish, as if enjoying their power to stop traffic.

This enraged the man in spandex. He thrust his hand through the partition and waved a five-dollar bill in my face.

"Turn off the meter! I'm getting *out!*"

I looked at him, all narrow eyes and flared nostrils. The wrinkles on his forehead and around his mouth turned white as the skin around them went from pink to scarlet. "I'm not going to take your money," I said, waving away the five dollars.

After the shift, and every time I opened the door to the apartment on 29th Street, the smell of the three litter boxes hit me like a smack in the face. I would rush down the hall, breathing through my mouth, wave hello to Rebekka if she was there (most of the time she wasn't), drop my purse, and check my email. There was usually a message from Rumen, often about food: I just tryed Your köfte in Kottbusser Damm. You are right! They are really great! In the last days I also made Fotos from three Vietnamese Restaurants. For a pity I hadn't time to try one of them. I have always clients what is good too . . .

I would answer him right away. We weren't wooing each other, so there were no games, no rules, no long, coy pauses between messages. I liked being free to respond to him when I felt like it, taunting him with alluring descriptions of what I was eating, sending him pictures from the taxi, telling myself I had a friend in Berlin, and I was going back to Berlin, and writing him was an escape from the stench of the apartment and the deafening soundtrack outside my window, which ebbed and flowed but never stopped.

As the weeks went by, emails flying back and forth, I began to depend on the daily rhythm of our communication, as addicted to its frequency as I was to its intensity. And before long, as the conversation progressed from food and taxi driving to cities and books and German philosophers, it seemed to me that Rumen and I were carrying on a twenty-first-century version of a nineteenth-century correspondence: I want to notice one thing by Nietzsche, he wrote. You can take it as Your first German lesson: "Du musst nicht nur mit dem Munde, sondern auch mit dem Kopfe essen, damit dich nicht die Naschhaftigkeit des Mundes zugrunde richtet." (You must not eat only with your mouth but also with your head, or your mouth's gluttony will destroy you.)

He sent photos of what he was reading and rereading—*Bay Ganyo*, by his favorite Bulgarian writer, Aleko Konstantinov, and *Berlin: Fate of a World City*, by Walter Kiaulehn—propped against a tall glass of *Milchkaffee*. He explained his devotion to Bob Dylan: He always do what nobody expect from him! Therefore I respect him! He expounded on *Lebenskunst* and *Lebenskünstlern:* For me the problem is that many people don't understand the idea of Lebenskünstler, he wrote. If you try to find your own way, what is a little bit different from the mainstream, always you have to explain why you are different, and sometimes this makes people not comfortable . . .

In Berlin, I'd caught hints of his substance, and more than a hint of his passion—I didn't know if I'd ever met a person so naturally passionate. But now, even though he wasn't writing in his native language, I felt as if I were dialoguing with a kindred spirit.

And isn't this, I would think, when I closed my laptop, *the beginning of a beautiful friendship?*

"Look at you!" I said, when Isabel walked out the door of her office on West 39th Street. She was elegant, as always, in a burgundy pea-coat, cinched at the waist, and knee-high boots the color of dark chocolate. I hugged her the way I learned to hug in the *milonga,* pressing my heart to hers. "How are you?"

She hugged me back like a real *milonguera.* "I'm OK," she said. "What about you, lady? How does it feel to be back?"

"Weird."

"I bet."

We walked toward Times Square, unlinking our arms as we ducked under some scaffolding on Seventh Avenue, stopping to listen to a man near the entrance to the 7 train who was playing a slow version of "My Favorite Things" on a trumpet.

"I think," I said, as we dug around in our purses for change, "I'm starting to understand the way you feel about New York."

"You are?"

"Mmmhmm."

We descended the stairs to the subway. The wind in the tunnel displaced a few of her short auburn hairs. She smoothed them back into the sleek sphere framing her heart-shaped face.

It wasn't just Isabel's elegance that struck me whenever I saw her. It was her joy. Her boyfriend may have been mired in an existential crisis, her job as a project manager boring, her green card trapped in some clogged bureaucratic maze, but in her presence I always sensed the (rare) contentment of a person who was exactly where she wanted to be.

We stood up on the subway to Queens, craning our necks and peeking out the windows as the 7 surfaced in Long Island City, trying to catch glimpses of the Manhattan skyline as the train rumbled north, scraping along the tracks between Jackson Avenue and Queensboro Plaza.

"Where are we getting off?" said Isabel.

"Eighty-second Street."

We were on our way to a Colombian place recommended by a pair of cabbies I'd met in the Team waiting room.

"You haven't tried *bandeja paisa*?" said Hernán, who was born in Barranquilla.

"It's our national dish," said José, who came from Bogotá, "from the northwestern part of Colombia. The people there, they call them *'paisas.'* "

Pollos a la Brasa Mario was where Hernán and José liked to eat *bandeja paisa* in New York. The restaurant, crowned with a red-and-yellow sign (ESPECIALIDAD EN MARISCOS ★ ASADOS ★ COMIDA TIPICA, FREE DELIVERY), glowed under a double halo of floodlights on the corner of 37th Avenue and 83rd Street in Jackson Heights. Isabel and I looked over the picture menu taped to the window before we went inside: *bandeja paisa* was the first dish on the list.

We chose a table in the middle of the dining room, under a fake ficus plant someone had stuffed into a tall, papier-mâché trunk, transforming it into a palm tree. My red Formica chair didn't budge when I tried to move it closer to the yellow Formica table—both were soldered to the floor. When we ordered *bandeja paisa,* with *mazamorra* (corn stew) to start, our waiter, a pint-sized man in a maroon waist apron, looked puzzled.

"So, lady," said Isabel, as the waiter set the *mazamorra* on the table, along with a plate of sliced lime and a bowl of green salsa, "how is it, driving the taxi now?"

"Hmm . . ." I squeezed lime and stirred some salsa into the *mazamorra,* which looked like a bowl of milk with a few dollops of mashed corn. "Well—"

"Ay, no!" said the waiter, rushing to our table before we could take a bite. Isabel and I looked up at him, our spoons in midair.

"This is for your *bandeja,"* said the waiter, moving the limes and salsa out of my reach. "This"—he pointed under the bowl of *mazamorra,* to some irregular chunks of brown sugar that resembled spoon-sized asteroids—"this is *panela,"* he said. "This we eat with *mazamorra.* And mostly," he added, smiling, "we have *mazamorra* for breakfast."

"Oh!" I blushed.

"No te preocupes," said the waiter. Don't worry. He whisked away the defiled corn stew and brought us a fresh bowl.

"Muchas gracias."

Isabel giggled as she stirred a chunk of *panela* into the *mazamorra.*

"Remember how burned-out I was, driving the taxi? Before I went to Berlin?"

"I remember Mr. 4:29," said Isabel, still stirring. The *panela* melted into the milky corn in cinnamon-colored swirls.

I pictured the strung-out businessman I'd barely dropped off at JFK on time. "Poor Mr. 4:29." I tasted the *mazamorra.* It was bland, but soothing, settling over my stomach like a starchy blanket. "But you know what?" I rested my spoon on the rim of the bowl. "If he got in my cab now, I think it'd be different." I told Isabel about the man in spandex, about being oddly detached from his tantrum over the garbage truck blocking our way on West 88th Street. "It think it's Berlin," I said. "The taxi drivers there, at least the ones I met, they just approach it—or at least they *seem* to approach it, in a totally different way. Like it's an opportunity." I gazed up at the fake ficus-palm. "Or even an art form."

"Are you talking about that Zorba guy?"

"Yeah." I smiled. Isabel had read my blog posts about Rumen. "We've been writing since I got back."

"Really?"

The waiter brought our *bandeja paisa*. We sat back, gaping, daunted, as he positioned the super-sized platter in the middle of the table. This was abundance approaching the obscene: fried sweet plantains, a slab of carne asada, half an avocado, an *arepa* (corn cake), a hunk of *chicharrón* (fried pork belly), rice, beans, and a fried egg.

"*¡Buen provecho!*" said the waiter, before he scurried back to the kitchen.

"Oh, my God," said Isabel, eyeing the *bandeja* with a mixture of excitement and alarm.

"Maybe you're supposed to spend the day working in the mountains before you eat this," I said. I spooned green salsa onto our serving plates.

Isabel laughed and started squeezing lime on everything. "So you guys are keeping in touch?"

I nodded, slicing off a hunk of carne asada, pounded thin, and a little tough, but still juicy, and sprinkled with lots of pepper. I told her what happened after the Dead Grandma tour, everything leading up to our sad goodbye. "Now we're friends," I said, smashing some beans under my fork. But our emails seemed to be getting more intimate, and more ambiguous: Now, at Rumen's suggestion, we were reading the same book, Erich Fromm's *To Have or to Be*. For the past week, we'd been sending our favorite passages from Fromm back and forth. (Me: "What is spent is not lost, but on the contrary, what is kept is lost." Him: "Knowing does not mean to be in possession of the truth; it means to penetrate the surface and to strive . . . to approach truth ever more closely.") You know what I like best? he wrote in one of his last messages. We understand each other very well.

It was Fromm, but of course it was more than Fromm, though Fromm was a kind of culmination—in any case, it was becoming harder for me to disguise the longing between my lines: for Rumen, for Berlin. It was also impossible not to get anxious when it took more than half a day for him to respond to my messages. But I told

myself there was nothing to be gained in rushing to resolve the unre-
solved. I was still searching for something here: I needed to keep
driving the taxi, to stay here a little longer, even though Rebekka's
cat had taken to doing her business outside my door, even if every
blog post felt like a prelude to another goodbye, another move.

Isabel and I got through half the *bandeja paisa* before we finally
asked the waiter if he could wrap up the rest of the pork belly.

"One thing I forgot to tell you," I said, as we walked side by side
on 83rd Street, back to the 7 train, squaring our shoulders against the
late October wind. "You know how Rumen was supposed to take
me to the airport, but I told you how we got in a fight, and I ended
up having to take another taxi?"

"Uh-huh."

"You know what that taxi driver told me?"

"What?" She tucked her chin in the collar of her coat.

"Berlin has ten years left before it becomes one big gentrified
SoHo. But you know what?" I said. "I don't care! If Berlin has ten
years left, I want to spend those ten years with Berlin." The city
might be going mainstream, and Rumen's golden nineties were over,
but even from a distance, it was still Elektropolis to me.

"Sounds like love," said Isabel, her voice catching.

I touched her shoulder. "I know you know what I mean, New
Yorker."

We rode the 7 in silence. I glanced at Isabel, biting her cheek.
Why didn't I want to live in New York, where, unlike my friend, I
could come and go as I pleased? Maybe, I thought, while the subway
plowed westward, we were both drawn to places where we had to
continually renew our migratory vows, where we had to keep asking ourselves, year after year, day after day, if wherever we were was
where we wanted to be. I gave Isabel a long hug before she got off to
transfer to the R. "Take the pork belly," I said.

"Are you sure?"

"You can make stew." I pushed the plastic bag into her hands,
and she slipped out just before the robot announcer finished saying
"Stand clear of the closing doors, please." She waited on the platform,
facing the train, clutching the pork belly. I waved at her through the

scratched windows as the 7 pulled away. *You are my sister,* her sad smile seemed to say, *and I know you have to go.*

At the end of my next taxi shift, driving back to the garage, stranded in a traffic jam on the Queensboro Bridge, I drummed my fingers on the steering wheel and turned up the volume on Celia Cruz, sighing at the sea of brake lights ahead.

It had been a good shift, aside from all the usual trips to the bathroom: two fares to JFK without incident, 193 miles driven, lamb over rice with green chili sauce at the Kwik Meal cart on West 45th Street (where they always served cab drivers first), $95 in my pocket, and 24 fares, one of whom happened to be a little girl named Alice, who got in the cab with her two dads and told me they were on their way to visit her ninety-nine-year-old grandma in Connecticut. Alice was a tiny vision in purple, down to her fingernails, worldly in the way of New York children, more cosmopolitan at seven than I was at thirty-six: "My favorite food in the universe," said Alice, as we sailed up Sixth Avenue, past the West 4th Street Courts, "is soup dumplings at Grand Szechuan." She blew me a kiss when she got out of the cab. "Please pay her a lot of money," she said to her dads before she pranced through the brass doors at Grand Central Terminal.

Now it was four o'clock in the afternoon. Alice was probably in Connecticut, and no one was making forward progress on the eastbound side of the lower deck of the Queensboro Bridge. I put the taxi in Park and sat up taller, trying to peer over the cab in front of me. All I could see were solid brake lights. I rolled down the passenger-side window and looked outside: the afternoon sun was glittering on the west bank of the East River, backlighting Manhattan, which looked like a Legoland silhouette. I thought about Rumen's last email: Do you remember the Bob Dylan CD Cover with the old NYC taxi?! he wrote. It was MODERN TIMES. Again I listen often to Bob Dylan and think about You and NY. I should see the city once, sometime.

Yes, you should. I fished my camera out of my purse and snapped some pictures of the skyline, and the trees puffing out at the tip of

Roosevelt Island, and an empty cargo ship crossing the East River, until the traffic started to move again.

I wrote Rumen as soon as I got back to 29th Street. Here are some photos of New York, New York. I knew what the next line was. I'd composed it in the cab. I trailed my finger around the rim of the keyboard, brushing away dust and crumbs. Maybe it was too forward. Maybe it was ill-timed? I typed it anyway and read it aloud, wondering how the words would sound to him: If you ever decide to come for a visit, you're welcome! I hit Send before I could think it through any longer.

35

I hope You are serious! Rumen wrote, the morning after I sent him the photo of the skyline. Maybe I'll decide—

The N train grated over the tracks outside. I glanced through the spotty window of my room on 29th Street as the subway slowed to a stop at Queensboro Plaza. I looked down at the computer again, reading the message to the end, eyes widening at the screen: Maybe I'll decide to come to New York for a visit . . .

I jumped off my stool. Maybe? I started to spin around the room. Maybe, yes? I hadn't known, when I'd sent my open invitation, that even the slightest chance of him coming here would set off something ecstatic in me.

Of course I'm serious! I could already envision Rumen eating a peppercorn catfish banh mi on the Staten Island Ferry. Rumen drinking Belgian ale at the rooftop bar of the La Quinta Motel in Koreatown. Rumen having his first taste of sweet potato pie from RCL Enterprises on Rockaway Boulevard. Rumen eating a harissa falafel from Taïm on the benches overlooking Tenth Avenue on the High Line. Rumen unwrapping Bukharan samsas from Tandoori Food & Bakery in the passenger seat of my taxi . . .

Imagine you're at the airport, embracing someone you love after they've come back from a long trip . . . The uninhibited embrace had been the most terrifying part of my first tango lessons, and of almost every tango I danced after that, even if it lasted only three minutes. And now? I could do nothing but fling my arms around the possibility of Rumen coming to New York. *And if he doesn't come?* It would shatter me. But part of me, call it the wizened share of my instincts, knew I could put myself back together.

. . .

"Do you think he'll come?" said Isabel. We were at the corner of 68th and Park, waiting for the light to change. I pulled out my notebook to double-check the address of the Americas Society, where we were going to hear Maria Kodama, Jorge Luis Borges's widow, read some new translations of his essays.

"I don't know."

I looked up at the penthouses, as out of reach as heaven, then down at the street, which was thick with taxis, most of them empty, driving north, farther into the Upper East Side.

"You know what he told me?" I said as we crossed the eastern half of Park Avenue.

"What?" A gust of November wind swept across the street. Isabel pulled her wine-colored scarf over her chin. Every time we saw each other now, it felt like the next to the last time.

"Everyone in East Germany used to say, 'See Paris, and die,'" I said. "But he didn't care about Paris. He would always say, 'See New York, and die.' His dream was New York."

"I can understand that."

"I know you can."

She laughed. "And *if* he comes?" She lifted her chin above her scarf. "Are you guys friends? Or . . . ?"

I thought about Rumen's latest email: I think about the best time to come to NY. Thats why I want to ask You serious: Can I stay at You? I'll pay You! I think about one week. What do You think?

Pay me? My heart sank when I read it. Of course, you can stay here!, I wrote back, frowning as I typed. We have a sofabed. BUT, no!! You don't need to pay me. I won't take your money . . .

"I'm trying to be enlightened about it," I said. "It would be amazing if he came. No matter what we are."

Isabel and I leaned forward, rapt, listening to Maria Kodama read from an essay called "The Full Extent of My Hope." "And let's be clear," she said, delivering Borges's words in a soft but eager voice, as though relieved to be sharing a long-held secret, "the future never has the nerve to be the present completely without first trying things out, and that trying things out is hope."

I looked over at Isabel. She squeezed my hand.

At last, after dozens of emails, after weeks of going back and forth on possible dates for his possible visit that didn't fall on the busiest weekends for taxi drivers in Berlin (First I have to have a plan with the dates of BERLINALE and the INTERNATIONALE TOURISMUS-BÖRSE and the FRUIT LOGISTICA . . .), Rumen sent me an itinerary—his itinerary:

> I AM COMING TO NY, NY!
>   Here are all the details:
>   HINFLUG Dienstag 11.Januar TXL ab 11:50am JFK an 2:59pm Delta 079 Nonstop
>   RÜCKFLUG Dienstag 18.Januar JFK ab 7:25pm Delta 078 Nonstop
>   I'll bring my brandnew sleeping bag. He/It is already happy to see something from the world!
>   PS—Do You know some place where we could find some "Dylan feeling"? ;-)

Hinflug! Rückflug! Yes, yes, yes! Rumen feasting on fried okra at Rockaway West Indian Roti Shop. Rumen appraising the Bosnian sausage at Cevabdzinica Sarajevo. Rumen eating black-eyed pea curry at Punjabi Grocery & Deli at three a.m. . . .

I ran into the living room, beaming. Rebekka looked up from the pamphlet she was studying, blinking hard. The cat leapt off the couch and streaked down the hall.

"What's up?" she said. Her shoulders were drooping more than usual, as if someone were kneeling on them.

I'd told Rebekka a little about Rumen, weeks ago, when his visit was still a maybe. "Oh, yeah," she'd said, after I'd described his dream to "See New York, and die." "He can totally stay here if he comes." She'd christened him Mr. Nietzsche.

"Um"—I cleared my throat—"so you remember Mr. Nietzsche?"

Rebekka lifted the amber glass vial containing what I guessed was the cat's new medicine off her lap and peered down the hall. "Huh?"

"Mr. Nietzsche . . . My taxi driver friend from Berlin?"

"Mr. Nietzsche . . . ?"

"He actually wants to come in January—"

"Mr. Nietzsche." She folded up the medication pamphlet and stuffed it back in its box. "January? OK. Cool."

"I can move the sofa to my room, if you want."

"You don't have to move the sofa." She stood up and started down the hall, hiding the amber vial behind her back. "Here, kitty, kitty, kitty . . ."

Rumen and I kept writing, every day, sometimes two or three times a day, now that he was coming to New York: Now I want to prepare you but not scare you and tell you about where I live, I wrote. Don't worry about me! he answered. I like cats—but not in my sleeping bag. ☺

I continued to think about what I'd told Isabel: "It would be amazing if he came, no matter what we are." Yes: he was an extraordinary person—the more I learned about him, the more apparent this was. But when I thought about Dead Grandma and *Milchkaffee* and listening to "Love Sick" at the taxi stand on Weserstrasse and dancing to Peter Fox and collapsing onto his sheepskin-covered futon and Nietzsche and Fromm and *Zorba the Greek* (which I still needed to read), I knew I wanted more than a beautiful friendship with Rumen. At the same time, despite (or because of?) all our virtual communication, the closer his arrival date drew, the more confused I became, about what our boundaries were, where the upper limit was, and what might happen when he arrived.

I even kept his visit a secret from my parents, who, for better or worse, usually had some sense of what was going on in my love life.

"Meet any nice guys in your taxi lately?" said Mom. She figured the taxi was the only place I would ever meet someone.

"Nope. Not lately."

"I guess it's kinda hard to hit a moving target," said Dad.

I knew that if Mom and Dad knew that some cab driver from Berlin was coming to stay with me for a week, *Lebenskünstler* or no, they would worry themselves into insomnia ("Is he a communist?"), or concoct some romantic fairy tale even more purple than I was capable of ("Maybe your kids will be taxi drivers!"), or at the very least ask me questions I wouldn't be able to answer ("Where's he going to sleep?").

Saturday or Sunday when you're here I'll drive the taxi, I wrote him, a week before he was due to arrive, and you can come with me for a couple of hours—if you want . . .

The true is, he wrote back, one of my dreams would come true! I have no words . . . I'll try anyway: This would be bigger than GREAT!!! (I don't want to say "amazing." After the Wall came down people say "amazing" too often . . .) But what about your taxi license? Could you have some trouble?

Don't worry! I answered. I have a plan. All we need is your taxi license . . . Technically it was illegal to have him, or any person, in the taxi if the meter wasn't on, but I wanted to do for Rumen in New York what he'd done for me in Berlin—especially when I understood what it meant to him.

But how will we say hello? I wondered, driving around in the cab searching for a passenger at eight o'clock on a Sunday morning. I looked up at the Christmas snowflake suspended over 57th Street, sparkling and precarious, trying to anticipate every possible scenario when I met Rumen at JFK: An awkward handshake, a friendly hug, a peck on the cheek . . . And after that? Every day I added something new to our New York itinerary—there was no way we could get through everything I wanted him to eat and see in a week. Hot chili chili crab at Szechuan Gourmet or Manchurian chow mein at Tangra Masala? Burgers at Shake Shack or fried chicken at Amy Ruth's? Chicken Jalfrezi at Curry in a Hurry or spinach and ricotta focaccia at Lorusso's? Trying to map them out only made the days with him seem blurrier.

The only thing I could envision with any clarity was the taxi shift. I could imagine Rumen in the passenger seat. I could picture us crossing the Queensboro Bridge, driving into Manhattan at the beginning of the shift, listening to "Balada para un loco" ("Ballad for a Crazy Man"), my favorite Astor Piazzolla tango: *Let's go flying, my dear / Get on my super sport illusion / let's run on the edge / with a swallow in the engine . . .*

The Delta International Arrivals area at John F. Kennedy Airport looked like a bomb shelter under construction. There were no flap display timetables or frosted glass or sliding doors or people lining up behind restraining ropes with signs and balloons and flowers like I remembered from LAX, where as a kid I loved to watch the people walk off the planes from Manila or London or Mexico City, and into the arms of madly sobbing relatives. Here, there was raw concrete on the floor, damp with dirty snow footprints, a pair of fluorescent lights on a drop ceiling, flickering under blackened bulbs, and one man in a rumpled suit, straddling a briefcase in front of the unmarked steel doors that must have been where the arriving passengers would make their entrance.

I'd been refreshing the Delta flight status page all morning with shaky fingers: "ARRIVAL ON TIME," it said, every time. Rumen had written me one last email before he left for the airport.

> Guten Morgen Layne,
>> I just stand up!
>> Everything is fine!
>> I'll bring my taxi license to New York, just in case!
>> And I'll waer my warm clothes!
>> To the luggage!

His plane was scheduled to land in thirty minutes. It was twenty degrees outside and someone had turned the heater in the arrivals area to a tropical setting. I started to sweat inside my puffy coat.

"Are you waiting for the flight from Berlin?" I asked the man in the rumpled suit. There was no logo, no sign, no electronic arrivals monitor anywhere.

"I hope so," he said, sighing at the steel doors.

I unzipped my coat and blotted my nose, trying to take deep breaths. The air kept getting stuck in my chest, refusing to go down any further. The man in the rumpled suit pulled out his cell phone and punched in a number. I walked outside, retracing my steps to the AirTrain, double-checking the signs to make sure I was actually in the Delta International Arrivals area. Blasts of icy wind did unfortunate things to my hair, erasing whatever traces of glamour I might have had after a sleepless night and an interminable hour on the E train and then on the AirTrain, agonizing every time we paused too long at a stop.

I followed the signs from the AirTrain back to the arrivals area—bleak as it was, this had to be the right place. The man in the rumpled suit was mumbling into his cell phone, and now clusters of people, some of them speaking German, were waiting in front of the steel doors, which were still barred shut. What would happen when Rumen stepped through those doors? I closed my eyes, trying to imagine the scenario one more time—hug? handshake? peck on the cheek . . . ?—and opened them again when I started to get dizzy. Someone lifted the bar on the doors.

"Oh, God," I whispered, blotting my nose again. *Why is it so hot?* The first passenger, a woman in her fifties in a gray turtleneck, pushed through the doors, which groaned and squeaked as they opened in front of her. She headed straight for the exit as if being chased, not looking for anyone to greet her. I stared at her suitcase as she hurried past, searching for the airport code on her luggage tag. I barely spotted it: TXL. *Berlin Tegel! Rumen Vassillevski has landed!*

I pictured him standing in line, waiting for the immigration officer to stamp his passport: "What is the reason for your visit to the United States?" How would he answer? "See New York, and die"?

I shifted my weight from one foot to the other, hoisting my purse higher on my shoulder. Where was the line between panic and euphoria? When was the last time I'd been so afraid and so excited at the same time? Dancing tango? Driving the taxi? Landing in Buenos Aires, New York, Berlin, not knowing a soul? Yes. No. This was a new sort of limbo—as thrilling as it was terrifying. What would happen when he walked through those doors? Anything was possible.

Anything. I stood there, sweating in my puffy coat, and I laughed. There was a kind of exhilaration in not knowing. *To be in suspense,* I thought, *is to be alive.* To dwell in uncertainty, as Keats put it, without an irritable reaching for certainty.

There's a tall guy who's ready to trek through Siberia, or so I supposed, when I saw a red-eyed man in hiking boots and a coffee-colored parka with a fur-lined hood burst through the double steel doors. It took me a few seconds to realize it was Rumen. I held my breath, watching him rush toward me, pulling a metal suitcase that looked like it was struggling to keep up with him. The suitcase toppled over before he made it to where I was standing. He grabbed it by the handle, stepped in front of me, parked the suitcase on the ground next to him, and pulled me into his parka, kissing me, carefully at first, as if he wanted to make sure it was what I wanted. I kissed him back until we were the only ones left in the arrivals area.

It was one of the coldest weeks of winter, so cold the subways were half empty, so cold our ears smarted, and our fingers ached, even in our gloves, as the crosstown winds sliced through our socks. Rumen hardly took off his goofy navy-blue snow cap with the ear flaps and the gold stripes—but I still liked looking at him, eating cold skin noodles at Xi'an Famous Foods in Chinatown, hiking through the snow in Central Park on the way to Spanish Harlem and slices at the original Patsy's, and oxtails at Walkerswood, eating peanut butter and jelly sandwiches ("I want to eat what the Americans eat!") on the Staten Island Ferry, sitting on his lap on the subway, sharing the headphones on his MP3 player, bobbing our heads to Mikis Theodorakis and Bob Dylan and Canned Heat, his favorite blues-rock band. I'd never had more fun in New York.

He gave me the present he'd wanted to give me on my last day in Berlin: ten CDs he had burned with music mixes for the taxi, a certified piece of the Berlin Wall, and English translations of his five all-time favorite books: *Zorba the Greek, Atomised, Narcissus and Gold-mund, Siddhartha,* and *Thus Spoke Zarathustra.*

The night we walked over the Brooklyn Bridge, passing his flask of Jameson back and forth, Manhattan looked like a pop-up-book image in the subzero air. "I can come to New York now," he said, opening his arms toward the skyscrapers. "Before, this was impossible." He lifted me up in a crushing hug. *"Das ist schon grossartig!"*

We wandered the slushy streets of the Village, visiting Bob Dylan landmarks I'd been unaware of until I'd researched them for him: the Village Gate, where Dylan wrote "A Hard Rain's A-Gonna Fall" in the basement, Gerde's Folk City, where he made his first professional appearance, the Fat Black Pussycat, where he allegedly wrote "Blowin' in the Wind" over a cup of coffee, Café Wha?, where he played a set of Woody Guthrie songs the day he arrived in New York, and Jones Street, where he posed for the cover of *Freewheelin' Bob Dylan,* walking arm in arm with Suze Rotolo, his love at the time.

"Come here!" said Rumen, standing in the middle of Jones Street, pulling out his camera.

"Want me to take your photo?" said a white-haired lady in a purple cape coat, smiling at us as she walked by. She snapped three pictures of Rumen and me, clinging to each other in the snow.

"I want to tell you serious," he said, after our Dylan tour, as we sat at a table across from the espresso machine at Café Grumpy, drinking late-morning cappuccinos, "I'm very sorry about your last night in Berlin. It was stupid from my side."

"I'm sorry, too," I said, wrapping my hands around the thick brown cup, "but I was so sad to be leaving—"

"When you'll come to Berlin exactly?"

"April." April was when my informal rental contract with Rebekka would end. It was also the first month I would be allowed to reenter Germany on a tourist visa.

"And then?" He stirred his cappuccino. "What is your plan?"

"To stay, indefinitely."

"You really love Berlin so much?"

"I do." I took a spoonful of foam. "But maybe I'm still in the honeymoon period."

He reached for my hand. "How will it end, this honeymoon period?"

I told him what the taxi driver told me on the way to Tegel, about Berlin having ten years left.

"Maybe we have to fight back together," he said, taking my other hand. "What do you say?"

I smiled. "This would be bigger than great."

We finished our cappuccinos and walked up Seventh Avenue, toward Times Square. Rumen shook his head as he observed the traffic, scowling at the taxis cutting each other off, fighting for fares like sharks battling for prey. "They are crazy!" he said, stopping in the middle of the sidewalk. "In Berlin you shouldn't take a passenger from another driver! It's—how do you say? An unwritten law!"

"In New York even taxi drivers don't respect taxi drivers," I said, "sometimes."

"But they drive like cannibals!"

"If you want to make money here, you have to be aggressive."

"Are you aggressive?"

"No."

He grinned. "So you are a vegetarian."

"Huh?"

"A vegetarian among cannibals!"

"Maybe." I laughed. "Or maybe a vegan."

"A what?"

"Never mind."

"Tomorrow we will see." He brushed my hair out of the way and kissed me on the cheek. "I can't wait."

I was usually half conscious, even after two cups of coffee, when I showed up at Team at four o'clock in the morning to pick up a taxi. Not on January 16, 2011. One day shy of the one-year anniversary of my first taxi driving shift, my eyes were wide open, even though Rumen and I had stayed up past midnight watching the New York City segment of *Night on Earth:* "Hey, man!" said the Brooklynite named Yo-Yo to the East German clown at the wheel, "You gotta put it in 'Drive.' 'D'! 'D' is to drive!" We laughed until our stomachs hurt, though we'd both seen the movie more times than we could count. "Put the motherfucker in 'Drive'!" We agreed: This was poetry.

The waiting room at Team was empty except for me and two cabbies I didn't recognize, who were engrossed in the TV, which was tuned to a rebroadcast of *Adventures in Babysitting.* I sat on the bench against the cinderblock wall and began to think about all the things that could go wrong in the next twelve hours: It was twenty-three degrees with a chance of snow, according to the weather report on WNYC. What if I got in an accident? Rumen was such a good driver. *How embarrassing would that be?* What if I got lost? Would today finally be the day I got a fare to Staten Island? And what if the Taxi & Limousine Commission discovered we were driving together? Could they—would they—really take away my hack license?

Elizabeth Shue was almost finished singing the "Babysitting Blues" when Mike, the dispatcher, called my name. *To hell with the risks,* I thought, rushing over to the intake window. I'd never been so glad to get a cab.

"It's on the pump!" said Mike.

"Thanks!"

My breath came out in puffs as I hurried through the rituals I usually prolonged before I started a taxi shift: stowing carrots and almonds and slices of cheddar in the pocket on the driver's side door, opening my *New York City 5-Borough Street Atlas* to the map of lower Manhattan, wedging my hack license—still in Boris's plastic sleeve—into the Plexiglas holder behind my head. I pulled out the Astor Piazzolla CD I'd made—"Balada para un loco" was song number one—ready to slip it into the CD player. But there was no CD player. There was no radio in the cab, period—someone had ripped it out of the dashboard. *Well,* I thought, stuffing the CD back in my purse, *that's that.*

Rumen was right where I'd told him to meet me, on the corner of 29th Street and 40th Avenue, jogging in place in his coffee-colored parka. When I honked at him, he raised his arms, shaking his fists in victory in the five a.m. darkness.

I rolled down the passenger-side window. "Good morning, sir." I smiled. "Would you like a ride?"

"Take me to Manhattan!" he said, jumping into the passenger seat like he was hopping a border. He took off his snow hat and kissed me. "Heee-heeee!" He drummed his hands on the dashboard. "D!" he said. "D is to drive!" He nodded at the taxi meter. "Ha!"

"You have your license, right?"

He fished a keychain necklace out of his sweater with his Berlin taxi license in a laminated pouch. If the Taxi & Limousine Commission caught us, we had a plan: Rumen would show his license, and I would say something like "This is a taxi driver from Berlin, and he's in New York doing a comparative research project." In the end, we were on a noble mission—I was almost sure I could talk us out of trouble.

I drove around the block so he could get a good view of the taxi garage and the night drivers lining up to turn in their cabs. He stared out the window, holding on to his taxi license. When he turned to me, there were tears in his eyes.

"I cannot believe you do this for me."

"Believe it," I said, tearing up, too, as I turned onto Northern Boulevard. I drove between the construction barricades on Queens Plaza North, slowing down over the potholes, clearing the last signal before the entrance to the upper deck of the Queensboro Bridge.

Rumen pointed at the hole in the dashboard where the radio was supposed to be. "No music!"

"We make the music."

"We?" He laughed. *Thunk-thunk, thunk-thunk* went the taxi as we rode over the creases in the asphalt. "OK!" He reached into his messenger bag. "Wait . . ." He pulled out his MP3 player, pressing one of the earbuds in my ear and one in his as we rounded the curves of the on-ramp. "Just for one song!" he said.

We came around the last curve and he let out a rebel yell. "YEEEE haaaaa!" There was Manhattan, cutting a dazzling outline in the inky, frigid air. "It looks so good from the taxi!"

"Doesn't it?" The city, as it sometimes did when I crossed the Queensboro Bridge at the start of a shift, seemed to be pulling on the sky.

"OK!" he said, thumb poised on the MP3 player. "Are you ready for some Canned Heat?"

"Oh, yeah!"

" 'On the Road Again,' " said Rumen, reciting the intro line in unison with the band leader, snapping his fingers as harmonica and drums and piano and rhythm guitar tore into the song all at once while we drove the taxi up and over the incline of the span, both singing at the skyline, "Well I'm so tired of cryin', but I'm out on the road again, I'm on the road a*gain* . . ."

"Hey!" He turned to me. "Are you hungry?"

"I'm always hungry," I said, as we coasted off the bridge, onto Second Avenue, dancing in our seats. "Do you like Punjabi food?"

Acknowledgments

———————————•———————————

Taxi drivers of Buenos Aires, New York City, and Berlin, this book is for you as well as for my parents. Sally McGrane, for helping me bring this book into being; for your honesty, generosity, and sensibility; for all those hours in the Volksbühne cantina, you will have my gratitude until the end of my days. Eleanor Jackson, thank you for finding me, for seeing through my futile attempts, for being my champion. Tim O'Connell, you grew this project from its infancy, and you continue to make it grow—how can I thank you enough? Tom Pold, I appreciate you driving me to the edge of sanity with your editorial suggestions. Michiko Clark, Sara Eagle, Jordan Rodman, I'm so grateful to you for being passionate about this book, for spreading the word. Johannes Dianovich Claerbout, your memory is part of every adventure. Matt Chesterton, I'm indebted to you for writing that beautiful piece about *Taxi Gourmet* and taking the time to read the Buenos Aires part of the manuscript. Vicky Baker, Vera Block, Jessica Bridger, Joanne Camas, Jory Des Jardins, Leah Douglas, Andy Eckardt, Geraldine Eisendrath, Jorge Luis Fernández, Emily Flake, Verena Hasel, Thiago Guimaraes, Nina Anika Klotz, Simon McCormack, Joshua Partlow, Olivier Pratte, Aaron Rutkoff, David Gordon Smith, Heike Vowinkel, Julia Washausen, and Claudio Weissfeld, thank you for joining me on the food quests, and for sharing the story. Fabián Peralta, Mariangeles Rodriguez, Natacha Poberaj, Oliver Kolker, Pato y Luis, I'll never forget your valiant attempts to teach me to tango. Iris and Constance Marie, you are my heroines—drive on, ladies. Daniel Beccaria, Joe Hennessey, Mike Katz, Allen, Jake, and the rest of the team at Team Systems Taxi Garage, you are the salt of the earth. Maria Teresa Mauro of Palma (Trapani), Italy, and Emil Dimitrov and the citizens of Spanchevtsi, Bulgaria, thank you for building beautiful places to finish a book. Querida Adriana Romano, *vos sos un regalo.* Thank you, Alberto Bernardino Paz and Julie Taylor, for your gorgeous translations, and to Valorie Hart for allowing Alberto's words to appear here. Maxine Brown, Elis Graifman, Debra Russell, I am indebted to you for your wisdom, tango and otherwise. Lisa Barelli, Ryan Bird and Christine Fannon, Gabriela Hallas, Rodrigo Varela Perarnau, Brainy Smurf, thank you for following *Taxi Gourmet* through thick and thin. Lilian Moreira, you showed me what it is to love a city. Julia Fischer, thank you for being my first friend in Berlin. Wonderful Kickstarter backers—Autumn Arnold, Bob Barad, Clement Barrera-Ng, Ann Bernard, Dave Bloch, Erik Boertjes, Jano Cabrera, Wanda Cairns, Patrick Campbell, Armando Carmona, Laura Chinen, Jon and Diane Claerbout, Lucy Cousins, Don Eash, Ben Emmel, Cheryl Ennis, Oriana Fowler, Terry Michael Gammon, Joshua Goldfein, Steven Goldman, Carolina Gomez-Jones, Caroline Hendrix, Patti Horikawa, Teresa Hernandez Nimmo, Marisa Elana James, Ira Kaplan, Craig Katerberg, Kent Keltner, Kira Lerner, Jongyu Lin, Paul Mariz, Robin Martinazzi, Frank and Joyce Miner, Lilian Moreira, Frank Mosler, James Mosler, Shirley Nakao, Daniel Neilson, René Clausen Nielsen, Ken and Ann Palmer, Salem Pasha, Karen Plise, Carolynn Pawluk, Sangeetha Raghunathan, Megan Rich, Amy Scott, Audrey Scott, Ed Scott, Matthias Schwab, Brant Smith, Richard Stahler-Sholk, Veronica V-V, Andrew Vollo, and Julie Wakelee-Lynch—you made Berlin possible, and you led me home. Enrique, Godfred, Zille, I'm so glad we met on the road. Mom and Dad, you'll never get to the end of the road . . . Rumen, *Du bist mein Zorbas.*